THE BELGIAN ECONOMY
IN THE TWENTIETH CENTURY

By the end of the nineteenth century Belgium was enjoying considerable economic success. However, the economic experience has proved significantly less stable in the twentieth century.

The Belgian Economy in the Twentieth Century offers a detailed study of one of the small economies constituting the Benelux group. Professor André Mommen describes and analyses the changing fortunes of the Belgian economy throughout this century. He traces the Belgian experience from the state regulation of the interwar period to its current difficulties.

Central to the discussion is the innate problem of Belgian dependence on international trade due to the country's small domestic market. Professor Mommen places this examination within its political context by confronting the problems which have arisen since the first oil crisis and the effect they have had on Belgian politics and society.

This volume explains how a small but industrialized European nation succeeded in preserving its competitiveness only to succumb to a devastating debt crisis in the last decade. The Belgian experience as discussed in *The Belgian Economy in the Twentieth Century* perfectly illustrates the volatility of European economic trends this century.

André Mommen is Scientific Librarian and Professor of Political Science at the University of Amsterdam. He has extensive research experience in Belgian political and economic history.

CONTEMPORARY ECONOMIC HISTORY OF EUROPE SERIES
Edited by Derek Aldcroft

THE
BELGIAN ECONOMY
IN THE TWENTIETH
CENTURY

André Mommen

London and New York

First published 1994
by Routledge
11 New Fetter Lane, London, EC4P 4EE

Simultaneously published in the USA and Canada
by Routledge
29 West 35th Street, New York, NY 10001

© André Mommen

Typset in Garamond by Florencetype Ltd, Kewstoke, Avon
Printed and bound in Great Britain by
Mackays of Chatham PLC, Chatham, Kent

British Library Cataloguing in Publication Data
A catalogue record for this book is available
from the British Library.

Library of Congress Cataloguing in Publication Data
Mommen, André.
The Belgian economy in the twentieth century/
André Mommen.
p. cm.
Includes bibliographical references and index.
1. Belgium—Economic conditions—20th century. 2. Belgium
—Economic policy. 3. Belgium—Commerce. 4. Competition,
International. I. Title.
HC315.M59   1994
330.9493′043–dc20
93–34914
CIP

ISBN 0–415–01936–2

CONTENTS

TABLES

ACRONYMS AND ABBREVIATIONS

Below is an alphabetical listing of acronyms and abbreviations used throughout the text for the names of companies, organizations and institutions.

ABR	Ateliers Belge Réunis
ACEC	Ateliers de Constructions Electriques de Charleroi
ACVW	Algemeen Christelijk Verbond van Werkgevers
AEG	Allgemeine Electrizitäts Gesellschaft
AFV	Avantages Fiscaux – Fiscale Voordelen
AG	Assurances Générales
AGF	Assurances Générales de France
AKZO	Algemene Kunstzijde Unie – Koninklijke Zout-Organon
ALMABO	Algemene Maatschappij Boel
ALMANIJ	Algemene Maatschappij Voor Nijverheidskrediet
ALZ	Allegheny–Longdoz
AMAX	American Metal Climax
AMEV	Algemene Maatschappij tot Exploitatie van Vezekeringen
ANIC	Association Nationale des Industriels et Commerçants
APIC	Association des Patrons et Ingénieurs Catholiques de Belgique
ARBED	Aciéries Réunies de Burbach–Eich–Dudelange
ASED	Ammoniaque Synthétique et Dérivés
ASTRAL	SA Ammoniaque Synthétique Trieu-Kaisin, Ressaix, Anderlues, La Louvière-Sart
ATEA	Ateliers Téléphoniques d'Electricité en Anvers
AT&T	American Telephone & Telegraph
BASF	Badische Anilin- und Sodafabrik AG Ludwigshafen
BBL	Banque Bruxelles Lambert
BBT–BBA	Banque Belge du Travail – Belgische Bank van de Arbeid

BCK	Compagnie des Chemins de Fer du Bas-Congo au Katanga
BELCHIM	SA Belge de Chimie Nucléaire
BELFIN	Compagnie Belge de Financement de l'Industrie
BELGIC-ATOM	Association Belge pour le Développement Pacifique de l'Energie Atomique
BELGO-NUCLEAIRE	Société Belge pour l'Industrie Nucléaire
BLEU	Belgian Luxembourg Economic Union
BN	Brugeoise et Nivelles
BP	British Petroleum
BPE	Bureau de Programmation Economique
BRUFINA	Société de Bruxelles pour la Finance et l'Industrie
BSN	Boussois–Souchon–Neuvesel
BUB	Böhmische Union-Bank
CABV	Creditanstalt–Bankverein
CAP	Common Agricultural Policy
CARCOKE	SA Société Carolorégienne de Cokéfaction
CARFIL	SA Société Carolorégienne de Tréfilerie
CARFROID	SA Société Carolorégienne de Laminage à Froid
CARLAM	SA Société Carolorégienne de Laminage
CBHK–OCCH	Centraal Bureau voor Hypothecair Krediet – Office Central du Crédit Hypothécaire
CBI	Compagnie Belge pour l'Industrie
CBL	Compagnie Bruxelles Lambert
CBMC	Compagnie Belge Maritime du Congo
CBR	Cimenteries et Briqueteries Réunies de Belgique
CCCI	Compagnie du Congo pour le Commerce et l'Industrie
CCI	Comité Central Industriel
CDI	Compagnie Coppée de Développement Industriel
CEAN	Centre d'Etude des Applications de l'Energie Nucléaire
CEDEE	Compagnie Européenne pour le Développement Electrique et Electronique
CEN	Centre d'Etude Nucléaire
CER–CCE	Centraal Economische Raad–Conseil Central de l'Economie
CERE	Centre d'Etudes pour la Réforme de l'Etat– Strudiecentrum tot Hervorming van de Staat
CFAO	Compagnie Française de l'Afrique Occidentale
CFE	Compagnie François d'Entreprises
CGE	Compagnie Générale d'Electricité
CGER–ASLK	Caisse Générale d'Epargne et de Retraite–Algemene Spaar- en Lijfrentekas
CIA	Convention de l'Industrie de l'Azote

CIG	Centre d'Information Générale
CIP	Compagnie Industrielle et Financière des Produits Amylacés
CMB	Compagnie Maritime Belge
CNA	Compagnie Néerlandaise de l'Azote
CNC	Conseil National des Charbonnages
CNEE–NCEE	Comité National d'Expansion Economique – Nationaal Comité voor Economische Expansie
CNPC	Comité National de Planification et de Contrôle
COBECHAR	Comptoir Belge du Charbon
COBELAZ	Comptoir Belge de l'Azote
COBEPA	Compagnie Belge des Participations
CODITEL	Compagnie Générale pour la Diffusion de la Télévision
COFIMINES	Compagnie Financière, Minière et Industrielle
COFININDUS	Compagnie Financière et Industrielle
COFINTER	Compagnie Financière Internationale
COMINIERE	Société Commerciale et Minière du Congo
CONTIBEL	Compagnie Belge et Continentale de Gaz et d'Electricité
COSIBEL	Comptoir de Vente de la Sidérurgie
CPCA	Comité Permanent de Coordination de l'Autoproduction
CSC–ACV	Confédération des Syndicats Chrétiens – Algemeen Christelijk Vakverbond
CSK	Comité Spécial du Katanga
DIAMANG	Diamond Company of Angola
DBLG	Drexel Burnham Lambert Group
DEGUSSA	Deutsche Gold- und Silberscheideanstalt AG
DEN	Deutschland–England–Norwegen
DSM	De Staatsmijnen
EAGGF	European Agricultural Guidance and Guarantee Fund
EBES	Société Réunie d'Energie du Basin de l'Escaut – Verenigde Energiebedrijven van het Scheldeland
EC	European Community
ECA	Economic Co-operation Administration
ECSC	European Coal and Steel Community
EEC	European Economic Community
EIA	Entente Internationale de l'Acier
ELECTROBEL	Compagnie Générale d'Entreprises Electriques et Industrielles
ELECTRORAIL	Compagnies Réunies d'Electricité et de Transports
EMGO	SA Osram Belgium
EMS	European Monetary System

ENCI	Eerste Nederlandse Cement Industrie
EPU	European Payment Union
EXMAR	Compagnie Belge d'Expansion Maritime
FABELTA	Union des Fabriques Belges de Textiles Artificiels
FABRICOM	SA pour la Commerce et les Fabrications Industrielles
FABRIMETAL	Fédération de l'Industrie des Fabrications Métalliques
FAGAZ	Société pour la Fabrication du Gaz
FDF	Font Démocratique des Francophones
FEDECHAR	Fédération Charbonnière Belge
FEER	Fonds d'Expansion Economique et de Reconversion – Fonds voor Economische Expansie en Reconversie
FERBLATIL	Laminoirs à Froid de Fer-blanc à Tilleur
FGTB–ABVV	Fédération Générale du Travail Belge – Algemeen Belgisch Vakverbond
FIB	Fédération de l'Industrie Belge
FINABEL	Compagnie Financière et Industrielle de Belgique
FIT	SA Financière de l'Industrie Textile
FN	Fabrique Nationale d'Armes de Guerre
FORMINIERE	Société Interntionale Forestière et Minière du Congo
FRAMATOME	Société Franco-Américaine de Constructions Atomiques
FRI–FIV	Fonds de Rénovation Industrielle – Fonds voor Industriële Vernieuwing
GBC	General Biscuit Company
GBL	Groupe Bruxelles Lambert
GECOMIN	Société Générale Congolaise des Minerais
GIAT	Groupement des Industries d'Armements Terrestres
GIB	Grand Bazar–Innovation–Bon Marché
GLAVER	Société Glaces et Verres
GPP	Gevaert Photo-Producten
GTE	General Telephone & Electronics Corp.
HADIR	SA des Hauts-Fourneaux et Aciéries de Differdange, St-Ingbert, Rumelange
HMZ	Hayen–Mommen Zepperen
IBEL	Inversterings- en Beleggingsmaatschappij Lacourt – Financière Lacourt
IBRAMCO	Iranian Belgian Refining and Marketing Co.
ICI	Imperial Chemical Industries
IISN	Institut Inter-universitaire des Sciences Nucléaires
ILO	International Labour Organization
IMF	International Monetary Fund

INCA–NILK	Institut National du Crédit Agricole – Nationaal Instituut voor Landbouwkrediet
INTERCOM	Intercommunale Belge de Gaz et d'Electricité
IRG-HWI	Institut de Réescompte et de Garantie – Herdisconterings- en Waarborginstituut
IRI	Istituto per la Ricostruzione Industriale
ITCB	Institut pour la Textile et la Confection – Instituut voor Textiel en Confectie
ITT	International Telephone & Telegraph
KIO	Kuwait Investment Office
KS	Kempense Steenkolenmijnen
LVD	Lefebvre–Vanneste–Dewulf
MBLE	Manufacture Belge de Lampes Electriques
MECANIVER	Union des Verrieries Mécaniques Belges
MECHIM	Génie Métallurgique et Chimique
MMN	SA Métallurgique et Mécanique Nucléaires
MMR	Métallurgie et Minière de Rodange
MPW	Mouvement Populaire Wallon
NAR–CNT	Nationale Arbeidsraad – Conseil National du Travail
NCE–CNE	Nationaal Comité voor de Energie – Comité National pour l'Energie
OECD	Organization for Economic Co-operation and Development
OEEC	Organization for European Economic Co-operation
ONSS–RMZ	Office National de Sécurité Sociale – Rijksdienst voor Maatschappelijke Zekerheid
OPEC	Organization of Petroleum Exporting Countries
OREC	Office National du Redressement Economique
PLP	Parti de la Liberté et du Progrès
POB	Parti Ouvrier Belge
PRB	Poudreries Réunies de Belgique
RBP	Raffinerie Belge de Pétroles
SABCA	Société Belge de Constructions Aéronautiques
SABENA	SA Belge d'Exploitation et de Navigation Aérienne
SADACEM	Société d'Applications de la Chimie, de l'Electricité et des Métaux
SAFEA	SA pour la Fabrication des Engrais Azotés
SAG	Schlesische AG für Bergbau und Zinkhüttenbetrieb
SAMITRI	Sociedade Mineração de Trinidade
SARMA	SA pour la Revente d'Articles en Masse

SAUTRAC	Société Auxiliaire pour la Fourniture d'Energie de Traction
SBR	Société Belge des Radios
SCHLESAG	Schlesische Bergwerke & Hütten AG
SCRE	Société de Cooperation à la Reconversion des Entreprises
SEEE	Société d'Electricité d'Eupen et Extensions
SEEN	Syndicat d'Etude de l'Energie Nucléaire
SFS	Société Financière de la Sidérurgie – Staalfinancieringsmaatschappij
SGB	Société Générale de Belgique
SGM	Société Générale des Minerais
SIBP	Société Industrielle Belge des Pétroles
SIDAC	Société Industrielle de la Cellulose
SIDMAR	Sidérurgie Maritime
SIDRO	Société Internationale d'Energie Hydro-Electrique
SIPEF	Société Internationale de Plantations et de Finance
SNCB–NMBS	Société Nationale de Chemins de Fer Belges – Nationale Maatschappij der Belgische Spoorwegen
SNCI–NMKN	Société Nationale de Crédit à l'Industrie – Nationale Maatschappij voor Krediet aan de Nijverheid
SNECMA	Société Nationale d'Etudes et de Construction de Moteurs d'Aviation
SNI–NIM	Société Nationale d'Investissement – Nationale Investeringsmaatschappij
SNSN–NMNS	Société Nationale de Restructuration des Secteurs Nationaux – Nationale Maatschappij voor de Herstructurering van de Nationale Sectoren
SNT–NMT	Société Nationale pour la Textile et la Confection – Nationale Maatschappij voor Textiel en Confectie
SOBAKI	Compagnie Belgo-Africaine du Kivu
SOBELVER	Société Belge des Verreries
SOCFIN	Société Financière des Caoutchoucs
SOFINA	Société Financière de Transports et d'Entreprises Industrielles
SOGECHIM	Société Générale Industrielle et Chimique du Katanga
SOLVIC	SA pour l'Industrie des Matières Plastiques
SOPARA	Société de Participations de la Rayonne
SOPRINA	Société Privée d'Investissement
SPEP	Société Parisienne d'Entreprises et de Participations
SPIE	Société Parisienne pour l'Industrie Electrique
SRIs–GIMs	Sociétés Régionales d'Investissement – Gewestelijke Investeringsmaatschappijen
STAB	Svenska Tändsticks Aktie Bolaget

SYBELAC	Syndicat Belge de l'Acier
SYBETRA	Syndicat Belge des Travaux
TABACOFINA	Union Financière Belge des Tabacs
TANKS	Tanganyika Concessions Ltd
TMM	Forges de Thy-Marcinelle et Monceau
TRACTEBEL	Verenigde Maatschappijen Electrobel en Tractionel
TRACTIONEL	Société de Traction et d'Electricité
UAP	Union des Assurances de Paris
UCB	Union Chimique Belge
UCE–LINALUX	Union de Centrales Electriques – Liège–Namur–Luxembourg–Hainaut
UCO	Union Cotonnière
UCOSIDER	Union Commerciale de la Sidérurgie Belge
UFIL	Union Financière et Industrielle Liégeoise
UFIMAR	Société Union Financière et Maritime
UNEBECE	Union des Utilisateurs et Négociants Belges de Charbon
UNRRA	United Nations Relief and Rehabilitation Administration
UTEXBEL	Usines Textiles Réunies de Belgique
UTM	Usines à Tubes de la Meuse
VEV	Vlaamsch Economisch Verbond
VNU	Verenigde Nederlandse Uitgeversbedrijven NV
VU	Volksunie

EDITOR'S INTRODUCTION

By comparison with the nineteenth century, the twentieth has been very much more turbulent, both economically and politically. Two world wars and a great depression are sufficient to substantiate this claim without invoking the problems of more recent times. Yet despite these setbacks Europe's economic performance in the present century has been very much better than anything recorded in the historical past, thanks largely to the super-boom conditions following the post-Second World War reconstruction period. Thus in the period 1946–75, or 1950–73, the annual increase in total European GNP per capita was 4.8 and 4.5 per cent respectively, as against a compound rate of just under 1 per cent in the nineteenth century (1800–1913) and the same during the troubled years between 1913–50. As Bairoch points out, within a generation or so European per capita income rose slightly more than in the previous 150 years (1947–75 by 250 per cent, 1800–1948 by 225 per cent) and, on rough estimates for the half-century before 1800, by about as much as in the preceding two centuries.[1]

The dynamic growth and relative stability of the 1950s and 1960s may however belie the natural order of things as the events of the later 1970s and early 1980s demonstrate. Certainly it would seem unlikely that the European economy, or the world economy for that matter, will see a lasting return to the relatively stable conditions of the nineteenth century. No doubt the experience of the present century can easily lead to an exaggerated idea about the stability of the previous one. Nevertheless, one may justifiably claim that for much of the nineteenth century there was a degree of harmony in the economic development of the major powers and between the metropolitan economies and the periphery which has been noticeably absent since 1914. Indeed, one of the reasons for the apparent success of the gold standard after 1870, despite the aura of stability it allegedly shed, was the absence of serious external disturbances and imbalance in development among the major participating powers. As Triffin writes, 'the residual harmonization of national monetary and credit policies depended far less on *ex post* corrective action, requiring an extreme flexibility, downward as well as upward, of national price and wage levels, than on an *ex ante* avoidance of substantial disparities in cost competitiveness and the monetary policies that would allow them to develop'.[2]

Whatever the reasons for the absence of serious economic and political conflict, the fact remains that up to 1914 international development and political relations, though subject to strains of a minor nature from time to time, were never exposed to internal and external shocks of the magnitude experienced in the twentieth century. Not surprisingly therefore, the First World War rudely shattered the liberal tranquility of the later nineteenth and early twentieth centuries. At the time few people realized that it was going to be a lengthy war and, even more important, fewer still had any conception of the enormous impact it would have on economic and social relationships. Moreover, there was a general feeling, readily accepted in establishment circles, that following the period of hostilities it would be possible to resume where one had left off – in short, to recreate the conditions of the pre-war era.

For obvious reasons this was clearly an impossible task, though for nearly a decade statesmen strove to get back to what they regarded as 'normalcy', or the natural order of things. In itself this was one of the profound mistakes of the first postwar decade since it should have been clear, even at that time, that the war and post-war clearing-up operations had undermined Europe's former equipoise and sapped her strength to a point where the economic system had become very sensitive to external shocks. The map of Europe had been redrawn under the political settlements following the war and this further weakened the economic viability of the continent and left a dangerous political vacuum in its wake. Moreover, it was not only in the economic sphere that Europe's strength had been reduced; in political and social terms the European continent was seriously weakened and many countries in the early postwar years were in a state of social ferment and upheaval.[3]

Generally speaking, Europe's economic and political fragility was ignored in the 1920s, probably more out of ignorance than intent. In their efforts to resurrect the pre-war system statesmen believed they were providing a viable solution to the problems of the day, and the fact that Europe shared in the prosperity of the later 1920s seemed to vindicate their judgement. But the postwar problems – war debts, external imbalances, currency issues, structural distortions and the like – defied solutions along traditional lines. The most notable of these was the attempt to restore a semblance of the gold standard in the belief that it had been responsible for the former stability. The upshot was a set of haphazard and inconsistent currency stabilization policies which took no account of the changes in relative costs and prices among countries since 1914. Consequently, despite the apparent prosperity of the latter half of the decade, Europe remained in a state of unstable equilibrium, and therefore vulnerable to any external shocks. The collapse of American foreign lending from the middle of 1928 and the subsequent downturn of the American economy a year later exposed the weaknesses of the European economy. The structural supports were too weak to withstand violent shocks and so the edifice disintegrated.

That the years 1929–1932/33 experienced one of the worst depressions and financial crises in history is not altogether surprising given the convergence of many unfavourable forces at that point in time. Moreover, the fact that a cyclical downturn occurred against the backdrop of structural disequilibrium only served to exacerbate the problem, while the inherent weakness of certain financial institutions in Europe and the USA led to extreme instability. The intensity of the crisis varied a great deal but few countries, apart from the USSR, were unaffected. The action of governments tended to aggravate rather than ease the situation. Such policies included expenditure cuts, monetary contraction, the abandonment of the gold standard and protective measures designed to insulate domestic economies from external events. In effect these policies, while sometimes affording temporary relief to hard-pressed countries, in the end led to income destruction rather than income creation. When recovery finally began in the winter of 1932/33 it owed little to policy contributions, though subsequently some western governments did attempt more ambitious programmes of stimulation, while many of the poorer eastern European countries adopted autarchic policies in an effort to push forward industrialization. Apart from some notable exceptions, Germany and Sweden in particular, recovery from the slump, especially in terms of employment generation, was slow and patchy and even at the peak of the upswing in 1937 many countries were still operating below their resource capacity. A combination of weak real growth forces and structural imbalances in development would no doubt have ensured a continuation of resource under-utilization had not rearmament and the outbreak of war served to close the gap.

Thus, on the eve of the Second World War Europe as a whole was in a much weaker state economically than it had been in 1914, with her shares of world income and trade notably reduced. Worse still, she emerged from the war in 1945 in a more prostrate condition than in 1918, with output levels well down on those of the pre-war period. In terms of the loss of life, physical destruction and decline in living standards Europe's position was much worse than after the First World War. On the other hand, recovery from wartime destruction was stronger and more secure than in the previous case. In part this can be attributed to the fact that in the reconstruction phase of the later 1940s some of the mistakes and blunders of the earlier experience were avoided. Inflation, for example, was contained more readily between 1939 and 1945 and the violent inflations of the early 1920s were not for the most part perpetuated after the Second World War. With the exception of Berlin, the map of Europe was divided much more cleanly and neatly than after 1918. Though it resulted in two ideological power blocs, the East and the West, it did nevertheless dispose of the power vacuum in Central/ Eastern Europe which had been a source of friction and contention in the interwar years. Moreover, the fact that each bloc was dominated or backed by a wealthy and rival super-power meant that support was forthcoming for the satellite countries. The vanquished powers were not, with the exception of East Germany, burdened by unreasonable exactions which had been the cause of so much bitterness and squabbling during the 1920s. Finally, governments no longer hankered after the 'halcyon' pre-war days, not surprisingly given the rugged conditions of the 1930s. This time it was to be planning for the future which occupied their attention, and which found expression in the commitment to maintain full employment and all that entailed in terms of growth and stability, together with a conscious desire to build upon the earlier social welfare foundations. In wider perspective, the new initiatives found positive expression in terms of readiness to co-operate internationally, particularly in trade and monetary matters. The liberal American aid programme for the West in the later 1940s was a concrete manifestation of this new approach.

Thus despite the enormity of the reconstruction task facing

Europe at the end of the war, the recovery effort, after some initial difficulties, was both strong and sustained, and by the early 1950s Europe had reached a point where she could look to the future with some confidence. During the next two decades or so virtually every European country, in keeping with the buoyant conditions in the world economy as a whole, expanded very much more rapidly than in the past. This was the super-growth phase during which Europe regained a large part of the relative losses incurred between 1914 and 1945. The Eastern bloc countries forged ahead the most rapidly under their planned regimes, while the western democracies achieved their success under mixed enterprise systems with varying degrees of market freedom. In both cases the state played a far more important role than hitherto, and neither system could be said to be without its problems. The planning mechanism in Eastern Europe never functioned as smoothly as originally anticipated by its proponents, and in due course most of the socialist countries were forced to make modifications to their systems of control Similarly, the semi-market systems of the West did not always produce the right results so that governments were obliged to intervene to an increasing extent. One of the major problems encountered by the demand-managed economies of the West was that of trying to achieve a series of basically incompatible objectives simultaneously – namely full employment, price stability, growth and stability and external equilibrium. Given the limited policy weapons available to governments this proved an impossible task to accomplish in most cases, though West Germany managed to achieve the seemingly impossible for much of the period.

Although these incompatible objectives proved elusive *in toto*, there was, throughout most of the period to the early 1970s, little cause for serious alarm. It is true that there were minor lapses from full employment; fluctuations still occurred but they were very moderate and took the form of growth cycles; some countries experienced periodic balance of payments problems while prices generally rose continuously though at fairly modest annual rates. But such lapses could readily be accommodated, even with the limited policy choices, within an economic system that was growing rapidly. And there was some consolation from the fact that the planned socialist economies were not immune from some of these problems, especially later on in the period. By the later 1960s, despite some warning signs that conditions might be deteriorating, it seemed that Europe had entered a phase of perpetual prosperity not dissimilar to the one the Americans had conceived in the 1920s. Unfortunately, as in the earlier case, this illusion was to be rudely shattered in the first half of the 1970s. The super-growth phase of the postwar period culminated in the somewhat feverish and speculative boom of 1972–3. By the following year the growth trend had been reversed, the old business cycle had reappeared and most countries were experiencing inflation at higher rates than at any time in the past half-century. From that time onwards, according to Samuel Brittan, 'everything seems to have gone sour and we have had slower growth, rising unemployment, faster inflation, creeping trade restrictions and all the symptoms of stagflation'.[4] In fact, compared with the relatively placid and successful decades of the 1950s and 1960s, the later 1970s and early 1980s were extremely turbulent, reminiscent in some respects of the interwar years.

It should of course be stressed that by comparison with the interwar years or even with the nineteenth century, economic growth has been quite respectable since the sharp boom and contraction in the first half of the 1970s. It only appears poor in relation to the rapid growth between 1950 and 1973 and the question arises as to whether this period should be regarded as somewhat abnormal with the shift to a lower growth profile in the 1970s being the inevitable consequence of long-term forces invoking some reversal of the special growth promoting factors of the previous decades. In effect this would imply some weakening of real growth forces in the 1970s which was aggravated by specific factors, for example energy crises and policy variables.

The most disturbing feature of this later period was not simply that growth slowed down but that it became more erratic, with longer recessionary periods involving absolute contractions in output, and that it was accompanied by mounting unemployment and high inflation. Traditional Keynesian demand management policies were unable to cope with these problems and, in an effort to deal with them, particularly inflation, governments resorted to ultra-defensive policies and monetary control. These were not very successful either since the need for social and political compromise in policy-making meant that they were not applied rigorously enough to eradicate inflation, yet at the same time their influence was sufficiently strong to dampen the rate of growth thereby exacerbating unemployment. In other words, economic management was faced with an awkward policy dilemma in the prevailing situation of high unemployment and rapid inflation. Policy action to deal with either one tended to make the other worse, while the constraint of the political concensus produced an uneasy compromise in an effort to 'minimise macroeconomic misery'.[5] Rostow has neatly summarized the constraints involved in this context: 'Taxes, public expenditure, interest rates, and the supply of money are not determined antiseptically by men free to move economies along a Phillips curve to an otpimum trade-off between the rate of unemployment and the rate of inflation. Fiscal and monetary policy are, inevitably, living parts of the democratic political process.'[6]

Since the 1970s governments have had to wrestle with a host of problems including inflation, budgetary deficits, unemployment and renewed recession, but they have not been able to recreate the success of the immediate postwar decades. Indeed, it may be that governments are powerless, as they were in the 1930s, to solve such problems if the underlying forces of growth remain weak and at a time when the expectations of people in terms of income growth and the provision of collective goods and welfare services exceeds the delivery potential of the economies in question. In a different context the former socialist economies of Eastern Europe had their problems and eventually these resulted in the disintegration of the regimes. In view of the current problems of western nations the transition to market capitalism may not have come at the most propitious time.

It is not however the purpose of the volumes in this series to speculate about the future. The series is designed to provide clear and balanced surveys of the economic development and problems of individual European countries from the end of the First World War through to the present, against the background of the general economic and political trends of the time. Though most of the European countries have shared a common experience for much of the period, it is nonetheless true that there has been considerable variation among countries in the rate of development and the manner in which they have sought to regulate and control their economies. The problems encountered have also varied widely, in part reflecting disparities in levels of development. While most European countries had, by the end of the First World War, achieved some measure of industrialization and made the initial breakthrough into modern economic growth, there nevertheless existed a wide gulf between the richer and poorer nations. At the beginning of the period northwest Europe, including Scandinavia, was by far the most advanced region and as one moved south and east so the level of development and per capita income declined. In some cases, notably Bulgaria, Yugoslavia and Portugal, income levels were a third or less of those in the more advanced countries and barely one half the European average. The gap has tended to narrow over time but the general pattern remains basically the same. Between 1913 and the early 1970s most of the poorer countries in the south and east (apart from Spain) raised their real per capita income levels relative to the European average, with most of the improvement taking place after 1950. Even so, many countries still fell below the European average which in the case of Spain, Portugal, Romania and Yugoslavia was as much as 35–45 per cent.[7]

The present volume deals with a country which industrialized early and achieved a high level of income by 1913. Belgium's experience in the twentieth century has been more chequered however. Because of the small domestic market Belgium has been very dependent on international trade. With a trade income ratio of 55 per cent in 1980 comparative efficiency was of crucial importance in maintaining market share. In this context the interwar period was not a happy time for the Belgian economy given the stagnation in international trade and the fact that the economy suffered from dependence on traditional low-value, cyclically prone heavy sectors and misguided government policy in the 1930s which adversely affected their competitiveness. Performance in the super boom years of the 1950s and 1960s was somewhat weaker than that of her main European trading partners, which can be partly attributed to lack of competitiveness due to the slow adaptation of the industrial structure and high wage levels. In some respects Belgium's problems were not dissimilar to those of contemporary Great Britain.

NOTES

1 P. Bairoch, 'Europe's Gross National Product: 1800–1975', *The Journal of European Economic History* (Fall, 1976), pp. 298–9.
2 R. Triffin, *Our International Monetary System: Yesterday, Today and Tomorrow* (New York: Random House, 1968), p. 14; see also D.H. Aldcroft, *From Versailles to Wall Street, 1919–1929* (London: Allen Lane, 1977), pp. 162–4. Some of the costs of the gold standard system may however have been borne by the countries of the periphery, for example Latin America.
3 See P.N. Stearns, *European Society in Upheaval* (New York: Macmillan, 1967).
4 *Financial Times*, 14 February 1980.

5 J.O.N. Perkins, *The Macroeconomic Mix to Stop Stagflation* (London: Macmillian, 1980).
6 W.W. Rostow, *Getting From Here to There* (London: Macmillian, 1979).
7 See Bairoch op. cit., pp. 297, 307.

INTRODUCTION

O friends, not these sounds!
Let us sing something more pleasant,
more full of gladness.

> Friedrich von Schiller

With its 30,500 square km and its 10 million inhabitants Belgium belongs to the category of the small European powers. Since the foundation of the Belgian State in 1830 the total population has doubled and the agrarian character of the nation has disappeared. Nowadays less than 3 per cent of the population works in agriculture

In September 1830 a liberal revolution swept away the Dutch king's autocratic power. Because the revolutionary leaders had opted for a constitutional monarchy Belgium's political and economic reforms soon reflected its capitalist transformation. As industry developed, imports of raw materials (wool, cotton, iron and zinc ore) increased. Meanwhile coal became the very backbone of heavy industry in Wallonia where blast furnaces and rolling mills were built in the Meuse and Sambre Basins. This industrial development was generously financed by big banks with a 'mixed character'. Of them, the Société Générale de Belgique and the Banque de Belgique played a dominant role in the metal and coal industries.

The Société Générale, founded in 1822 by the Dutch King Willem I, constituted an important centre of decision in Belgian politics. After the Revolution of 1830 Willem's bank remained the only Belgian bank of national importance, issuing notes and playing the role of Treasurer. Liberal politicians and bankers fearing this concentration of so much power founded the competing Banque de Belgique in 1839. But the cyclical business made both 'mixed banks' vulnerable to liquidity crises, making it difficult for banks to convert their 'frozen loans' into shares. During the slump of the 1840s both banks had to be floated by the Belgian government. Then the Liberal government led by Walthère Frère-Orban established the National Bank of Belgium, a circulation bank discounting commercial paper.

Belgian industrialists specializing in steel and heavy equipment were interested in exporting their products to the more developed areas of the capitalist periphery instead of looking for protected colonial markets in Africa where King Léopold II had built his empire. Describing Belgian entrepreneurship in Russia the American historian John P. McKay describes how Belgian tramway companies operated when acquiring concessions:

> The streetcar companies, normally Belgian, were all based upon concessions from Russian municipalities to operate either horse-drawn tramways in the early 1880s or, more importantly, electrically powered trams from 1890 onward. Almost invariably entrepreneurship involved the following steps. First, representatives of leading Belgian equipment makers, who were very disposed to foreign investment, received leads from Russian businessmen (or city councilmen). Then promising opportunities were investigated thoroughly. Finally after more negotiating a concession was perhaps granted and a separate firm was founded to exploit it. By 1911 this process resulted in twenty-three Belgian streetcar companies in Russia with annual revenues of 38,000,000 francs.
>
> (McKay 1970: 100)

Banking syndicates provided enterprises with expensive underwriting guarantees and floated holding companies specializing in promoting and controlling city services companies and industrial firms abroad. Although all these undertakings promised high profits to their shareholders, only a minority of them were paying high annual dividends. Because all these shares were highly speculative and the companies in question were practically all established in Belgium, this portfolio investment promised their holders both a high return on investment and a high degree of liquidity. The Brussels Stock Exchange was the place where all these financial ties came together and speculators could make a fortune within a few years. Entrepreneurship abroad and unlimited speculation shaped a dynamic form of capitalism which was rather unique in the world. But stability in industrial affairs was granted by industrial firms, management and bankers who provided this system with enough innovative and creative talents. Between 1890 and 1914 this form of capitalist expansion acquired its highest stage and shaped the very structure of Belgian capitalism based on heavy industry, rolling-stock factories and a continuous capital flux to industrializing countries, promoted by banking syndicates, financial intermediaries and specialist holding companies. Directors of big industrial firms and bankers were controlling these operations and constituted networks of agents prospecting for investment opportunities.

The Société Générale de Belgique was still the largest and most powerful of all banks. The Banque de Belgique did not survive the slump of the 1870s and was liquidated in the 1880s. Although the Société had acquired a real influence in the steel and coal industries its influence on management remained rather limited. A mixed bank like the Société was especially interested in dividends paid by the affiliated industrial firms, not in exercising a daily influence on management decisions. This explains why directors of large industrial firms were able to decide quasi-autonomously when investing in additional production capacity or modernizing their production units. Specialist holding companies operated as financial intermediaries and delegated their representatives to the board of directors of the firms in which they held a stake. But in general all these firms remained independent and directives coming from the shareholders only concerned dividend payments. The Brussels-based holding companies were headed by professional directors or freshly recruited engineers aware of the many technical and managerial problems they had to meet when directing expansion abroad. These holding companies and banks operated with a small administrative and technical staff. They generally appointed a delegated director (*administrateur délégué*) at home and a plant superintendent abroad. As technical problems increased and investment decisions necessitated elaborated projects and planning activities, specialist engineering firms appeared, especially in the city services sector, mining activities and turnkey projects. Most of them developed as departments of holding companies and industrial firms specializing in tramway and electricity companies.

The existence of the holding companies and mixed banks favoured financial control over a multitude of rather small factories and city services companies. Where American-style enterprise allocated resources and controlled company performance, the Belgian version raised capital for financial integration without effectively controlling production and marketing. As the American historian Richard F. Kuisel has ascertained for the case of France, many Belgian industrial conglomerates (Solvay, Empain, Cockerill) also operated as manufacturers and holding companies. As in France, holding companies were most common in chemicals, electricity, metals, and heavy industry, 'and they appeared mainly as a response to financial needs at a time of scarce capital resources . . . The holding company, however, did not represent best management practice' (Kuisel 1981: 87–8).

This is also the opinion of the Belgian economist Herman Daems who remarked that 'the holding companies are institutions for organising and structuring the corporate control market. These institutions are able to gain and hold such control because they issue securities to buy and hold "substantial" blocks of stocks (controlling interest) in operating companies and other holding companies' (Daems 1978: 3). Because the holding companies issue shares in order to hold claims in other companies, 'they offer the Belgian saver a substitution of securities: the securities of the controlled companies substituted for the holding companies' own securities' (Daems 1978: 3).

Much has been written on Belgian economic and social history, especially of the interwar period, but many aspects remain unexplored. One still has to consult the volumes written by the Belgian economist and business historian Fernand Baudhuin. However, scholars like I. Cassiers, J. Gillingham, R.L. Hogg, P. Scholliers and G. Vanthemsche have considerably enhanced our understanding of recent economic history.

ACKNOWLEDGEMENTS

Many people have contributed to the realization of this book. Marc Francken, René Lamy, Léon Masset, Jean-Baptiste Nothomb, and M. Schartz read parts of the first draft and/or gave useful comments on special topics. Without Raoul Schildmeijer's technical assistance life would have been more complicated. They all merit my gratitude.

André Mommen

1

STATE REGULATION DURING THE INTERWAR PERIOD

The First World War meant a rupture with the previous period of classical liberalism. Important changes were the generalization of social legislation, the establishment of unemployment benefits and the recognition of the principle of social justice as formulated in part XIII of the Versailles Treaty concerning universal peace and the organization of labour. Fiscal reforms completed postwar reconstruction. Meanwhile the Belgian government was confronted with monetary instability, high public debt and speculation against the Belgian franc. All these problems must be considered within the realm of a small open economy producing industrial products which had to find an outlet on the world market. Like the other European countries Belgium was striving for a rapid normalization and a return to the gold standard and pre-war currency stability.

AN OPEN ECONOMY

From the mid-nineteenth century the Belgian economy produced industrial products far in excess of the relatively small domestic market (4.3 million inhabitants in 1846; 6.7 million in 1900; 7.4 million in 1920; 8 million in 1930).

After the turn of the century products like steel, matches, dyes, rayon, rolling stock, glass and textiles were exported at a high percentage of their total output and these industries employed a large labour force (Hogg 1986: 108). The Belgian balance of trade always showed a trade deficit, but this deficit was easily compensated by returns on foreign investment, services and transit trade. After the stabilization of the Belgian franc in 1926 at a low exchange rate an export-led boom lasted until 1929. Then the economic crisis in combination with an overvalued national currency had a negative

1

impact on Belgian export chances. Again, after the devaluation of the Belgian franc in 1935 exports immediately picked up (see Table 1.1).

The Belgian government could not avoid protectionist measures, but compared with other countries, Belgian tariffs remained relatively low (see Table 1.2), except for agricultural products. After 1931 protectionist measures continued to multiply and in June 1931 legislation was passed on quotas for sugar, fertilizers and coal. Quotas were extended in 1932–3 to a wide range of agricultural products and in 1933–4 to textiles. After the devaluation of 1935 most of these protectionist measures were cancelled, but soon re-established (Hogg 1986: 112).

The Belgian historian Isabelle Cassiers points out the exceptionally high degree of openness of the Belgian economy when compared with other countries. This obliged many sectors to find an outlet for their products abroad, especially in neighbouring European and North American markets. Until 1932 the UK was Belgium's main export market, but the fall of the pound sterling narrowed Belgium's export advantages and obliged steel, glass and textile producers to slash their prices. France, with its less competitive industry, served as an outlet for Belgian products, but during the Great Depression the French government returned to protectionism. In 1932 France cancelled the 1924 trade agreement with Belgium.

Meanwhile, the development of a domestic market for products destined for mass consumption was neglected (Cassiers 1989: 207), while the deflationary policy of the early 1930s combined with mass unemployment led to underconsumption and poverty. During the early 1930s, because of deflationary measures, gross prices fell by 44 per cent, nominal costs of living by 24 per cent and wages by 23 per cent (Cassiers 1989: 162).

The international sector was heavily over-capitalized and felt the constraints of fierce competition on the world market, which obliged the entrepreneurs to compress expenditures (wages) and the big banks to finance their losses. The protected sector was less-capitalized and operated on the domestic market, where competition from imports was quasi-absent. During the Great Depression the international sector was obliged to reconquer the domestic market and to adapt its output to local demand. But in the meantime the international sector was waiting for new opportunities in order to export its semi-finished products.

Table 1.1 The Belgian balance of trade, 1919–38
(in million Belgian francs and million tonnes)

	Import		Export	
	Weight	Value	Weight	Value
1919	4,769	5,246	6,908	2,300
1920	13,347	12,942	10,623	8,862
1921	17,765	10,198	17,257	7,273
1922	21,074	9,229	16,436	6,234
1923	26,603	13,205	16,974	9,725
1924	33,412	17,712	20,368	13,865
1925	33,265	17,881	20,924	14,807
1926	34,305	23,063	23,203	19,999
1927	38,061	29,139	24,222	26,697
1928	39,868	32,060	26,749	30,954
1929	45,074	35,624	25,840	31,880
1930	42,227	31,094	23,768	26,159
1931	38,722	23,971	24,617	23,178
1932	31,376	16,424	19,558	15,130
1933	30,697	15,243	19,936	14,288
1934	31,726	14,021	19,986	13,698
1935	30,590	17,446	20,300	16,126
1936	32,858	21,506	21,841	19,944
1937	38,985	27,893	25,010	25,516
1938	31,555	23,167	22,008	21,724

Sources: Tableau annuel (1919–31); *Bulletin mensuel du commerce avec les pays étrangers* (1932–8)

SOCIAL REFORMS

After the First World War employers and the government recognized the existence of trade unions. The Act of 24 May 1921 declared article 310 of the Penal Code abrogated, and strikes were no longer considered as criminal acts. But another act promulgated on the same day declared illegal any attempt to install compulsory membership in a trade union or in an entrepreneurial organization. The Law of 14 June 1921 introduced the 8-hour working day and the 48-hour working week. It was not until the General Strike of June 1936 that the government agreed on the principle of the 40-hour week in those industries where working conditions were characterized as unhealthy and difficult (Neuville 1981: *passim*). Until the First World War there was no comprehensive social security system, but the introduction of a system of full social

Table 1.2 Absolute height of potential tariff levels, 1927–31
(in percentages of prices)

	(1)		(2)		(3)		(4)	
	1927	1931	1927	1931	1927	1931	1927	1931
Germany	27.4	82.5	14.5	23.4	19.0	18.3	20.4	40.7
France	19.1	53.0	24.3	31.8	25.8	29.0	23.0	38.0
Italy	24.5	66.0	28.6	49.5	28.3	41.8	27.8	48.3
Belgium	11.8	23.7	10.5	15.5	11.6	13.0	11.0	17.4
Switzerland	21.5	42.2	11.5	15.2	17.6	22.0	16.8	26.4
Sweden	21.5	39.0	18.0	18.0	20.8	23.5	20.0	26.8

(1) Foodstuffs
(2) Semi-manufactured goods
(3) Industrial manufactured goods
(4) General

Source: Hogg 1986: 111

insurance had already been studied, starting from the idea of a compulsory insurance system based on a triple contribution scheme (State, employers, employees). After 1919 several bills were passed in order to cover practically all the major social risks (Chlepner 1972: 300–14).

During the First World War a Comité de Secours et d'Alimentation had functioned in order to provide the poor with food. After the war this relief fund had to stop its activities, but the principle of public assistance to the poor or the unemployed had gained acceptance justifying an increased intervention of the State in social affairs (Vanthemsche 1989: 19–25). In June 1920 a bill standardizing a compulsory system of unemployment insurance based on the existing union unemployment funds was passed. The entire benefit system was headed by a National Crisis Fund (Fonds National de Crise). Non-union unemployment funds also emerged and public sector funds were established, but the union funds accounted for 97 per cent of all insured workers (Vanthemsche 1990: 349–76). There was also a steady growth of union membership. On the eve of the Great Depression one-third of the 1,850,000 manual and non-manual workers was unionized (Chlepner 1972: 257–81; Vanthemsche 1989: 27).

Towards the end of the 1920s Belgium experienced an economic upturn. As a result of the booming economy unemployment was very low and the costs of unemployment insurance were insignificant. This changed after 1930 because the state had to allocate huge sums to the unemployment insurance system. The employers' organization Comité Central Industriel (CCI), which represented heavy industry in Wallonia, was pressing the government for the reduction of benefits payments and a tightening of conditions for eligibility. The municipal unemployment funds were replaced by regional funds which stood under the direct control of the central government. At the end of 1934 some 23 per cent of all insured workers were unemployed (see Table 1.3).

Table 1.3 Unemployment: daily averages of secured unemployed, 1921–39 (in December)

Year	(1)	%	(2)	%	(3)	(4)
1921	49,851	6.6	36,232	4.8	86,083	756,516
1922	11,743	1.7	14,312	2.1	26,055	686,429
1923	11,017	1.7	12,550	1.9	23,567	656,708
1924	9,844	1.5	23,410	3.6	33,254	642,695
1925	16,897	2.8	27,494	4.6	44,391	600,571
1926	15,804	2.6	17,889	3.0	33,693	604,589
1927	22,526	3.6	35,006	5.6	57,532	621,355
1928	11,988	1.9	28,218	4.5	40,206	631,379
1929	15,761	2.5	29,309	4.6	45,070	640,375
1930	63,540	9.2	117,519	17.0	181,059	693,045
1931	129,380	17.0	164,099	21.6	293,479	761,239
1932	171,028	18.6	155,699	16.9	326,727	919,873
1933	194,279	19.8	163,537	16.7	357,816	980,406
1934	212,713	22.3	167,562	17.5	380,275	955,464
1935	162,166	18.0	102,174	11.3	264,340	901,104
1936	131,565	14.4	92,619	10.2	224,184	911,146
1937	136,298	14.9	147,510	16.1	283,808	916,463
1938	167,145	16.9	232,788	23.6	399,933	986,956
1939	175,644	17.3	136,434	13.4	312,078	1,015,514

(1) Completely unemployed
(2) Partly unemployed
(3) Total unemployed
(4) Total insured people
Source: Vanthemsche 1989: 277–83

Conservatives and Liberals then discussed the abolition of the union unemployment funds, but the Christian Democrats refused. In 1935, when a coalition government led by Paul Van Zeeland came to power with the help of the Socialists, the debate on the suppression of the trade union unemployment funds suddenly lost its political opportunity. After the General Strike of June 1936 the government appointed the Socialist Henri Fuss as Royal Commissioner for Unemployment and asked him to study the unemployment problem. In 1937 Fuss reported in favour of a state insurance system, but in Parliament a clear majority passed a bill confirming the role of the trade union unemployment funds as the pivotal institution of a compulsory system. Due to the opposition by the Conservatives and the employer organizations the bill was blocked in the Senate. Thus, at the outbreak of the Second World War, the problem of the unemployment funds remained unsolved (Vanthemsche 1989: 153–82).

REGULATING PRICES AND WAGES

During the period immediately after the First World War the Belgian government was confronted with high prices and bad social conditions. Controlling prices and wages became an urgent question and in 1919 the Minister of Industry, Labour and Food Supply, the Socialist Joseph Wauters immediately promulgated a decree establishing maximum prices for all important food products. Another decree protected the tenants from their landlords and kept rents lower than the inflation rate until a Conservative government liberated the market in 1929 and provoked a phenomenal rents explosion. Aiming to lower the rhythm of inflation, the government also abolished all duties on the import of cattle and meat and imposed high taxes on alcoholic beverages. The overall effect was a slowing-down of the inflationary trend. The government and the trade unions co-operated in order to prevent a wage explosion by pressing the entrepreneurs to accept a system of collective bargaining and collective agreements fixing wages for all industrial and clerical workers, because collective agreements could protect the workers from the consequences of a sudden recession (Scholliers 1985: *passim*).

Notwithstanding all these stabilizing institutional mechanisms the wage-earners were threatened by inflation and the subsequent erosion of their purchasing power. The answer to that danger was the indexation of wages to retail prices. Although the indexation of wages to fluctuating prices became a technique in order to avoid strikes and to contain social demands within the limits of market fluctuations, the employers did not react with great enthusiasm when the system was first introduced in 1920. It was only a few years later that they adhered to the system of indexation of wages to retail prices. Thus a consensus grew that systemic stabilizers such as automatic price compensation could prevent the economy from wage inflation and growing sectoral imbalances. The government, which was also the largest employer, played a major role in this process of consensus building. In fact the system conquered its own dynamic, taming the trade unions and making the workers more dependent on their delegates in the bipartite committees. The government, which remained de facto an outsider in this process of collective bargaining, played a technical role by defining and discussing modalities of the indexation (Scholliers 1985: *passim*).

Bipartite bargaining and indexation of wages did not alter the distribution of national income. Research has shown that during the 1920s capital income grew extremely fast in comparison to wage income and to entrepreneurial income (Peeters et al. 1986: *passim*). Among farmers, livestock producers doubled their income while the income of producers of crops stagnated or decreased. Income from dividends, rents, deposits, and property tripled. Wages and pensions of all categories of workers and employees kept pace with the increase of income from capital and real estate (Peeters et al. 1986: *passim*). But after 1930 income from labour and professional activities declined sharply while capital income accrued to private persons maintained its pre-crisis level until 1935. Between 1928 and 1933 income from rent doubled and income from dividends, bonuses and donations increased by 40 per cent. These figures prove that the boom of the 1920s was due to a speculative move fed by indebtedness. The owners of bonds, real estate and bank deposits easily increased their income during the first years of the Depression, while the entrepreneurs, peasants, wage-earners and civil servants lost ground. After 1935 a new equilibrium was reached when the government broke with the policy of deflation (Peeters et al. 1986: *passim*).

GERMAN REPARATION PAYMENTS

During the First World War the gold reserves and the securities of the National Bank were transferred to London. Meanwhile the German Governor General in Brussels had dismissed the Governor of the National Bank and withdrew the right of issue. The expenses of the German administration and German soldiers brought a considerable amount of Reichsbank notes into Belgium, payable in marks and issued at the rate of 1.25 francs for 1 mark. After the

Armistice the total circulation of Belgian notes reached 2,800 million francs. But there were also the German marks in circulation issued at the rate of 1.25 francs. The Belgian government stipulated that the redemption of these marks should occur at the rate of 1.25 francs. With the view to a reduction of the fiduciary circulation, the government decided to issue a loan in order to absorb the marks in circulation in Belgium. The exact figure of the marks exchanged for francs reached 6,109 million marks at the rate of 1.25 francs. The government was hoping that the Germans would repay at the original rate and accept any exchange losses which might result (Hogg 1986: 15; Van der Wee and Tavernier 1975: 35–9). But the exchange operation was soon considered to be a monetary disaster. People could present their marks for reimbursement during a one-month period. This resulted in fraudulent operations, with the bringing of marks into Belgium (Lemoine 1929: 194–9).

At Versailles the Belgian government tried to have the repayment of the marks held by the National Bank recognized by the Allies (Marks 1981: *passim*). But the British government remained hostile to the Belgian demands. The result was that the Belgian government introduced war inflation into its economy (Van der Wee and Tavernier 1975: 40). There was also the question of the German reparation payments due to the destruction of the communications channels and the seizure and transportation into Germany of all Belgian industrial equipment. The total of damages caused by German war activities in Belgium amounted to 19,982 million francs (Depoortere 1989: 748–69). Meanwhile the Belgian government began the reconstruction of the country on a large scale, implemented social legislation, the 8-hour day, pension schemes and wage increases. But the conviction that the Germans would pay for the reconstruction of the country received a severe blow in 1923 when the Ruhr occupation made it clear that the affair of the reparation payments would reinforce the monetary instability of Belgium (Van der Wee and Tavernier 1975: 54–8). Although spending programmes designed to restore the capital infrastructure could be financed by loans, the Belgian government preferred to transfer items of its current expenditures to the investment budget. Meanwhile short-term borrowing grew from 3,900 million Belgian francs in 1922 to 5,400 million Belgian francs in 1925 and 6,000 million Belgian francs in 1926. In order to raise higher tax incomes, the government shifted from indirect taxation to personal income taxes, which constituted a fiscal revolution (Van der Wee and

Tavernier 1975: 34). The government was striving to balance the ordinary budget while incorporating therein expenditures that, on account of peculiar postwar circumstances, had been incorporated in the budget of recoverable expenses, or in the special budget. The budget of recoverable expenses consisted of the advances of the Belgian State to the war victims.

THE MONETARY CRISIS OF 1926

The Belgian franc having stabilized at 107 to the British pound, the Poullet–Vandervelde government (a coalition government of Socialists and Christian Democrats) submitted a bill on 12 November 1925 to strengthen fiduciary circulation and monetary stabilization. The bill was based economically on a de facto establishment of the gold exchange standard. To furnish sufficient cover for fiduciary circulation, the Belgian government contracted a foreign loan of 150 million US dollars, which, converted into foreign exchange, served both to redeem the national debt to the National Bank and to meet demands for gold or foreign currency for foreign payments. The balance of the debt to the State was to be paid through an accounting operation: the revaluation of the gold reserve of the institution of issue. The bill stipulated that the stabilization rate would be fixed by royal decree determined in the cabinet, as well as a prolongation of the privilege of the bank of issue. The course of the respective exchanges made it possible to make the Belgian franc independent of the French franc. The attempt failed. The foreign loan promised by J.P. Morgan was not granted. Under circumstances that have remained obscure, panic spread abroad and J.P. Morgan reasoned that the Belgian government had to balance the budget before a stabilization programme could be launched (Burk 1989: 136–9) at a time when the Belgian government was confronted with increasing difficulties to finance its expenditures even on a short-term basis (Vanthemsche 1978: *passim*; Van der Wee and Tavernier 1975: 120–1; Hogg 1986: 17–18).

The Belgian government failed to stabilize the floating debt. This failure was caused by a campaign against it led by the political Right and the reluctance expressed by Belgian private bankers to consolidate Belgium's floating debt. Belgian private banks were also responsible for the heavy selling of Treasury bills at the moment when the government was trying to stabilize the Belgian franc. It was widely known that the private bankers simply opposed the

9

existence of a coalition government of Socialists and Christian Democrats. The Poullet–Vandervelde government had no other choice than to resign (Vanthemsche 1978: 165–214). On 25 May 1926 a new coalition government was formed. This was a government of National Unity including politicians from the Liberal Party and the Catholic Right, formed with the help of the Belgian banks. The key minister was the banker Emile Francqui (Société Générale de Belgique – SGB) who proposed a new stabilization programme. The Francqui government decided to raise 1,500 million Belgian francs in new taxes, to be placed in a sinking fund for the public debt. As it was necessary to insure resources for the sinking fund immediately, it was decided to use one of the State's assets: the railways which heretofore were state-managed. The Société Nationale des Chemins de Fer Belges – Nationale Maatschappij der Belgische Spoorwegen (SNCB–NMBS) was formed, responsible for the operation of the State railways, with a capital of 11 billion Belgian francs, 10 billion Belgian francs of which was represented by preferred stock and 1 billion Belgian francs by registered and non-transferable common stock. The total stock was returned to the State in remuneration for the right of operation granted to the association; it kept the common stock, but transferred the preferred stock to the sinking fund, with instructions to negotiate it or exchange it for Treasury bonds (Ranieri 1985: 214–18: Van der Wee and Tavernier 1975: 149–212).

Francqui did not want to stabilize the exchange rate of the Belgian franc until his monetary reform had been completed. On 31 July 1926 the Treasury Minister, a new post which duplicated that of Minister of Finance and which was held by Francqui, decided on the forced consolidation of the six-month Treasury bonds and five-year bonds maturing on 1 December 1926 into preferred stock of the SNCB–NMBS. The National Bank of Belgium at the same time restored and increased its exchange reserve, and the government redeemed certain provisory credits (Hogg 1986: 20). The politicians of the Right accepted all the measures Francqui proposed and on 23 October 1926 a loan of a 100 million dollars was obtained. On 25 October 1926 a royal decree stabilized the franc at 175 Belgian francs to the pound sterling. As a consequence of the devaluation Belgian industry received a competitive advantage in export markets. Because demand for Belgian industrial products was elastic and the markets were growing, profits could rise and generate cash to be invested in industry. But the boom that followed the devaluation of 1926 did not provoke substantial qualitative mutations. Belgian industry prospered without adapting its structure to new technologies because ineffiencies were not penalized at a time when the public preferred investing its savings in shares instead of State bonds (Hogg 1986: 21).

Francqui's policy rested equally on the principle of the gold exchange standard, on the repayment of the national debt to the National Bank by means of a loan in foreign currencies intended to reinforce the cover of the notes, and on a revaluation of the gold held in the vaults of the National Bank. A loan of 100 million US dollars was negotiated with an international group including Baring Brothers, the Westminster Bank, J.P. Morgan and Co., Hope and Co., the Swiss Banking Association and the Stockholm Enskilda Bank (Lemoine 1929: 204).

THE BANKS AND THE BELGIAN ECONOMY

The Belgian banking system could be characterized by the preponderance of banks established in Brussels, by the complete absence of concentration and their individualism, by the mixed character of their operations and their relations to industry. Most of the Belgian banks granted advances liberally to their industrial customers on current accounts and the most important of them also participated in their stock capital. Banks were represented on the boards of directors of the industrial companies and were in permanent contact with their customers (Chlepner 1930: *passim*; Daems 1978: 3–5; Durviaux 1947: *passim*; Van der Valk 1932: *passim*).

In Brussels a few big banks monopolized all important financial transactions and they left regional commercial operations to a large number of provincial banks. Apart from the banks, financial trusts or holding companies (for the most part offshoots of the banks) helped industry to expand abroad. Because Belgian banks possessed only a relatively insignificant number of branches in foreign countries, several Belgian banks created holding companies when investing in urban transportation, railway companies, lighting, etc. Financial services for these holding companies were carried on in Belgium by the parent banks.

Before the First World War only the powerful SGB had created a chain of dependent banks or banks that it supported in the provincial towns and that enabled the bank to reconcile its interests with those of the industrialists. Meanwhile the Crédit Anversois and the

Crédit Général Liégeois chose to establish local branches. Medium-sized local banks, notaries and stockbrokers played an important role in mortgage loans and issues of securities, either on their own account or as intermediaries of the banks. After the First World War this situation changed because co-operative savings banks spread throughout the country on the initiative of the Catholic Boerenbond (Peasants' League). Brokers and private banks adopted the corporate form. Meanwhile the SGB, the Banque de Bruxelles and the Caisse Centrale de Crédit of the Boerenbond became the 'Big Three' and their agencies spread throughout the country in order to collect savings and to place issues of public securities. Some important merchant banks like J.J. Le Grelle, Nagelmackers Fils and F.M. Philippson remained private banks and specialized in the management of funds of rich clients. Rural savings went directly to a savings bank instead of being kept at home in an old sock. Security portfolios and investments rose from 730 million Belgian francs to 4,234 million Belgian francs, due to numerous increases of capital of industrial organizations in which the banks took shares when not being able to turn the securities over to the public immediately. The shares issued by colonial firms were very successful. In the Belgian Congo some 170 colonial companies were active, with a total capital of more than 3 billion Belgian francs. But colonial expansion was largely due to the financial power of the SGB investing in mining companies and railroads. The total amount of the issues of the colonial companies reached 1 billion Belgian francs. In 1926 the income of the Belgian colonial firms in the Belgian Congo rose to 200 million Belgian francs, although many of these companies were of only recent foundation and were still in the process of organization (Lemoine 1929: 244).

Already before the First World War the portfolios of the large banks comprised numerous securities of companies with activities abroad. But the necessity to increase the capital of the national companies and international political and monetary difficulties now forced the banks to pursue a domestic strategy with increased attention to the steel industry in Belgium and in Luxembourg, where the elimination of German influence was of the highest importance.

FOREIGN BANKS

Foreign banks establishing their subsidiaries in Belgium had conquered an important part of the discount market. After the Franco-German War of 1870, a subsidiary of the Banque de Paris et des Pays-Bas (Paribas), established in Brussels, played an outstanding role as financial intermediary for the payment of the war indemnity by France to Germany. But during the interwar period the importance of Paribas declined considerably. Before the First World War German capitalists played an active role in the Belgian economy. They were devoted to large commerce in Antwerp and involved in industrial activities. In 1898 the Banque Internationale de Belgique was formed by Bleichröder and the Disconto Gesellschaft, while the Crédit Anversois was partly owned by the Darmstädter Bank. The Allgemeine Electrizitäts Gesellschaft (AEG) had conquered a predominant place in Belgium by establishing close ties with the Société Financière de Transports et d'Entreprises Industrielles (SOFINA) of Brussels. SOFINA was founded in 1898 by the Disconto Gesellschaft, the Dresdner Bank and the Gesellschaft für Electrische Unternehmungen (Liefmann 1932: 266, 270; De Boeck 1989: 21–40) and the Compagnie Hydro-électrique Anversoise was established by the Schuckert–Schaaffhausener Bankverein group.

After the First World War Belgium saw the proliferation of English and American banks, devoting themselves to discounting Belgian bankers' acceptances outside of the banks, as well as to operations regulating the exchange rate. They disposed of capital for their compatriots purchasing industrial stock and undervalued State securities. The role played by the foreign banks was considerable: grants were made to the Belgian bankers as well as to manufacturers and merchants, advances on merchandise and bank credits and banking facilities were provided, documentary acceptance credits, advances on documentary drafts, discount or rediscount Belgian commercial paper, and they entrusted deposits in Belgian francs to the local banks and facilitated the accomplishment of operations to cover the risk of changes in exchange rates. They gave their support to big industry and helped enterprises in undertaking business abroad by furnishing them with working funds, either in the form of renewable acceptance credits or by advances on current accounts. The foreign banks absorbed hundreds of millions in Treasury bonds (Lemoine 1929: 250–2). After the stabilization of the Belgian franc in 1926 American and British banks strived to develop permanent business with Belgian manufacturers. Wool and cotton manufacturers, the tobacco and chocolate industries, as well as breweries, were offered credit by British banks. Dutch banks participated in issues of capital of new companies and floated loans to Belgian steel plants, while the American automobile firms General Motors and Ford Motor Co. dealt in credit sales via British banks (Lemoine 1929: 255).

After the disappearance of German financial institutions, Belgian industrialists formed investment trusts with the help of American bankers. Solvay's Mutuelle Mobilière, Lee, Higginson and Co., White, Weld and Co., Clark, Dodge, and Co., and the Banque Philippson founded the American–Belgian Financial Corp. Similarly W.A. Harriman of New York, Niederösterreichische Skontogesellschaft of Vienna, the Banque de Bruxelles, the Union Européenne Industrielle et Foncière de Paris, and the Comptoire d'Escompte de Genève founded the Central European Investment Company (a holding company issuing bonds in the USA). Total American industrial investment in Belgium amounted to between 50 and 60 million dollars at that time (Lemoine 1929: 255).

THE BELGIAN HOLDING COMPANIES

The development of the Belgian holding companies was intimately connected with the export of rolling stock and street railway systems. A considerable number of street railway and lighting companies founded by Belgian stockholders had proliferated abroad. These companies were utilizing Belgian engineers and technology and their profits were paid in the form of dividends to the Belgian stockholders. Belgian capital was invested in heavy industry in Tsarist Russia, in oil companies in Russia and Romania, and plantations in the Dutch Indies (Banque des Colonies).

The reason why mortgage operations of Belgians abroad were so popular was because of the high income from loans to developing countries. South America, and to a lesser degree Canada, received special attention from some twenty large real estate loan companies.

Founded in 1909, the Banque du Congo Belge was provided with the right of issue and a charter similar to that of the National Bank (Van de Velde 1936, 219). When the charter was granted by the Belgian government in 1911, the Banque du Congo Belge had to relinquish certain operations, such as promoting colonial firms. A

14

new bank, the Banque Commerciale du Congo took them over. Both banks retained a close relationship, establishing their branches in the same office buildings and sharing a common staff in their headquarters. In reality the Banque du Congo Belge was a subsidiary of the large Belgian private banks which preserved as founders their dominant position on its board of directors. The bank had the monopoly of issue in the colony (Van de Velde 1936: 218–26) and all decisions were taken in Brussels. The notes were not legal tender in Belgium but they could be redeemed in Brussels by the purchase of demand drafts on the Congo. A branch of the Banque du Congo Belge was established in London as early as 1914 (Van der Wee and Tavernier 1975: 50–1). The Banque du Congo Belge borrowed in London in pounds sterling and here the Colonial Treasury sold the gold from the Kilo-Moto mines. The transfers from London to the Congo amounted to about 15,500,000 pounds sterling. After the war the Congolese franc again followed the exchange rate of the Belgian franc. During the interwar period banking activities in the Belgian Congo remained of minor importance because the Belgian colonial firms kept their administrative seats in Brussels and Antwerp (Lemoine 1929: 261).

During the 1920s the idea of investing savings in stock had acquired some popularity. Although some failures had occurred during the crisis of 1926, when the fluctuation of the Belgian franc led to numerous withdrawals of deposits, everybody believed that the position of the banks was safe. In reality most of them had invested their deposits in industrial securities of firms which were also their clients. Because during the panic of 1926 many banks had been able to liquidate important parts of their industrial portfolio by selling on the stock market, the Belgian banking system had gained more prestige.

POPULAR CAPITALISM

Popular capitalism gained the favours of the peasantry and the working-class organizations and two banks now symbolized the freshly acquired vitality of the lower classes: the savings banks of the Catholic Boerenbond and the Socialist Banque Belge du Travail – Belgische Bank van de Arbeid (BBT–BBA). After the First World War the Boerenbond became an important financial and commercial trust grouping the agricultural interests of the smallholders in Flanders. Bureaux for buying and selling agricultural products spread throughout the country, making the organization of mutual credit indispensable and feasible. During the 1920s the Boerenbond had more than 100,000 members and some 900 local banks affiliated with the Boerenbond collected the savings of the Belgian farmers and financed the modernization of agricultural enterprises, the construction of low-priced dwellings, etc. The Caisse Centrale de Crédit centralized the deposits of the local branches and invested the surplus in negotiable securities (i.e. Treasury bonds). Because secrecy was the consequence of the symbiosis of the Catholic Party and the Boerenbond the public was kept uninformed of the investment policy the directors of the Boerenbond had chosen. But it was widely known that the Caisse Centrale de Crédit had a close alliance with other Catholic banks (the Volksbank van Leuven and the Algemeene Bank Vereeniging) owned by the Group of Louvain (Baudhuin 1946 (II): 184–94; Van der Wee and Verbreyt 1985: 1–147).

The co-operative groups belonging to the Belgian Labour Party (Parti Ouvrier Belge – POB) could bring their savings to the BBT–BBA, founded in 1913 by Edward Anseele. The BBT–BBA took the form of a capitalist bank and its capital was subscribed for the most part by the co-operative society Vooruit in Ghent. The role of the BBT–BBA was to create new opportunities for the savings of the co-operative organizations, the trade unions and the mutual societies of the POB. The BBT–BBA built up a significant security portfolio, including the securities of companies (colonial affairs and cotton spinning-mills) belonging to the group. It also subscribed to national loans and issued stock in the companies of its group. The expansion of the BBT–BBA depended on the confidence the local branches of the POB kept in their leaders and the profitability of the textile firms belonging to the group. In 1934 the BBT–BBA was liquidated (Baudhuin 1946 (II): 174–83).

INDUSTRIAL CREDIT

After the First World War there was a need to divert credit with medium maturity in order to finance industrial projects. The attention of Belgian bankers and industrialists was drawn to this point, especially since before the war German brokers located in Hamburg had organized the export of Belgian products. The lack of credit with medium maturity, the need for which was so great, obliged the National Bank to accept paper subject to renewal and to meet the requirements of industry to a certain extent. Medium-term credit appealed little to the private banks and in 1919 the National Bank solved the problem of furnishing the necessary capital (25 million Belgian francs) for a National Bank for Industrial Credit (Société Nationale de Crédit à l'Industrie – Nationale Maatschappij voor Krediet aan de Nijverheid – SNCI–NMKN). Until October 1926 the relations between the SNCI–NMKN and the National Bank were extremely close. The private banks entrusted to the SNCI–NMKN on a time deposit a part of their assets for which they found no use in short-term operations, and which they could not utilize for long-term investments. Due to this practice by the private banks the SNCI–NMKN had abundant funds at its disposal (Hogg 1986: 156; Lemoine 1929: 262–7).

The promotors of the SNCI–NMKN did not particularly foresee its eventual intervention in financing the indemnities to be awarded to war victims. But the government soon asked the new institution in 1919 to consent to mobilize the 5-year registered securities issued to represent advances granted on the German requisition notes. In 1924 a conference between war victims, the government and the SNCI–NMKN resulted in the creation of the Association Nationale des Industriels et Commerçants (ANIC), which had to finance the reparations for war damages by the issue of bonds. In the balance sheets of the SNCI–NMKN these bonds replaced promisory notes signed by the war victims to represent advances made to them. The SNCI–NMKN undertook the financing of several important shipments of railway equipment to foreign countries (Greece, Latin America). At a moment when the Belgian capital market was very tight, the SNCI–NMKN put its signature at the disposal of exporters, who could thus obtain advances from foreign banks. In 1926 the legal position of the SNCI–NMKN was modified under pressure by the private banks. It was separated from the National Bank and its capital was tripled. A block of 50 million shares of new stock was subscribed by the private bankers who were represented on its board. The bonds of the ANIC were taken over to the account of the State. Thus the original activity of the SNCI–NMKN was restored: financing foreign trade. Because the private bankers held a firm majority on the board of directors the SNCI–NMKN was reduced to the status of an auxiliary bank (Lemoine 1929: 262–7; Dierckx 1989: 121–86).

BUDGETARY PROBLEMS IN THE EARLY 1930s

Because the Belgian franc had been stabilized at a very low level in comparison to the pound sterling, an export-led boom occurred. The big banks gained large profits and were eager to underwrite the shares issued by the industrial firms they controlled. Between 1926 and 1929 the Belgian Treasury easily balanced its financial policy. Current expenditures were paid out of fiscal income provided by direct and indirect taxes. Public debt was consolidated and reduced to 52 billion Belgian francs and financial orthodoxy was imposed by Francqui (Ranieri 1985: 214–18). In January and July 1930 the government decided to alleviate the tax burden by some 1,600 million Belgian francs. New pension schemes for civil servants, white-collar workers, industrial workers and miners were established and two Royal Commissions prepared the launch of an investment programme aimed towards a thoroughgoing modernization of canals and roads.

But the economic crisis obliged the government to revise its budgetary policy. During 1930 the budgetary deficit rose to 1,382 million Belgian francs or 13.5 per cent of national expenditure. The Hoover moratorium of 20 June 1931 caused a severe setback for the Belgian budget. In 1929 German payments had reached some 1,072 million Belgian francs or 10 per cent of the budget. In 1932 German payments had dropped to 204 million Belgian francs. This forced the Belgian government to consider higher taxes and import duties in order to balance the budget. But the step to increased taxation was largely insufficient because of the declining economic activity and the unwillingness of people to pay more taxes. Indirect taxation had the virtue of generating a steady flow of tax income, but the government, which feared an inflatory push, was not eager to decide a substantial increase of the level of indirect taxation.

On 27 February 1932 the Renkin government decided a cut of 10 per cent on pensions and wages and the level of all taxes increased by 10 per cent, measures which were presented as 'provisional' (Van Audenhove 1980: 8). Because the government was not able to balance the budget, a new coalition government of Catholics and Liberals led by the old Conservative Comte Charles de Brocqueville was formed. In December 1932 a new act stressed the deflationary policy the government had chosen. In May 1933 de Brocqueville obtained 'special powers' from Parliament in order to introduce budgetary measures. Again, higher taxes and severe cuts were to

Table 1.4 State budget, 1929–40 (in million Belgian francs)

Year	Tax revenues	Expenditures	Balance
1929	13,802	12,278	+ 1,524
1930	11,725	13,857	− 2,132
1931	11,081	12,078	− 997
1932	10,470	11,653	− 1,183
1933	11,908	11,187	+ 721
1934	10,661	11,272	− 611
1935	15,998	13,568	+ 2,430
1936	13,502	13,847	− 345
1937	14,359	14,175	+ 184
1938	12,900	14,485	− 1,585
1939	11,417	13,798	− 2,381
1940	11,067	23,833	− 12,766

Source: Cassiers 1989: 186

balance the budget within a year, but in the summer of 1934 the government discovered that its deflationary policy had failed and that the economic crisis undermined its fiscal capacities to raise more tax income. In June 1934 the Minister of Finance, Henri Jaspar, resigned, but de Brocqueville only reformed his coalition. Again he asked for 'special powers' from Parliament. It would be de Broqueville's last term, because in November 1934 Georges Theunis formed the so-called 'government of the bankers', which aimed to defend the parity of the Belgian franc. Again this government sharpened its deflationary policy by lowering pensions and wages of civil servants. The Minister of Finance, the banker Camille Gutt, campaigned with the slogan *dégrever ou crever* (Van Audenhove 1980: 10), which referred to his basic philosophy that deflation was the pre-condition for a successful export policy (Vanthemsche 1987: 133).

Nevertheless, expenditures were stabilized at an annual level of 11 billion Belgian francs and in 1933 registered a small surplus in the current budget (see Table 1.4). But the major problem the government was confronted with was the extremely high level of unemployment and the low level of industrial activity. Further deflation at the expense of wages and pensions could lead to a social explosion. The stabilization of the Belgian franc at too high an exchange rate caused problems that could have been solved by a devaluation of the national currency. Some 80 per cent of all foreign trade payments were registered in pounds sterling. But, instead of following the exchange rate of the pound sterling the Belgian government chose a 'hard currency strategy', imitating the other countries of the Gold Block (France, Italy, Switzerland, the Netherlands).

The budgetary problems of the Belgian government forced it to borrow heavily on the capital market. But here the government was confronted with the problems the banks had to preserve their liquidity. Savings decreased by some 30 per cent between 1930 and 1933 (Van Audenhove 1980: 11). Foreign loans were contracted after 1932 and the Treasury had to issue short-term bonds in order to cover its daily expenditures. For instance, at the end of 1934 the government had to contract a short-term loan of some 100 million Dutch guilders provided by the Mendelssohn Bank in Amsterdam. The collapse of the deflationary policy was announced by the breakdown of the Belgian credit system. In 1933 some small banks went bankrupt. In 1934 two important banks operating in Flanders, the Socialist BBT–BBA and the Catholic Algemeene Bankvereeniging, were closed, leaving a significant deficit. Both banks had invested in industrial projects or speculated on the stock market. The position of the other big banks was also precarious because of the short-term deposits they had invested in shares of virtually bankrupt industrial conglomerates. Savers withdrew their savings provoking a disastrous credit contraction and high interest rates. During the period 1930–3 bank deposits decreased from 33,153 million Belgian francs to 25,254 million Belgian francs (−31 per cent). Although the National Bank lowered the interest rates to the extremely low level of 2 per cent just before the devaluation of 1935, there was no economic upswing. The whole credit system was undermined by a lack of confidence. The banks were reluctant to provide the industrial firms with new loans and confined themselves to commercial operations involving no risks. While the major part of their credit balance was frozen, they were forced to discount their commercial paper with the connivance of the National Bank and the SNCI–NMKN. A new decree on bank liquidity was promulgated on 22 August 1934 regulating credit expansion within the realm of the SNCI–NMKN. The latter was empowered to convert all 'sound' loans the banks had conceded to enterprises into bonds issued by the SNCI–NMKN. This operation led to an enormous credit expansion, because these bonds were granted by the government and could be purchased by the National Bank. In March 1935 the SNCI–NMKN issued bonds for a total amount of 1,630 million Belgian francs which were discounted by the banks. Because the discount rate for these bonds was established at 4.25 per cent the financial burden of enterprises decreased by some 200 million francs (Van Audenhove 1980: 11–14; Hogg 1986: 145–9; Vanthemsche 1980: 31–50; Vanthemsche 1987: 139–40).

THE BANKING REGULATION ACT
OF 22 AUGUST 1934

Until the mid-1930s the Belgian banks were of a mixed character, supplying industry short-term and long-term credit. The Belgian banking system was dominated by two large banks, the SGB and the Banque de Bruxelles, both heading industrial and colonial conglomerates. Although both banks dominated the economy, a large number of small provincial banks existed because the liberal rediscounting policy of the National Bank had stimulated this dispersed banking system. Until 1935 there were no legal controls over the banks and even a practice of standardized accounting was lacking. The role of the National Bank was kept to a strict minimum and confined to its rediscounting activities. The two main banks had no interest in letting the National Bank play a major role as supervisor of the banking system (Vanthemsche 1978: *passim*). During the 1930s dividends paid in relation to paid-up capital fell sharply when the industrial firms were making heavy losses, but in general dividend payments were not halted. This practice of the dividend-paying firms provoked an investment crisis, leading to reinforced industrial Malthusianism, because the dividend-receiving shareholders refused to re-invest their dividends.

The widely accepted practice of advances enabled the firms to invest in fixed capital out of banking credit. But advances linked the banks directly with industry and kept the small and medium-sized firms away from the stock market. Because advances permitted the banks to yield higher profits and to gain more influence over the firms than by accepting their commercial paper, the mixed banks preferred to convert these advances into shares which subsequently could be sold to the public. There were also significant disadvantages. Advances could not be discounted at the National Bank, which only accepted commercial paper to be discounted. As long as the economy was booming this practice of substituting commercial paper by advances was extremely profitable to the banks. But in a period of recession advances dangerously diminished the liquidity

21

rate of the banks and they could set in motion a chain of failures even if the banks had covered a large portion of the advances by their own resources. This happened during the crisis of the Great Depression of the 1930s when many banks had to convert their advances into shares because industrial firms were unable to repay their loans. Thus the value of advances fell, and the insolvency of the banks grew correspondingly with the depreciation of their share portfolio. The banks sometimes tried to maintain the value by buying their own shares and those they held in portfolio, creating a situation of artificial confidence in the solidity of the banks and their investments held in portfolio. But any attempt to sell even small quantities of them on the stock market could provoke panic and the final collapse of the entire banking system.

Another factor of instability was the existence of financial holding companies founded and controlled by mixed banks and their subsidiaries. During the 1920s the mixed banks had set up specialist financial holding companies in order to boost investment in some key sectors (electricity and municipal services) of the economy. The Société Union Financière et Maritime (UFIMAR) developed significant shipping activities. Others, such as the Union Financière Belge des Tabacs (TABACOFINA), organized mergers of smaller family-owned tobacco firms.

When the pound sterling left the gold exchange standard in 1931, the British export market was lost to Belgian products. Immediately several banks ran into difficulties when simultaneous withdrawals of deposits increased and many firms accumulated losses. The bankruptcy of the BBT–BBA in March 1934 forced the government to save the whole credit system. On 22 August 1934 the government decided to separate the deposit activities of the banks from their investment activities and empowered the SNCI–NMKN to accept frozen assets offered by the banks in return for bonds discountable at the National Bank. But the sum involved, some 2,000 million Belgian francs, was nowhere near enough to float the mixed banks. Then the government had to bring down the discount rate of the National Bank. Although both measures ran against the current policy of deflation, these reforms were applauded by the banks. The new Banking Regulation Act enabled the mixed banks to hide their losses and granted them substantial tax concessions when splitting off the investment portfolio from the deposit bank. Thus the mixed banks transformed themselves into holding companies heading deposit banks and many sub-holdings and industrial firms. The major psychological effect of the Act was that the banks regained peoples' confidence. The Socialists, who were pleading for nationalization of the whole credit system, immediately lost an important argument in favour of state-owned investment and deposit banks. But the Act could not prevent the Catholic Algemeene Bankvereeniging from running into difficulties. Just like the other mixed banks, the Algemeene Bankvereeniging had invested short-term deposits in advances and shares. Because the liquidation of the Algemeene Bankvereeniging also would have meant the collapse of the Catholic Boerenbond and the bankruptcy of thousands of Catholic peasants, governmental intervention was very necessary. The Boerenbond merged the bankrupt Algemeene Bankvereeniging with the Bank voor Handel en Nijverheid van Kortrijk forming the Kredietbank voor Handel en Nijverheid. A holding company (Algemene Maatschappij voor Nijverheidskrediet – ALMANIJ) inherited the practically worthless investment portfolio of the former Algemeene Bankvereeniging (Van der Wee and Verbreyt 1985: 148–86).

THE DEVALUATION OF 1935

Outward flows of capital already had taken place in the summer of 1934, but then had been stopped. Because the speculation against the Belgian franc had been financed by withdrawals of deposits from the banks, any new speculative move against the exchange rate of the Belgian franc would threaten the liquidity of the banks. A weakening of the position of the pound sterling at the beginning of 1935 provoked speculation against the Belgian franc which could not be stopped by classical methods. Thus, on 18 March 1935 the Belgian government decided to introduce exchange controls and, on 30 March 1935, a new government led by the banker Paul Van Zeeland, devalued the Belgian franc by 28 per cent (Michel 1936: *passim*).

The question is why the Belgian government had waited such a long time to devalue the national currency. The idea has prevailed that the opponents of the devaluation had to be sought in the banking sector. This assumption lacks any evidence. The devaluation of 30 March 1935 actually saved the banks from a final collapse. The British historian Robert L. Hogg has argued that the devaluation of the Belgian franc had become a necessity long before the government had wanted to discuss it. As long as the speculation against the Belgian franc could be resisted by classical methods nobody would withdraw his deposits and transfer them abroad. But in February and March 1935 the situation was completely different. Now the banks were hard-pressed to cope with withdrawals, but they found themselves unable to realize sufficient quantities of their assets and recalling loans would depress economic activity further (Hogg 1986: 150). Lamed by the fear of a closing-down of all banks and confronted with insufficient support from other members of the Gold Block, the Belgian government finally decided to devalue the Belgian franc. The classical defence against the export of capital (i.e. a rise in the discount rate) was not feasible, because this would have squeezed the banks and thus the rest of industry. This made Belgium vulnerable to any speculative run against the Belgian franc. The decisive speculative wave was stirred up in February and March 1935 when gold outflow increased as a consequence of a further depreciation of the pound sterling, wiping out the effects of the past deflationary policy. The Bankcommissie – Commission Bancaire (Banking Commission) was created with the task of supervising the banking sector (*De Bankcommissie* 1960: *passim*). Although this measure undoubtedly announced a tendency towards more state control on the economy, the influence of the Bankcommissie was rather limited. The holding companies were exempt from all control. Even the traditional links between holding companies and deposit banks were not forbidden, because the deposit banks provided cheap credit to companies owned or controlled by the holding companies. The bankers preferred that a soft control be executed by a committee of wise men chosen from the bankers. Meanwhile the excesses committed by some banks during the boom of the 1920s harmed the reputation of the financial sector and led to fierce criticism from the Revolutionary Right and the Leftist parties. Finally the Bankcommissie had to open up its doors to a limited number of captains of industry.

THE TEMPTATION OF CORPORATISM

After the First World War the Socialists forced a dialogue between the representatives of capital and labour at the national and the sectoral levels. In principle, the modest role of the State was deliberately kept in this concerted action and pleased the trade union movement and the entrepreneurs. Of course, there was the corporatist ideology the Christian Democrats and some Social Catholics had adhered to, but they never could win a parliamentary majority.

The Liberal bourgeoisie opposed the idea of compulsory membership of professional organizations and the Socialists refused all projects that would instal a system of 'class collaboration'. The result was an offspring of bipartite committees, one for each industrial sector, where delegates of the trade unions could meet the delegates of the employers in order to bargain for contracts. Although the employers recognized the presence of the delegates of the trade unions as spokesmen of their employees, the bipartite committees confined themselves almost exclusively to the discussion of wage demands and conditions of work. To the employers this situation was satisfactory as long as the unions could discipline the workers. Nevertheless, the employers criticized the 'excessive' power held by the unions, indicating that they only tolerated the trade unions as long as the balance of power was unfavourable to the employers.

The Catholic unions, who gained more and more influence in Flanders and who were protected by some Catholic employers, stressed that solidarity and corporatist agreements would improve the condition of the working classes. The higher circles of the Catholic Party, the Church and the entrepreneurs believed that the bipartite committees could bring together on equal terms the delegates of capital and labour and create solidarity among the social classes and the producers. A series of papal encyclicals underpinned this reasoning (Luyten 1990: *passim*; Henau 1993: *passim*).

During the Depression discussions about a compulsory system of organized professions (i.e. corporations) shifted from corporatism to compulsory cartels organizing whole industrial branches (Luyten 1990: 95) because falling exports and over investment had brought Belgian industry into an uncomfortable position. So it was not surprising that the National Committee of Foreign Trade (Comité National du Commerce Extérieur) dependent on the Ministry of Foreign Affairs, pleaded for cartelization imposed by governmental decrees. These compulsory cartels had to ban exaggerated competition. How they could boost exports was not explained. Nonetheless, in November 1934 Minister Hendrik Heyman (Flemish Christian Democrat) proposed a bill introducing collective labour agreements, professional groupings and bipartite committees, all covered by a legal statute, in all branches of industry. Decisions would be compulsory for all parties and a Central Commission for Production was to head the whole system.

Heyman's proposals were killed at an early stage by industrial pressure groups representing heavy industry.

The spokesman of the corporatist Catholic employers' association (Association des Patrons et Ingénieurs Catholiques – APIC), Henri Velge, submitted a more detailed bill to Parliament. But this proposal was also rejected (Vanthemsche 1978: *passim*). Finally the government decided to recognize the existence of cartels (Royal Decree of 13 January 1935). If in any branch of industry the majority of producers reached agreement, they could apply for special regulatory powers over the entire branch. In reality this new legislation was destined to help the owners of the coal mines to organize a compulsory cartel. An argument against compulsory cartels was that they only would have a defensive character and exclude newcomers in the branch irrespective of their degree of efficiency. Another argument was that they were of little value if export promotion had to be organized. Successful cartels already existed well before this legislation, but they preferred to keep their private character. One of them was the Belgian steel cartel Comptoir de Vente de la Sidérurgie (COSIBEL), established in 1933 as a central selling organization. Finally, cartels could not assist ailing firms in high financial need (Luyten 1990: 98). Notwithstanding these criticisms, the corporatist ideology gained the approval of many journalists and younger politicians belonging to the Revolutionary Right and the Rexist party led by a former Catholic student, Léon Degrelle. In Flanders corporatism made inroads into Catholic opinion. The Flemish Nationalist Party started to move away from its democratic and romantic ideology and adopted a programme stressing 'solidarity' among all members of the Flemish community. Corporatism was an ideology many intellectuals in and outside of the Catholic Party (Luyten 1990: *passim*) adhered to in a period when the Socialists adopted corporatist ideas about the solidarity of workers and 'productive capital' in order to cope with the economic crisis. In the POB Hendrik de Man was undoubtedly the most outspoken protagonist of a form of authoritarian rule (Dodge 1966: *passim*). In his Labour Plan De Man conferred full power to the King and his ministers in order to regulate the economy and to execute a new fiscal policy (De Man 1935: *passim*). Corporatism and authoritarian political reforms became ideological twins when at the end of 1936 the Centre d'Etudes pour la Réforme de l'Etat – Studiecentrum voor Hervorming van de Staat (CERE) met for the first time and the participants tried to set up a number of committees representing the traditional political parties and the interest organizations in order to thrash out the complex problem of political and economic control in Belgium. In 1938 a bill pleading for authoritarian reforms presented in Parliament was denounced by the Comité Central Industriel (CCI) as beginning a slide towards etatism. In the event the government had to drop the bill.

THE DECLINE OF CLASSICAL LIBERALISM

The first 'think tanks' appeared in Belgium at the end of the nineteenth century when Ernest Solvay founded his Institut de Sociologie at the Free University of Brussels. This institute started research on the country's economic and social structure. In 1912 the Institute organized autumn meetings aiming at bringing together intellectuals from all political parties in order to discuss and study various social and economic problems. The prestige of the Institut Solvay was increased by the quality of its scientific management. In 1901 Emile Waxweiler became the first director of the Institut Solvay. He studied income distribution, wage formation and the living standards of the working classes in Belgium. His successor Ernest Mahaim was also a labour specialist and a man of high culture and great influence. In 1897 he presided over the International Congress of Labour Legislation and in 1900 he was one of the founders of the Association Internationale pour la Protection Légale des Travailleurs. In 1919 he was present at the Conference of Versailles and in 1931 he became president of the International Labour Organization (ILO). Mahaim and Waxweiler were both liberals articulating corporate liberal views on labour legislation. Finally there was Robert-J. Lemoine (1897–1938), who had studied at the Free University of Brussels. He became an influential staff member of the research department of the National Bank. When De Man became Minister of Public Works and Unemployment in 1935 he nominated Lemoine as director of his personal cabinet with the task of studying thoroughgoing reform of the Belgian economic system (Baudhuin 1946 (II): 378–81).

The Institut des Sciences Economiques of the University of Louvain, founded in 1928, gained influence because of a number of brilliant economists it attracted. Some of them (Van Zeeland and Gaston Eyskens) became leading Catholic politicians. There was also the Belgian American Educational Foundation, created in 1920, which sent Belgian students to American universities. These foundations and research institutes gradually surpassed the traditional learned societies created during the nineteenth century by the Liberal bourgeoisie (i.e. the Société d'Economie Politique de Belgique, the Société Belge d'Economie Sociale, the Société Scientifique de Bruxelles). Although the CCI constituted a decisive bulwark against corporatist reforms, its position was contested by the Flemish Economic Union (Vlaamsch Economisch Verbond – VEV) founded in 1926 (Baudhuin 1946 (II): 360–72). The VEV organized working committees, discussing economic development of Flanders in relation to cultural and linguistic problems and during the interwar period it operated as a pressure group (Luykx 1967: *passim* ; Vints 1989: 211). The APIC, with its headquarters in Brussels, was led by Theunis and supported by Walloon entrepreneurs like Evence Coppée and Edouard Empain, who openly opposed the idea of giving the trade unions more influence. In Flanders corporatism was strongly promoted by the Catholic Action Group (a group within the Catholic Church which promoted a Christianization of public life) and industrialists like Léon Bekaert and René Goris, both aspiring to leadership of the Flemish Catholic entrepreneurial organization, the Algemeen Christelijk Verbond van Werkgevers (ACVW). Finally, Bekaert became the uncontested leader of all Catholic entrepreneurs in Flanders. The second Van Zeeland government convened a national labour conference on 17 June 1936 in order to discuss economic and social reforms (Vandeputte 1979: 157–74). As an important producer of steel-wire, Bekaert found allies among the Walloon heavy industry (Ougrée–Marihay) and the banks (Banque de Bruxelles) (Deloof 1979: *passim*). In Bekaert's view the Church, the Catholic entrepreneurs and the Catholic trade unions could hope for a unified society growing from the bottom up to the top.

THE CRISIS OF PARLIAMENTARISM

The economic crisis had a devastating effect on social and political life in Belgium. Respect for parliamentary democracy diminished because of the political and financial scandals the political parties were involved in. In 1936 the three 'traditional' political parties lost many of their voters to parties of the extreme Left and Right. With the unfolding power of the political parties the virtues of the parliamentary system had disappeared. Meanwhile the inner circles of party officials and tycoons of the financial world had taken over power. Linguistic divisions moved suddenly to the forefront complicating political life. Thus governments of National Unity, which periodically were necessary to generate a broader consensus, did not express a strong feeling of harmony.

A 'democratic compromise' between the Socialists and the Christian Democrats (Catholic trade unions and peasants' organizations) could have given birth to an alliance of peasants and workers. But the fact that social progress (i.e. higher wages, the 8-hour day and old age pensions) had to be combined with agrarian protectionism, guaranteed prices for agricultural products and cheap credit for the peasants, was not perceived by all the political players as a basic condition for any economic programme implemented by a coalition of all democratic forces. Socialists and Catholics still believed in the virtues of free trade and financial orthodoxy. The government of National Unity formed after the fall of the Poullet–Vandervelde government (1925–6) buried the idea of a new political power block and re-established the predominance of the rich bourgeoisie in alliance with the petty bourgeoisie in the cities and the leaders of the Boerenbond. This coalition allying a power block led by the Right was not able to master the problems caused by the economic crisis of the 1930s. After the major banking crisis in 1934 and the devaluation of 1935 the influence of the bankers on state affairs waned considerably.

Meanwhile the economic crisis set in motion a process of political fragmentation making a democratic solution improbable. More than the Socialists and the Liberals, the Catholic Party was destroyed by internal struggles and repeated crises caused by its multi-class basis and by the pressure the Flemish Nationalists kept on the Flemish Christian Democrats (Gerard 1985: *passim*; Van Haver 1983: *passim*). Although the Christian Democrats now represented the strongest faction within the Catholic Party, they were handicapped by their organizational weakness. Christian Democratic politicians not only represented the growing importance of the Catholic trade union movement in Flanders, but also the aspirations of the Flemish bourgeoisie. Because the Catholic trade union movement lacked qualified leaders of working-class origin, the unions still had to lean on the organizational power of the Catholic Church and the expertise of bourgeois intellectuals. This made the Catholic trade union movement vulnerable to pressures coming from the Church and from the industrial lobby in the Catholic Party in a period when the Catholic trade unions only represented a minority of the working class. Although the POB was still influenced by Marxism, the Party as a whole lacked any form of ideological monolithism and the rather simplistic idea dominated that Socialism would be the combined result of capitalist development, proletarization of the majority of the population and electoral progress made by the Party. This strategy did not pay and when the Party was confronted with the devastating effects of the Great Depression, the Socialist leaders were not able to formulate an alternative policy. After the Socialists lost the parliamentary elections of 1932 and a miners' strike in Wallonia had shaken the party's rank-and-file, the Socialist leadership decided to draft a Labour Plan (Dodge 1966: 130–53). The theoretical father of the Labour Plan, De Man, pleaded for 'structural reforms' to be carried out by the State. The State had to control the financial sector and heavy industry. The rest of industry remained in private hands, but was subordinated to the State-run sector. De Man's idea was that public works launched by the government would reflate the economy. A programme of domestic expansion should absorb unemployment, a proposal enabling the Socialists to obtain the support of the Christian Democrats. Commissariats had to supervise the whole economy and economic power should be delegated to industrial organizations foreshadowing corporatism. At any rate, the Labour Plan had to be carried out by a government dominated by the Socialists.

REFORMING THE STATE

In March 1935, when the Conservative Theunis government had to resign, a devaluation of the Belgian franc became inevitable and the Socialists entered into a government of National Unity led by Van Zeeland without insisting on the option of forcing new elections which the Socialists stood to win. The Socialists found themselves in a government that was dominated by Liberals and Catholics and even the new Prime Minister Van Zeeland was not inclined to adopt the plan. The newly installed Office National du Redressement Economique (Organization for Economic Recovery – OREC) was only the shadow of the Economic Commission which should have supervised and applied the National Plan. Banks and basic industries were not nationalized. The Bankcommissie only received the status of a supervisory board where bankers and entrepreneurs met in order to reconcile the interests of industrial and banking capital. But OREC had no budget of its own to launch a programme of public works and depended on the goodwill of the other ministries when implementing new projects. De Man proposed that OREC make an inventory of the new products for which it had to intervene, but it was not very clear how OREC would realize its proposals. Some senior civil servants and advisors of OREC opposed the idea that the State play a leading role in choosing the products which should obtain special protection. Public works destined to reduce unemployment met stiff resistance from the Liberals and the Catholic Right, who feared big spending and inflation. Thus OREC was officially wound up in November 1939. From 1935 to 1939 OREC expenditure amounted to 2,866 million francs and its counter-cyclical effects were minimal. The minimal results OREC obtained were largely due to the minority position the Socialists accepted within the coalition governments of National Unity (Cassiers 1989: 187). The coalition government headed by Van Zeeland was weakened by electoral successes obtained in May 1936 by the two major Fascist parties, Rex in Wallonia and Brussels and the Flemish Nationalist Party. The Catholic Party fell back from 38.55 per cent of the vote in 1932 to 28.80 per cent in 1936. The recently founded Rexist Party collected 11.4 per cent. The progress of the Flemish Nationalists was important enough to warn the Catholics in Flanders that the 'Flemish Question' called for a more comprehensive solution. Although the Socialists lost votes and seats they became by far the strongest party in Parliament, which enabled them to claim a Socialist for Prime Minister. But the General Strike which broke out after the general elections of May 1936 was undoubtedly the reason why the Socialists hastily accepted again the formula of a government of National Unity in which they did not play a dominant role. On 24 June 1936 Van Zeeland presented his programme to Parliament. He promised a wide range of social reforms to the workers on strike that the trade unions had already accepted, plus governmental control on the armaments industry, electricity, the insurance companies and the credit sector. But there was no paragraph promising nationalization of the financial sector. Instead, the new Van Zeeland government only completed its project for establishing sectoral credit organizations funded by the State (Cassiers 1989: 180–4).

In June 1935 the first Van Zeeland government had already founded the Institut de Réescompte et de Garantie –

Herdisconterings- en Waarborginstituut (IRG–HWI) and in January 1936 the Centraal Bureau voor Hypothecair Krediet – Office Central du Crédit Hypothécaire (CBHK–OCCH) aimed at lowering the interest rates. Finally, the second Van Zeeland government created in September 1937 the Institut National de Crédit Agricole – Nationaal Institut voor Landbouwkrediet (INCA–NILK) and in October 1937 the Caisse Nationale de Crédit aux Classes Moyennes, both promising cheap credit to the middle classes and the peasants (Cassiers 1989: 191–2). The politics of cheap credit demonstrated the weakness of the Van Zeeland government when facing the economic problems and proved that they wanted to protect the petty bourgeoisie and the farmers in a period when the banks were reluctant to expand their activities. (Already in 1934 several royal decrees signed by the Conservative government of de Broqueville had to protect merchants and shop-keepers against their creditors. In January 1935 the Theunis government established the Office National du Ducroire (National Bureau for Credit Insurance) and in February 1935 a state bank providing cheap credit to smallholders (Van Audenhove 1980: 19).)

The position of the second Van Zeeland–De Man government was soon shaken by scandals and the incompetence of Minister of Finance De Man. On 25 October 1937 Van Zeeland resigned as Prime Minister. A new government of National Unity was constituted under the leftist Liberal Paul-Emile Janson. But in March 1938 De Man resigned because his tax reform proposals met increased opposition by the Catholic Right and some Liberals and the authorities returned to their policies of balanced budgets and financial orthodoxy. In February 1939 a short-lived coalition of Socialists and Catholics even proposed deflatory measures.

CONCLUSIONS

The 1920s and 1930s could be characterized as a transitory period from liberalism to a pressure-group democracy and corporatist interest intermediation. The economic crisis of the 1930s made clear that state intervention in the economy had become urgent. Because Belgium was largely dependent on industries producing semi-finished products for the world market and importing raw materials, all reforms that increased the costs of production had to be avoided. Within this narrow margin it was not easy to find appropriate solutions to the effects of the economic crisis. Falling prices on the world market automatically led to declining export opportunities, fierce competition on the domestic market, lower earnings for Belgian industry and, consequently, higher unemployment and a decline in the average purchasing power of the population. Remedies were difficult to find. Social tensions and political polarization finally undermined any form of consensus about economic, administrative and social reforms.

2

THE POLITICS OF
INDUSTRY

The Belgian economy was largely determined by its nineteenth-century origins. Coal and iron were, together with heavy machinery and railway equipment, still predominant during the interwar period. Because the big banks had acquired overwhelming interests in heavy industry, they were not really interested in promoting investment in new industries downstream. As long as Belgian capitalism was able to sustain foreign competition, the big banks had some good reasons to favour investment in regressive sectors such as the coal industry. Although Belgium suffered a relative decline of its coal industry in combination with an increased world supply and unfavourable effects on prices, the banks refused to reconsider their industrial policy. The steel industry offered them the argument that a more rational use of coal and energy would enable the Belgian economy to support the financial burden of marginal coal mines. Meanwhile the steel industry renewed its installations without concentrating all its efforts on a more rationalized organization of the production process. Other energy-intensive industrial activities, such as the heavy chemicals industry, cement and other processing industries were largely dependent upon the coal sector for their raw materials (industrial gas) and energy.

During the 1930s Belgian industry suffered from overcapacity, tariff barriers and quotas, a depreciated pound sterling and low prices paid for bulky industrial products. Soon Belgian industry was forced to conquer and organize the internal market with the help of cartels and central selling organizations. Meanwhile the Belgian government opted for a deflationary policy which finally ended in March 1935 with a devaluation of the Belgian franc.

THE POLITICS OF COAL

In the 1930s the import of cheap coal threatened the marginal domestic mines, a problem the mine-owners already had had to face before the First World War. The pits in Wallonia were producing coal at high costs because the seams were difficult to work and the concessions only allowed small-scale production. A large number of shafts had survived in Wallonia producing household coal. Rising expectations were met by the developing coalfields in Limburg, where the seams contained coal suitable for the coke ovens and the steel industry. The coalfield of Limburg required high capital investment with low returns. That was the reason why the Belgian banks and the steel companies had waited until 1901 to explore the geology of Limburg. The northern mines were more modern, larger and heavily mechanized, but several setbacks negatively influenced the financial results of the Limburg mines. They suffered from the fact that during the First World War and its direct aftermath investment had been slowing down and only an expensive programme of canal construction, which was completed only in the late 1930s, could connect the Limburg coalfields with the steel works in Wallonia. Another disadvantage was that the Limburg mines produced coal of lower quality ('fat coal'). Supply of cheap labour in huge quantities was also a problem. When industrial production rose elsewhere, the miners deserted the pits forcing the coal mining companies to pay relatively high wages and to provide cheap housing. In Limburg the mining companies countered this tendency by increased mechanization and by importing workers from other European countries (Poland, Italy).

The miners and the coal mining firms had established good relations through their professional organizations. After 1919 both pleaded for protection from foreign competition, a policy the Belgian government was not eager to implement. But the 170,000 miners and their families constituted a homogeneous and heavily concentrated population of voters always threatening a general strike. Thus in 1927 a Study Commission for the Coal Problem comprising delegates of the mining companies and the unions started to discuss the problems of the coal industry. Although the Commission was not able to propose an overall solution, in 1928 the government lowered taxes, a measure designed to facilitate the fusion of the smaller coal mining companies. Although many small mining firms resisted mergers, the number of pits in operation was reduced by 30 to 40 per cent.

The independent mining companies still constituted an influential lobby and successfully opposed the plan of the Belgian coal syndicate Comptoir Belge du Charbon (COBECHAR) founded in 1929 to organize the larger companies. Because large consumers, such as the steel firms and coke ovens owning their coal mines, inclined towards protectionism and the railway companies and the electricity companies operated on a protected internal market, the survival of the Belgian coal mines mobilized all support from those consumers who were able to pass the costs on to other consumers. But how to stop the import of cheap German coal, which came in freely as a result of the German–Belgian Trade Agreement? The mining companies called for a renunciation of the Agreement. Finally Germany agreed to limit its coal exports to Belgium, which sharpened the conflict between free traders and protectionists when the metallurgical sector denied the coal-mine owners the right to organize the market. Although a significant minority of the coal-mining firms was still making profits, the government was forced by the SGB and Coppée to subsidize the wages of the miners (Hogg 1986: 92) and to organize in January 1935 a compulsory national coal board, the Office National des Charbons, which also included the reluctant independent producers of household coal in Liège. The office had to control the production and the prices and introduced a new policy largely due to the effect of the devaluation and the upturn of the economy. From then on Belgium became a net exporter of heavily subsidized coal, while some small domestic consumers were complaining they could not obtain sufficient quantities of industrial coal (Hogg 1986: 92). The reason why the large banks had invested heavily in stocks of coal mines had its origins in the industrial strategy of these banks interested in developing heavy industry and controlling the energy sector. In 1931, out of a total production of 27 million tonnes, the SGB controlled an output of 5.5 million tons and the Banque de Bruxelles of 5.8 million tons (Hogg 1986: 95). Thus banks, coal mine owners and trade unions formed a broader class alliance to secure a special status for the mines and to help them to survive during the Depression of the 1930s. This alliance supported a defensive policy of rationalization and mechanization of coal production in Wallonia (Cassiers 1989: 58) and forced industry to buy Belgian coal.

Table 2.1 Financial results of the Belgian coal mines, 1919–39

Year	Profits of the Southern Basin (millions of BF)	Profits/tonne (in BF)	Profits of the Northern Basin (millions of BF)	Profits/tonne (in BF)
1919	+ 142.16	+ 1.36		
1920	+ 115.94	+ 7.75		
1921	− 2.86	− 0.14		
1922	+ 19.40	+ 0.14		
1923	+ 240.83	+ 10.89		
1924	+ 0.60	+ 0.03		
1925	− 124.46	− 5.66		
1926	+ 489.51	+ 20.84		
1927	+ 167.14	+ 6.65	− 50.69	− 20.83
1928	− 77.64	− 3.14	− 74.21	− 25.66
1929	+ 241.19	+ 10.18	− 36.72	− 26.76
1930	− 90.92	− 3.85	− 99.48	− 26.08
1931	− 283.42	− 12.39	− 99.65	− 23.85
1932	− 167.44	− 9.57	− 69.64	− 17.74
1933	− 130.62	− 6.36	− 21.78	− 4.57
1934	− 136.91	− 6.57	+ 5.09	+ 0.92
1935	+ 109.69	+ 5.27	+ 71.91	+ 12.66
1936	+ 172.75	+ 8.00	+ 124.40	+ 19.83
1937	+ 413.75	+ 17.84	+ 190.49	+ 28.61
1938	+ 135.40	+ 5.87	+ 68.58	+ 10.48
1939	+ 226.24	+ 10.01	+ 191.95	+ 26.52

Source: Baudhuin 1946: (II) 12–13

Table 2.2 Total coal production, 1920–38 (in tonnes)

Year	Southern Basin	Northern Basin
1920	22,143,000	246,000
1925	21,993,000	1,104,000
1930	23,600,000	3,813,000
1935	20,825,000	5,680,000
1938	23,049,000	6,536,000

Sources: Baudhuin 1946: (II) 10–19; Hogg 1986: 84

THE POLITICS OF STEEL

The absence of a sophisticated engineering sector and the narrowness of the domestic market inspired the steel firms to produce simple and bulky products destined for foreign markets. The crisis in the railway sector soon forced the Belgian steel companies to cut the production of rails. In the 1930s rail production had fallen to 100,000 tonnes a year, while in the pre-war period the average production had reached 350,000 tonnes a year.

The Belgian steel firms had numerous interests in common with French firms in order to share their mining interests and to ensure the supply of coke. Iron ore had to be imported from Spain, Sweden and Lorraine. Vertical integration was the normal way towards self-sufficiency as was shown by take-overs of coal mines by Cockerill and Ougrée–Marihaye. The banks financing these take-overs were mainly interested in rationalizing the production process. After the First World War a steel programme formulated by Jean Jadot, Governor of the SGB, proposed to merge all firms in one single company (*Société Générale de Belgique* 1972: 91; Jacobs 1988: 455–8). But the Jadot Plan was refused by the independent steel firms. They rebuilt the Belgian steel sector on pre-war standards: a large number of flexible small blast furnaces using low-quality ore (Bussière 1984: 308).

Helped by high prices for steel products and the depreciation of the Belgian franc Belgian steel firms made large profits. Cheap credit, inflation and a willing stock market had helped them to rebuild their plants within a few years. During this period of high prices the independent Belgian steel firms with their small blast furnaces produced steel on a very efficient basis and yielded higher profits than the big firms. But they failed to forecast the coming slump and during the Depression they had to reduce their prices in order to maintain the production of their newly established capacity.

Regulating the steel market was a very difficult task, because the Belgian steel firms behaved as independents. Thus the Comptoir des Aciéries collapsed in 1919 within a few months and the Groupement des Hauts Fournaux et des Aciéries Belges remained a loosely organized entrepreneurial pressure group. Because of conflicting interests of both the French and the German steel firms, only in March 1926 could the European Railmakers' Association spread its wings. In 1926 Emile Mayrisch of Aciéries Réunies de Burbach–Eich–Dudelange (ARBED) succeeded in building an international cartel (Entente Internationale de l'Acier – EIA) receiving support from the Belgian, French, Luxembourg and German producers of cast iron and steel. The cartel organized 30 per cent of the world steel production and 65 per cent of the world steel trade (Jacobs

1988: 495). But in October 1929 the German steel industry, feeling itself stronger than its competitors, left the EIA. Only the specialist cartels in the steel industry such as the International Tube Convention (1929) and the International Wire Cartel (1927) could survive. It was significant that some Belgian, French and Luxembourg steel firms (Ougrée–Marihaye, Steinford, ARBED, SA des Hauts-Fourneaux et Aciéries de Differdange, St-Ingbert, Rumelange-HADIR) with interests in Lorraine and Luxembourg set up the Comptoir Franco–Belge–Luxembourgeois des Fontes Phosphoreuses de Moulage with its headquarters in Brussels and Paris.

The problem with the Belgian steel firms was that they could not agree on the necessity to organize themselves in a national cartel. The banks could have forced the steel firms to join the international cartels, but they failed to do so. During the Great Depression the banks were forced to convert their frozen loans to the steel firms into shares. Finally the banks imposed the formation of COSIBEL. Bankers presided over COSIBEL and represented the Comptoir on an international level. But, notwithstanding the growing authority of the banks, rebellious tendencies did not disappear. After the devaluation of the Belgian franc in 1935, when exporting prices had become more attractive, some Belgian steel firms clearly challenged the authority of COSIBEL. With its existence threatened COSIBEL informed the government that only the introduction of a system of export licences could prevent the cartel from dissolution. The Van Zeeland government complied and COSIBEL became a working instrument in the hands of the big banks.

The Belgian firms lacked both capital and markets to invest in wide strip mills. Even specialization in higher-quality steels was out of the question because of a lack of demand on the domestic market. Special steel alloys were bought by the engineering sector, but the steel firms were unwilling to invest in special steels and they displayed a marked preference for the mass production and exporting of crude products often even at the expense of the needs of the domestic market. Preference for fulfilling export orders rather than domestic ones meant that delivery dates on the domestic market were seriously delayed. Even COSIBEL listened to the voice of the export interests and, in 1937, withdrew from the domestic market for finished steel products. The crisis and the devaluation of 1935 had not inspired another industrial and commercial strategy. The steel works limited their investment programmes and capital raised

Table 2.3 Total production and total export of crude steel, 1925–37
(in '000 tonnes) (BLEU)

Year	Production of ingots and castings	Exports of semi-finished and finished products
1925	4,633	2,847
1927	6,151	4,152
1929	6,811	4,123
1931	5,140	3,326
1933	4,576	2,957
1935	4,860	2,984
1937	6,379	3,626

Source: Hogg 1986: 41

on the stock market was destined to pay off outstanding debts. In the meantime technical progress was slowed down by the absence of a large-scale investment programme financed by public funds. Thus the Belgian steel industry fell into something of a trap, because it was saddled with huge productive capacity which represented massive investment. In order to survive, the steel firms depended on a large output of comparatively low-value steel (Hogg 1986: 48).

THE AUTOMOBILE INDUSTRY

Although Belgium was an important producer of metal products and steel, its engineering industry was a general failure and its automobile industry specialized in making heavy and expensive luxury cars, leaving the expanding branch of popular models to American and French firms who established their assembly units in Belgium. In 1927 the two remaining Belgian automobile firms Minerva in Antwerp and the Fabrique Nationale d'Armes de Guerre (FN) in Herstal (Liège) were forced into a production agreement (Baudhuin 1946 (II): 61). Until the advent of the Depression Minerva was making heavy luxury cars for the export markets in the UK and the USA. But with the outbreak of the economic crisis and rising world tariffs on car imports Minerva got into trouble. A series of liquidity crises forced Minerva to rely on governmental aid and loans from the SGB. In order to help Minerva, in 1932 the Belgian government decided to raise import tariffs on cars and car components. But higher prices of imported cars were not of great help for Minerva which now was forced to switch to the domestic market. The Belgian firm lacked enough capital to invest in new equipment and in a new popular model. In November 1934 Minerva had to stop all activities (Baudhuin 1946 (I): 304). After the devaluation of the franc in 1935 the Belgian government lowered the import duties on car parts to be assembled by the American firms established in Belgium. It was a concession made to the American government in order to boost the Belgian export of ordinary steel and textile products to the American market (Baudhuin 1946 (II): 64–5).

ELECTRICAL ENGINEERING

Belgian industry was more successful in the production of heavy equipment and rolling stock. In the pre-war period Belgian firms held a fair share in the booming railway sector in the colonies and in Latin America. In the interwar period production of railway equipment stagnated and became dependent on governmental help. Government agencies, such as the Export Credit Guarantee Department, had to finance exports during the Depression. But the nationalized railway companies in Belgium and abroad became increasingly critical and even reluctant to invest in new rolling stock. During the Depression the Belgian Government decided to replace its wooden coaches with metal ones and forced the numerous independent railway equipment firms to modernize their plants. Some big companies, like Cockerill and others, owned important railway divisions, producing steam engines. But the ill-equipped independent small firms were still numerous. In 1939 fourteen companies manufacturing rolling stock had to share the domestic market. In order to help the rolling stock sector, the government was forced to subsidize the national railway company and to provide funds for a programme of electrification of the main railway lines.

In the 1920s electricity was relatively cheap and available to practically the whole population. Electricity was produced by the large steel firms and coal mines at low costs in order to secure their own demand for electricity, while at the same time supplying the population with electricity. Not only did the expansion in the electricity sector depend on the large industrial producers and on the price of fuel, but also on the colonial mining companies supplying the sector with copper and on engineering firms able to construct power stations and transport systems. The ACEC (Ateliers de Constructions Electriques de Charleroi) specialized in the field of heavy equipment and electrical cables after having acquired patents from Bell Telephone in 1922. Foreign firms also competed on the Belgian market. In 1920 General Electric and Thomson–Houston reorganized the Ateliers Carels, a firm specializing in producing diesel and steam engines (Baudhuin 1946: (II) 55–7). A particular feature of the Belgian electrical engineering sector was that it depended heavily on foreign capital or patents and that it was frustrated by a lack of financial support by the Belgian banks. Compared with Siemens or other foreign competitors ACEC was a small firm.

High technological potential was held by the Bell Telephone Manufacturing Co. in Antwerp which employed in 1927 some 11,100 workers (*Bell* 1982). Bell Telephone specialized in telephone equipment and also in consumer durables such as refrigerators, phonographs, radios and other home appliances. The fast-growing market for light bulbs became the monopoly of Philips. Philips owned the SA La Lumière Electrique in Louvain (Bouman 1956: 99) and, later on, Philips and ACEC acquired Manufacture Belge de Lampes Electriques (MBLE). From the very beginning (1882) Bell Telephone was owned by the American shareholders of the Western Electric Company, itself a subsidiary of the American Telephone and Telegraph (AT&T). But in 1925 International Telephone and Telegraph (ITT) acquired a major stake in Bell Telephone. Notwithstanding these changes in ownership of its stock capital, Western Electric's influence as supplier of new technology remained (Baudhuin 1946: (II) 297).

NON-FERROUS METALS

Belgian capitalism confined itself within the limits of providing raw materials and metals (steel, copper, zinc) to the manufacturers of consumer durables and the engineering industries. The best example of this strategy was the specializiation chosen by the subsidiaries of the SGB in the sector of non-ferrous metals. The non-ferrous metal empire of the SGB had no direct links with the Walloon-based zinc industry. The zinc-producing firm Vieille Montagne had its already exhausted zinc mines in the eastern part of Belgium and refineries in Liège. At the end of the nineteenth century a new plant was opened in northern Belgium. The zinc industry was by no means an expansive sector. During the interwar years the production level stagnated at the pre-war level of 200,000 tons a year, while employment in this sector fell constantly from 5,677 workers in 1900 to 3,766 workers in 1939. This signified important productivity gains. But at the same time financial results were rather poor. Zinc ore had to be imported from Spain where the Asturienne des Mines operated (Baudhuin 1946: (II) 50). After the turn of the century the non-ferrous metals industry established itself near the port of Antwerp where ships with raw materials came in. In 1908 the Société Générale Métallurgique de Hoboken started up near Antwerp as a refiner of African copper. In 1913 the Métallurgique built a new chrome and radium refinery in Olen (Baudhuin 1946: (II) 49). After the First World War the SGB acquired the Métallurgique de Hoboken.

THE TEXTILE INDUSTRY

The Belgian textile sector was dominated by three large conglomerates: the Union Cotonnière (UCO), the Usines Cotonnières de Belgique and the Usines Textiles Réunies de Belgique (UTEXBEL). These firms were created out of mergers which occurred in the 1920s. Especially the owners of the cotton factories integrated their spinning, weaving, dyeing and finishing divisions without accepting the authority of the big banks. Their strategy consisted of making large profits by selling their cheap textiles on the world market. Low wages and cyclical demand were the main characteristics of this sector employing more than 50,000 workers. The branches of the woollen and linen textiles were less-mechanized and integrated than the cotton industry. The manufacture of woollen products was also geographically dispersed over Wallonia and Flanders and employed 40,000 workers. The depreciation of the Belgian franc gave the textile exporters an important competitive advantage during the 1920s and led to a substantial increase in the number of cotton spinners and looms. The major textile companies of Ghent were willing to sub-contract to other firms in the small towns, a practice which stimulated the growing importance of textile towns such as Renaix and Courtrai (Hogg 1986: 55; Baudhuin 1946 (II): 73).

Small-scale textile firms were neglected by the large banks and had to rely on local banks. Because numerous textile firms had only two or four looms, they specialized in weaving high-quality products or they went into the fast-growing markets of tufted carpets, knitwear and furniture textiles. These small firms kept their character of family-owned enterprises. Thus the Belgian textile industry preserved its nineteenth-century capitalist structure with, on one hand, a few families dominating cotton spinning and weaving and, on the other hand, a large number of small textile firms. In the woollen industry of Verviers three families (Peltzer, Zurstrassen and Simonis) dominated production. The linen industry was a declining branch producing luxury products destined for wealthier customers. The firms working in wool remained relatively small and backward during this period. Cheapness of the labour force here was the reason why introduction of automatic looms was postponed. The more advanced linen industry lost a good deal of its custom when during the Depression Russian exports reappeared on the world market. Demand slowed down because the important and lucrative Latin American export market was disturbed by monetary disorders, low prices paid for raw materials and protective tariff barriers (Hogg 1986: 57–60).

There was also very little specialization in weaving and most of the firms produced low-quality goods, selling them at any price on the world market. When exports declined, the textile industry tried to adjust its costs by lowering wages and buying cheaper raw materials. But during the Depression the textile firms were not able to reduce wages sufficiently and were condemned to regain the narrowing domestic market. The small firms had no other choice than to force down each other's prices. Marketing techniques were unknown to them and they preferred selling their produce based on price, not on quality. They also refused to concentrate their effort on the production of high-quality goods, and during that period the Japanese conquered a substantial part of the world market (Baudhuin 1946 (II): 75). As a consequence of this situation the textile industry was only interested in lowering wages and a depreciated Belgian franc. As export margins constantly narrowed the Belgian firms were not able to offer customer credit for more than one or two months. Here the government Export Credit Department was of little help to small Belgian textile companies lacking experience on foreign markets. Finally, in 1936 the government decided to protect the domestic textile market by introducing quotas (Hogg 1986: 112). Although the Belgian textile industry had to face difficulties, progress was made by a new generation of entrepreneurs looking for diversification downstream. This was not backed by the big wool and cotton yarn producers who preferred to specialize in particular qualities and specifications. As a consequence of these conflicting interests between spinners and domestic weavers, the latter had to import large quantities of the yarn they needed. During the Depression yarn prices fell sharply, obliging the spinners to produce higher-quality yarn for the domestic market. An overall disequilibrium between spinning and weaving capacity existed because the spinning activities had outgrown the importance of the weaving activities. That was the reason why attempts to organize the producers within cartels failed or were limited to a minority of the firms in the different textile branches. La Textile, a marketing organization of the spinners, never succeeded in monopolizing the domestic market. Thus the purchasing syndicates of the weavers easily forced down yarn prices. In 1935 the spinners organized themselves as the Association Belge des Filateurs and with the backing of the big banks they convinced the Belgian government of the necessity for a cartel for the whole textile sector. But the weaving companies opposed this project and they reacted with the setting up of the Association Belge de Tissage (Hogg 1986: 60).

HEAVY CHEMICALS

The Belgian chemical industry, which was closely attached to the Walloon heavy industry and the coal mines, produced soda ash and caustic soda. It was only after the First World War that investment was directed towards entirely new areas, such as fertilizers and rayon, and the paper and glass industries could leave their artisanal production methods. Before the First World War the Belgian chemical industry produced superphosphates, but these small factories could not keep up with new foreign competitors. New opportunities were found in the production of nitrogenous fertilizers, a byproduct of the coke ovens and gasworks. Coppée, who owned several coke ovens and who had acquired control over the steel firm Espérance–Longdoz in 1920, became with his Société Belge de l'Azote in Ougrée the biggest producer of artificial fertilizers. He also stood at the cradle of other chemical firms, such as the Ammoniaque Synthétique et Dérivés (ASED) in Willebroeck, the SA Ammoniaque Synthétique Trieu-Kaisin, Ressaix, Anderlues, La Louvière-Sart (ASTRAL) in Ressaix in Hainaut, and in 1929 he founded the Société des Produits Chimiques du Marly for the production of ammonia and nitrous acid. In 1929 Coppée joined Montecatini, Istituto per la Ricostruzione Industriale (IRI) and de Wendel, in order to establish the Compagnie Néerlandaise de l'Azote (CNA) in Sluiskil (in the Netherlands) (Dubois 1988: 206–8). Other financial groups tried to conquer a substantial part of the lucrative market for fertilizers. The Carbonisation Centrale, founded in 1928, with its marketing organization Coke et Sous-produits de Tertre, was controlled by the SGB. The latter also set up the Carbochimique in Tertre. The Union Chimique Belge (UCB) possessed factories in Zandvoorde and Houdeng, while the French group Kuhlmann owned a factory in Zelzate. Engrais et Produits Chimiques de la Meuse established a plant in Tilleur. Because of overinvestment the producers of fertilizers were obliged to set up a cartel (the Comptoir Belge de l'Azote – COBELAZ). This cartel became affiliated with the Convention de l'Industrie de l'Azote (CIA) and signed an agreement with the DEN cartel (Deutschland–England–Norwegen). A gentleman's agreement with American and Chilean producers lasted until 1941. In 1931 the Belgian government established a quota for the import of nitrogenous fertilizers.

Cartelization enabled the producers to reduce production capacity. Thus the large ASTRAL plant in Ressaix was closed and prices were adjusted. The agricultural interests protested, but the powerful Boerenbond refused to endorse this revolt by the small-holders because it was a shareholder of three large companies involved in the production of fertilizers (Société Carbochimique, Société Belge de l'Azote, Société Belge d'Electrochimie) (Van Molle 1990: 188, 243).

The production of rayon or 'artificial silk' required large quantities of cheap industrial alcohol. The Belgian sugar refineries were able to meet this demand. Meanwhile an advantageous tax regime encouraged Comte Hilaire Bernigaud de Chardonnet to establish in 1890 an 'artificial silk' processing factory in Tubize (near Brussels). At the outbreak of the First World War the sector employed some 6,000 people in several *celanese* factories of which Tubize had become the largest producer with subsidiaries in the USA (Tubize Articial Silk Company of America in Hopewell – Richmond), Poland (Tomaszow) and Hungary (Sárvár). After the First World War, Alfred Loewenstein, who led Tubize, joined with J. Henry Schroeder and Dannie Heinemann (Société Internationale d'Energie Hydro-Electrique (SIDRO) and SOFINA) to form the Hydro-Electric Securities holding company. But after his mysterious death (Norris 1987: *passim*) in 1928, the Loewenstein empire crumbled and his Belgian celanese firms (Tubize, Obourg, Viscose, Soieries de Ninove, Sadsa and Seta) came under the aegis of Solvay's UCB.

Because 95 per cent of the production had to be exported UCB was obliged to reorganize the sector. The Union des Fabriques Belges de Textiles Artificiels (FABELTA) was created. FABELTA survived the Depression and, after having retrenched behind tariff barriers, it increased its yearly total output of viscose from 4,350 tons in 1932 to 5,800 tons in 1939 (Baudhuin 1946: (II) 82).

The collieries and the quarries in Wallonia needed explosives, which were produced by small factories on the basis of Chilean saltpetre, carbon and sulphur. Dynamite produced by several Belgian firms from saltpetre, nitrate, nitrous acid or sulphate found an outlet in Africa and Latin America. But before the First World War all these firms were relatively small specialist producers. In 1919 under the impulse of the SGB and the Union Financière et Industrielle Liégoise several small firms merged into the Poudreries Réunies de Belgique (PRB).

In the safety matches industry concentration occurred just before the First World War when the Union Allumettière was founded. After the war the Svenska Tändsticks Aktie Bolaget (STAB) and the International Match Corporation reorganized the remaining independent firms under the aegis of SA Fabriques d'Allumettes. In 1929 both organizations merged their interests into the new Union Allumettière. Although Ivar Kreuger headed this empire because of his strong position on the British market and his control over the supply of Swedish wood, it was Paul de Launoit who led the holding company Union Allumettière (Belart et al. n.d.: 89–90: Joye 1960: 48–9). About 75 per cent of Belgian safety matches produced was exported, especially to the Belgian Congo, the UK and her colonies, the USA and Latin America. In 1926 the Belgian factories employed 8,000 people and produced 91 billion matches, but during the Depression the British export market was lost which forced the Union Allumettière to reduce its output.

In the early 1860s the brothers John and Ernest Solvay (De Leener 1946: *passim*; De Preter 1983: 71–8) developed and patented a new method for producing soda ash and with the help of their family they built up a multinational empire of soda firms. In 1913 Solvay employed worldwide some 20,000 workers. Patents generated enough royalties to finance this expansion. On the eve of the First World War Solvay produced more than 50 per cent of all soda on the European continent. Solvay's patents were used for the production of 90 per cent of all the soda in the world. Solvay avoided borrowing from the banks and Ernest Solvay, who survived his brother for several decades, grouped his holdings in the Mutuelle Mobilière et Immobilière SA (in 1927 Mutuelle Solvay). During the 1920s Solvay reached the apex of power by penetrating many industrial sectors of the soda industry and establishing financial ties with other holding companies and big banks. For instance, the Mutuelle Solvay helped to float the Union Financière et Industrielle Liégeoise (UFIL), Ougrée–Marihaye, the Banque Belge pour l'Etranger and the Banque Italo–Belge. Solvay became a major shareholder in HADIR, an important steel firm in the Grand Duchy of Luxembourg and of coal mining companies in the Campine (Charbonnages de Houthaelen, Charbonnages André Dumont). Alliances marking this drive towards diversification were concluded with airlines (SA Belge d'Exploitation et de Navigation Aérienne – SABENA), the producer of electrical home appliances (Société Belge des Radios – SBR), with mining firms (Société Minière de la Luebo, Miñas de Potasa de Suria SA in Spain), colonial trading firms and railway companies (Vicicongo, Compagnie des Chemins de Fer du Bas-Congo au Katanga – BCK), Latin American trading and banking activities (Bunge, Anglo South American Bank), colonial real estate and plantations (Société Internationale de Plantations et de Finance – SIPEF, Compagnie Sucrerière Congolaise) (*Morphologie* 1967: 200–4). Diversification in the direction of colonial and trading firms was important in order to establish closer links with sodium nitrate production and trade in Chile and to play a role in the international soda and nitrate cartels. Solvay became directly involved in the modernization of the glass industry when he founded the Compagnie Internationale pour la Fabrication Mécanique du Verre in 1921. When floating UFIL Solvay joined the Banque Nagelmackers (owner of the Compagnie Générale des Wagons-Lits) and the SGB in their attempt to control UFIL's industrial empire (FN, Société Métallurgique de Hoboken, Société Générale des Minerais – SGM).

Solvay acquired shares in a multitude of firms, such as the Société Belge de Constructions Aéronautiques (SABCA) (aviation), Ecrémeuses Mélotte, Ford Motor Co. (Belgium), Papeteries de Belgique (paper), Union de Centrales Electriques – Liège–Namur–Luxembourg–Hainaut (UCE–LINALUX (electricity)), Pharmacie Centrale de Belgique, Cophaco, Société Générale Industrielle et Chimique du Katanga (SOGECHIM), and the Columbia Gas and Electrical Corporation. The Mutuelle Solvay reorganized the rayon industry after having constituted the UCB. Furthermore, Solvay held a stake in the Carbochimique and had helped to found the SA pour la Fabrication des Engrais Azotés (SAFEA).

Political and economic difficulties prompted Solvay to establish several banks in Eastern Europe (the Crédit Foncier d'Autriche, the Banque Malopolski and the Banque de l'Union Yougoslave) which financed the local Solvay factories. In Belgium Solvay preferred to establish holding companies in which large banks were invited to hold shares in order to finance investment in industrial firms. With the Banque de Bruxelles and Coppée the Compagnie Belge pour l'Industrie (CBI) was founded. With the Lamarche (Ougrée–Marihay) and P. de Launoit (Union Allumettière, Banque de Bruxelles) families the Mutuelle Solvay created the Mutuelle Liégeoise. Solvay received the backing of the SGB when founding the UCB. In France Solvay allied with the Banque Vernes and Gillet (Rhône–Poulenc). Solvay was not exempt from financial and monetary difficulties caused by the sequels to the First World War. Therefore Solvay founded the Compagnie Financière et Industrielle de Belgique (FINABEL).

During the Depression Solvay was obliged to retreat from many non-core activities. Because of the Banking Regulation Act of 1934 the Mutuelle Solvay SA transformed itself into a *société en commandite simple* and the Société Belge de Banque became a commercial bank. Despite acute financial problems Solvay's industrial autonomy remained unshaken with important stakes in chemical firms in Germany, the UK and the USA (Van der Valk 1932: 87; Liefmann 1932: 269). The alliance with Imperial Chemical Industries (ICI) permitted Solvay to hold a privileged position in the expanding sector of non-ferrous metals, fibres, explosives and photographic paper industries. In 1927 the Solvay American Corp. and North American Solvay Corp. both became shareholders of the Allied Chemical Corp. (formerly the Allied Chemical & Dye Corp.). Solvay held a stake in the American glass industry (Owens Illinois Glass Corp.), in Monsanto and in the Plax Corp. Solvay invited Courtaulds and Monsanto to become shareholders in American Viscose, a Solvay subsidiary. In France Solvay allied with the Gillet family when founding the Mutuelle Industrielle (1927). This investment bank also served as a financial agency for Pricel, Progil and Rhône–Poulenc. Finally the Mutuelle Industrielle became a shareholder in the Société Privée d'Investissement (SOPRINA), a subsidiary of the Gillet Group. Gillet and Solvay owned the Société de Participations de la Rayonne (SOPARA), which controlled

Bemberg SpA in Italy, Ducilo SA in Argentina and SA de Fibres Artificielles in Spain. Although Solvay was not completely absent from Africa, its interests in the Belgian Congo were of minor importance.

In 1930 Solvay sold all chemical concerns apart from soda production to the UCB, making the latter chemical firm a conglomerate owning coke ovens, chemical and pharmaceutical producers, electrical power stations and non-ferrous metals refineries. In 1937 UCB acquired the shares the Mutuelle Solvay held in the Compagnie Chimique et Industrielle de Belgique. The latter holding company controlled the Société Glaces et Verres (GLAVER) (glass), the Société Industrielle de la Cellulose (SIDAC) and Entreprises et Construction (engineering firm).

THE OTHER PROCESSING INDUSTRIES

The glass industry developed in Belgium in the region of the coalfields of Charleroi. In the beginning there was little specialization in the sector, with many factories all producing window glass, plate glass, bottles and other containers. Window and plate glass were high-quality products and were exported to other countries. The famous crystal factories of Val Saint-Lambert (Liège) employed some 6,000 workers.

Before the First World War glass-making was dominated by small family-owned firms, when the SGB started concentrating window glass production within the Verreries de Mariemont. But a generalized technological breakthrough was delayed because the workers in the glass factories strongly opposed modernization. Finally, in 1923 a new firm set-up in Mol (Campine) started production of so-called 'float-glass' (by drawing it continuously onto a surface of molten metal for hardening from a molten state). The factory in Mol belonged to the Compagnie Internationale pour la Fabrication Mécanique du Verre with window glass factories in France, Spain, Switzerland and Germany.

The Belgian producers of plate glass exported 90 per cent of their produce, and already in 1904 they signed the Convention Internationale des Glaceries limiting production. Their central marketing organization (Union Continentale Commerciale des Glaceries) fixed prices. But after the First World War all international cartels collapsed (Berger 1925: 88–90).

During the Depression the overcapitalized producers of window

Table 2.4 Total output of the Belgian window glass factories, 1913–30
(in '000 m^2)

Year	Blown glass	Mechanically produced glass	Total
1913	39,687	–	39,687
1920	27,404	1,325	28,729
1922	29,973	1,563	31,536
1924	30,071	10,915	40,986
1926	23,984	25,467	49,451
1928	11,055	42,070	53,125
1930	3,500	31,107	34,607

Source: Olyslager 1947: 148–9

and plate glass were forced to reorganize; three Belgian producers of plate glass (Glaces de Charleroi, Glaces de Moustier-sur-Sambre and the Compagnie de Floreffe) formed GLAVER, while the Union des Verreries Mécaniques grouped the producers of window glass. Under the influence of Saint-Gobain the Glaceries de la Sambre grouped the Glaceries de Saint-Roch, Glaces d'Auvelais and Glaces de Sainte-Marie d'Oignies. But because of the existence of small independent firms, these cartels could not stabilize the glass market (Delaet 1986: 113–52).

The bottle, wine and beer glass factories only modernized after 1929 (using the Libbey–Owens principle, whereby semi-molten glass is shaped by machine and stretched into hollow forms) and spread throughout the country. Because the automobile industry had become an important client of the glassworks, new firms (Sécurit, Société Belge de Verreries (SOBELVER), Splintex, Gomglas, Indestructo) were founded.

Rubber factories were small and depended on the import of rubber from Malaysia, Java and the Belgian Congo. Synthetic rubber was imported from Canada. The Englebert factory in Liège was the only one that gained importance. The Belgian rubber companies held a strong position not in production of finished rubber products, but in plantations and the commercialization of raw materials. The Hallet Group owned the Plantations Nord-Sumatra and the Sennah Rubber Co. in the Dutch Indies and the Compagnie Congolaise de l'Hévéa and the Cultures Equatoriales in the Belgian Congo. Together with the French Rivaud Group Hallet established

51

plantations in Indochina and in French Africa. In the British colonies Hallet owned the Selangor Plantations Co. Ltd (Malaysia) and the Socfinal Co. Ltd (Kenya). Furthermore, Hallet controlled the Banque Hallet, a private bank investing funds provided by his wealthy friends (Solvay). Hallet's investment strategy was co-ordinated by the Société Financière des Caoutchoucs (SOCFIN) and the Financière des Colonies (Joye 1960: 170–1).

Before the First World War Belgium was already an important producer of cement. Soon artificial cement (Portland and scoria cement) supplanted natural cement. In 1929 production of natural cement had fallen to 650,000 tonnes, while the total output of Portland had increased to some 3,255,000 tons (Hulpiau 1945: 8–9). The development of the cement industry was fostered by cheap labour, rich natural marlstone layers, a large transport system and low freight prices at the port of Antwerp. During the 1920s total output of Portland cement doubled as a result of investment in new high-capacity ovens and the very low stabilization rate of the Belgian franc enabled the cement producers to conquer new foreign markets.

Two major companies – the Cimenteries et Briqueteries Réunies de Belgique (CBR) and the Ciments d'Obourg – dominated the cement sector. CBR was founded in 1924 by the SGB and absorbed several existing firms. Ciments d'Obourg was founded in 1911 by Swiss investors (Financière Glaris and the holding company Amiantus) and absorbed the Ciments de Lanay in 1930. As in other sectors cartels appeared. In 1919 the cement producers associated within the Association des Fabricants de Ciments Portland Artificiels, distributing orders among its members. This cartel collapsed during the crisis of 1921. A successor organization, the Union des Cimenteries, could only organize the cement producers of the north, while several other marketing organizations operated on the export markets (Hulpiau 1945: 11). Not all producers were won over to the idea of cartelization and even during the Depression all efforts in this direction failed until the government imposed a cartel on the producers of Portland cement in June 1935. Then the producers of slag cement were invited to join. The Depression had a devastating effect on the Belgian cement sector because of the prohibitive tariffs forcing the Belgian producers to narrow their margins. The important Latin American market was lost. In 1936 75 per cent of exports went to four countries: the Netherlands, the Republic of Ireland, the UK and the USA. The high exchange rate of the Belgian franc, fierce competition and low quality had a negative impact on export opportunities. In the Netherlands the Belgian firms had to withstand German dumping practices and competition from the Eerste Nederlandse Cement Industrie (ENCI), a subsidiary of the SGB.

With the growth in the demand for cheap paper, the paper industry came to depend increasingly on imported wood pulp. Hence new factories were built near the ports of Antwerp and Ghent or alongside the canals in Flanders. The SGB brought several paper mills together under the umbrella of the Papeteries de Belgique.

During the 1920s and 1930s many grain mills, breweries and sugar refineries disappeared, but, generally speaking, these family capital-based firms could withstand the crisis because their investment was written off.

Table 2.5 Concentration in the food industry, 1880–1947

	1880	1896	1910	1937	1947
Breweries	2,574	1,375	2,273	1,123	716
Breweries/Malt houses	–	1,543	981	81	34
Malt houses	–	73	109	100	102
Grain mills	4,077	3,922	3,501	2,925	3,111
Sugar refineries	40	7	13	12	8
Sugar mills	146	111	66	34	39
Canneries	–	16	41	141	121
Dairy factories	–	128	528	641	447
Margarine factories	–	10	10	22	9

Source: Van Molle 1986: 170

The grain mills remained rather small, but several important firms milling imported grain from the USA and Argentina existed in Antwerp and alongside the canals in Flanders. In the branch of the oil mills the Union Margarinière (Unilever) competed with Belgian butter produced by the innumerable small co-operatively owned dairies. Many types of grains, seeds and nuts were treated in large factories linked to the colonial trading and shipping houses in Antwerp. The grits were transformed into animal fodder. Flax seeds were used for the production of siccatives, linoleum and soap. Because import of all these raw materials (in 1938 280,000 tonnes) was destined to the factories producing for the domestic market, the falling prices of raw materials during the 1930s were advantageous to the Belgian producers of vegetable oil products. Although cane sugar was cheaper, the sugar-beet growers and beet-sugar refiners remained successful on a protected and cartelized internal market (Union Sucrière) dominated by the SA Raffinerie Tirlemontoise (Joye 1984: *passim*).

The situation in the tobacco industry was not dissimilar. The producers specialized in the production of cigarettes and formed trusts. Three firms, the Etablissements Gosset (Saint-Michel), Henri Vander Elst (Belga) and Odon Warland (Boule Nationale), held 80 per cent of the national market. The production of cigarettes required heavy investment in machinery, the import of huge amounts of tobacco of standard quality and advanced methods of packaging and distribution. In 1928 TABACOFINA was founded as a holding company controlling the tobacco factories owned by the Vander Elst and Van Zuylen families.

In the mid-nineteenth century there were some 2,700 breweries in Belgium employing 6,800 people. In the big cities industrial brewers specialized in lager beer. Concentration was slowed because freight costs and local traditions enabled small breweries to survive.

Biscuits, chocolates and pudding were produced in Antwerp and Brussels by small factories. Edouard de Beukelaer (biscuits), Imperial Products (British instant puddings), Meurisse (chocolates), and Edouard Parein (biscuits) established themselves in Antwerp, while Biscuiterie Paquot and Biscuits Delacre (both biscuits), Côte d'Or, Alimenta, Godiva and Neuhaus (all chocolates) had their factories in Brussels.

THE AGRARIAN SECTOR

The survival of a large class of smallholders (see Table 2.6) necessitated agrarian protectionism. Although tariffs protected the farmers from foreign competition, agrarian protectionism did not go as far as in some neighbouring countries. But because Belgian agriculture was slow in modernizing its output and in shifting from cereal production towards dairy farming and market gardening, protectionism hampered agricultural development. Furthermore, the use of fertilizers promised the smallholders a higher yield without changing their ways of farming. Apart from the Boerenbond, organizing more than 100,000 smallholders' families, agriculture remained rather poorly organized. Many farmers and gardeners preferred to have direct access to the urban markets instead of joining a co-operative organization distributing their products (Kruyt 1932: 56).

The Boerenbond operated as a central purchasing organization for eggs, butter, fruit and early potatoes and tried to sell these products on the London market. Selling of agrarian products made some progress compared with the pre-war period. The import of cheap Argentinian beef forced the farmers to specialize in milk cows and to buy milk-skimmers or to transport their milk to co-operative dairies. Production and consumption of butter was boosted. In 1929 Belgium produced 50 million kilos of butter and consumed 53 million kilos.

Table 2.6 Agrarian population, 1846–1947

Year	Agrarian population	Percentage of total population
1846	854,000	42
1880	953,000	36
1890	858,000	30
1900	836,000	26
1910	801,000	23
1920	604,399	18
1930	629,639	17
1947	412,026	12

Source: Van Molle, 1990: 365.

Table 2.7 The use of fertilizers in agriculture, 1925 (in kg/ha)

	Nitrates	Phosphates	Potassium
Germany	11.2	13.1	21.4
Belgium/Luxembourg	22.6	69.2	22.7
Netherlands	17.0	39.6	32.3

Source: Kruyt 1932: 30.

The competitiveness of Belgian agriculture has been depicted as poor, but if we compare its performance with the other European countries the overall result is rather good and even well above average (Kruyt 1932: 29). But the efficiency of Belgian agriculture depended on the use of fertilizers (phosphates and nitrates) (see Table 2.7).

During the 1920s Belgian farmers made substantial profits because high prices were paid for foodstuffs and the rapid inflation had freed them from their mortgages. Re-allotment could have been a method to rationalize farming, but the agrarian interest groups never proposed a comprehensive project of land reform. The final result was that the size of the farms decreased, forcing the smallholders to work harder, because the small plots precluded mechanization. Harsh competition among peasants to acquire additional plots of land meant that prices paid for real estate were constantly rising.

During the Depression wheat production rose at a steady rate while the production of rye and oats decreased, because the government had decided to favour wheat at the expense of the other crops. Thus the Belgian stock farmers and the producers of dairy products had an advantage in purchasing their cattle-fodder (oats, rye) by paying the world market price. Butter production was protected by imposition of quotas and high tariffs. Because the government had to keep down the general level of all agrarian prices (see Table 2.8), protectionism could not assist all peasants.

Table 2.8 Prices of some agrarian products on the Belgian market, 1926–35 (in Belgian francs/100 kg)

Year	Wheat	Rye	Oats	Potatoes	Butter
1926	174.38	131.79	125.25	60.30	2,077
1930	127.87	86.55	92.46	47.73	2,594
1934	62.09	56.58	61.64	36.00	1,828
1935	76.56	68.32	81.63	41.18	1,790

Source: 'De Invloed' 1968: 1630

The agrarian lobby gave a very pessimistic view on the income situation of the farmers, while it was widely known that rural savings remained relatively high during the Depression. The banks of the Boerenbond did not collapse at this time and agricultural land remained one of the safest investments for village dwellers. That agricultural concessions could be traded abroad for openings for industrial products was traditionally strongly opposed by the Boerenbond. Even the idea of a customs union with the Netherlands was described as an attempt to undermine the living conditions of the Belgian peasants. Although protective barriers were lowered in the period of prosperity which followed the devaluation of the Belgian franc they were soon raised again. As a result of protectionism Belgian farmers were annually costing around 2,500 million Belgian francs.

THE SHIPPING INTERESTS

Almost all overseas trade was concentrated in Antwerp, where raw materials came in and where finished goods went out. Because of their shipping activities in the Baltic Sea and transit trade to the western and southern part of Germany or to Latin America, rich German merchants like Bunge, Bracht, Kreglinger, Osterrieth and Born had made Antwerp a real cosmopolitan metropolis. Because the steamships had difficulty in entering the port of Antwerp, in 1906 the government decided to subsidize a modernization programme.

At the end of the nineteenth century the transatlantic lines departing from Antwerp were exclusively in the hands of foreign companies like the White Cross Line (Daniel Steinmann) or the Red Star Line (International Navigation Co., Philadelphia). The latter specialized in transatlantic passenger transport. Because the Belgian government had made its flag attractive to foreign companies, shipping companies specializing in the Latin American trade were established in Antwerp (Steinmann & Co., T.C. Engels & Co., Armement Deppe and the Compagnie Royale Belgo–Argentine). Deppe was financed by the Banque d'Anvers and the Argentinian wheat merchants Bunge & Born and his strategy consisted in shipping heavy railway equipment and building materials to Argentina, where Bunge & Born could provide his liners with wheat. On the eve of the First World War Armement Deppe owned thirty-five steamships (42 per cent of the Belgian merchant fleet capacity).

An act of 18 August 1907 gave a strong impetus to the development of a Belgian merchant fleet because it allowed Belgian shipping companies to borrow capital with advantageous conditions (the Belgian State guaranteed repayment of these loans). In 1911 a consortium of Belgian bankers and merchants led by Albert Thys took over the Compagnie Belge Maritime du Congo (CBMC) from British and German capitalists, but soon the SGB with its growing Congolese interests became the major shareholder of the CBMC (*Compagnie* 1947: 59).

In 1916 five minor Belgian ship-owners (Antwerpse Zeevaart-maatschappij, Scheepvaartmaatschappij Gylsen, SA de Commerce et de Navigation, Brys & Gylsen Ltd, Anglier Steamship Co. Ltd) merged their companies into the Lloyd Royal Belge (Luykx 1972: 176; Reuchlin 1978: 246) in order to facilitate the implementation of the foreign aid programme organized by the Commission for Relief in Belgium and the American government. At the end of the war the Belgian merchant fleet had lost 35 per cent of its pre-war shipping capacity. Because the postwar boom ended in 1921 in falling freight prices, many companies faced liquidity problems. The Belgian Lloyd, which had financed its growth (80 ships) by borrowing and expanding its activities far beyond the limits of its normal capacity, was forced to sell a significant part of its fleet and since the Belgian government had guaranteed loans for the purchase or construction of new ships, it had to convert all bad loans into Belgian Lloyd shares. Meanwhile a consortium of French and Belgian bankers, which had helped to float the company, acquired control of Belgian Lloyd. In 1929 Belgian Lloyd merged with the CBMC, forming Compagnie Maritime Belge (CMB) (*Compagnie* 1947: 94).

In 1932 the Belgian merchant fleet consisted of 118 vessels with a shipping capacity of 439,975 tons, but fifty-one of these ships (or 194,029 tonnes) had been laid up. Generous loans granted by the Belgian government enabled the shipping companies to modernize their fleet, but meanwhile total tonnage of the Belgian merchant fleet had declined to its pre-1914 level (Bogaert 1945: 13).

The problem of the Belgian shipowners was that they were not able to impose their rules on the stronger nations and therefore they relied on their ability to attract heavy freight from the Latin American and African ports towards Antwerp, knowing they could easily acquire return freight in their home port. But the very existence of the CMB in Antwerp also helped to break the power of the foreign shipowners united in conferences from imposing their terms (Bogaert 1945: 15).

Belgium was increasingly importing heavy raw materials and grain. If one calculates the average weight of the goods handled in Antwerp for the period 1936–8, grains, ores and fuel (oil and coal) constituted some 60 per cent of total imports. Metal products, coal, fertilizers and cement accounted for 70 per cent of total exports. This reflected the one-sided specialization of Belgian industry in heavy products of a low added value.

Although Belgium was an early industrialized country with an outstanding machinery industry and large steel factories, shipbuilding was of marginal importance. As early as 1829 John Cockerill established his first wharf in the neighbourhood of his iron and machinery factory in Liège, but soon he moved his wharf (Cockerill Yards) to Antwerp. In 1829 Joseph Boel founded a small wharf in Temse for the construction of barges. These two wharves became important firms. During the Depression the CMB became an important client of the Cockerill Yards in Hoboken, because the Belgian authorities launched an important relief programme destined for the wharves and the shipping companies (Bogaert 1945: 25–6). Thus the Cockerill Yards and the Boel Wharf in Temse obtained the opportunity of building modern ships for the Belgian merchant fleet. Despite this modernization programme the average age (19.25 years) of the Belgian merchant fleet remained rather high. (The average age of the Dutch fleet was 13.3 years.)

CONCLUSIONS

Although the Belgian economy suffered from the economic crisis, the authorities never made serious attempts to impose a centrally organized economy. The traditional sectors (coal and steel) remained the cornerstone of the economy. While the steel industry was heavily dependent upon export markets, the government was forced by the steel industry and the big banks to organize the coal industry. Sectors suffering from overcapacity and falling profits were in general characterized by concentration of capital. This occurred in the sectors of fertilizers, glass, cement, rayon, cotton, shipping, non-ferrous metals and paper. Meanwhile the Belgian economy as a whole suffered from a small domestic market. As a marginal supplier of bulky and cyclically dependent products and industrial products, the Belgian industry tended to compete on price, rather than on quality and stimulated a policy of defensive investment. The development of new products was neglected and modernization of industrial equipment was postponed as long as possible. This explains why all automobile firms disappeared and were replaced by foreign companies.

3

THE POLITICS OF PRODUCTION DURING THE SECOND WORLD WAR

As early as 1936, the Minister of Finance Camille Gutt (Gutt 1971: 14–15) started consultations with the Governor of the National Bank in order 'to protect Belgian financial interests regardless of the outcome of the war' (Gillingham 1977: 25). In the mind of the politicians a Belgian government in exile could be foreseen. The question was whether that government should reside in Paris or in London. The latter place would be a good location from which the Belgian Congo and the international interests of the financial groups could be managed, but most of the politicians preferred Paris, where the National Bank and the financial groups were preparing to establish their headquarters. But it was only several months after the outbreak of the Second World War that in February 1940 Georges Janssen, Governor of the National Bank, formed an economic committee to determine the measures to be taken after an invasion. The Belgian government now hesitated to decide whether the National Bank should be relocated in France or not. Thus there was no clear programme which could serve as a guideline for the government.

MILITÄRVERWALTUNG

During the confused days following the German invasion on 10 May 1940, a select group of three leading bankers (Alexandre Galopin of the SGB, Max-Léo Gérard of the Banque de Bruxelles and Fernand Collin of the Kredietbank) met Minister of Foreign Affairs Paul-Henri Spaak and Minister of Finance Gutt on 15 May 1940 in Spaak's office (Gérard-Libois and Gotovitch n.d.: 171) in order to determine their conduct after the Belgian government left Brussels. Although no official record was made of this important meeting, we know that the two ministers ordered the bankers to assure the payment of the civil servants' salaries during the occupation. During this important meeting ministers and bankers also discussed the problem of the economic future of the country during an occupation which probably would last for several years. After the war Collin reported that Minister Spaak finally pronounced the far-reaching sentence: 'Messieurs, nous vous confions la Belgique!'.

After the departure of the Belgian government a group of leading bankers and technocrats active in the narrow circle of the CERE made arrangements for an authoritarian reform of the State. Among the members of the CERE, the leading bankers and the delegates of the powerful entrepreneurial organization CCI had constituted an informal network, also named the Consortium of Bankers or the Galopin Committee, which developed the guidelines of economic and social policy implemented during the Second World War in occupied Belgium. At their head stood Alexandre Galopin, Governor of the SGB. Among the members were Max-Léo Gérard (Banque de Bruxelles), Fernand Collin (Kredietbank), Willy de Munck (SGB), Baron Albert-Edouard Janssen (Solvay), Emile Van Dievoet (Kredietbank), Paul Tschoffen (Ougrée–Marihaye), Baron Vaxelaire (Bon Marché), Albert Goffin (National Bank) and Léon Bekaert. During the war this committee acted as a *pouvoir de fait*, without a legal base and without a clear *ligne de conduite* designed by the Belgian government staying in London.

Meanwhile, the Germans established a *Militärverwaltung* (military administration). They contacted the Belgian economic élite and invited it to normalize the economic situation. The policy formulated by the Germans was mainly inspired by the material interest of preserving the Belgian production capacity from a collapse and letting it work to serve the economic needs of the German war effort. The *Militärverwaltung* was interested neither in destroying the Belgian economy nor in taking over the entire administration of the country. In that way the *Militärverwaltung* opposed in practice the ambitions of the local Nazis who were striving for an independent Flanders or an immediate integration of Belgium into the German Reich. Finally, this kind of 'realism' fitted well with the policy of accommodation the Belgian economic élite would adopt after May 1940. The leaders of Belgian business could be forced to collaborate because they depended on the import of raw materials and foodstuffs controlled by the Germans. The Belgian industrialists also had to find outlets for their products and here the Reich appeared as the 'natural' export market. This situation determined the attitude of both players in the war game.

The German government in Berlin was interested in strengthening the Belgian administrative system in order to smooth the economic collaboration. Therefore the *Militärverwaltung* tried to replace the administrative chiefs by local Fascists as faithful executors of German policy and reorganize the economic system on a Nazi model by imposing the '*Führer*-principle' and offices for each industrial sector. The first step of the Germans was to force the Belgian administration to implement its policy concerning food and agriculture, foreign trade and price regulation, employment, banks and insurance, social problems, and Jewish property.

THE POLITICS OF PLUNDERING

After a period of confusion the Germans assigned to the Belgian employers' organization CCI the responsibility of organizing Belgian industry into industrial groupings analogous to the German organizations. These organizations had to operate as central bodies for defining production and allocating raw materials. Hence the Belgian economy could be fitted into a German-controlled European economy. General Georg Thomas arrived from Berlin with the primary responsibility for the seizure and removal of raw materials and bringing under German control strategic production units, such as the large weaponry producer Fabrique Nationale d'Armes de Guerre in Herstal (Liège). German managers were appointed in the American-owned firms (Bell Telephone, Ateliers Téléphoniques d'Electricité en Anvers (ATEA), Ford Motor, General Motors). Meanwhile German heavy industry started plundering stocks and buying goods on the black market in the occupied countries.

There were also other plans and projects to unify 'Europe' under the flag of German heavy industry and the big banks (Deutsche Bank, Dresdner Bank). After having absorbed the Czech and Austrian steel firms, the Ruhr barons thought a cartel agreement with the Belgian and French firms would serve their interests better than a dismantling of the heavy industry in the occupied territories (Gillingham 1977: 48–9). The Ruhr barons obtained a dominant role in establishing contacts with the Belgian steel firms. The latter reconstituted their Syndicat Belge de l'Acier (SYBELAC) (Gillingham 1977: 51). The German coal-mine owners had a similar approach when discussing the future of their industry, but they failed to organize the European coal industry into an international cartel. The reason was that the coal-mine owners were in a weaker position and dominated by the steel industry and the IG Farben (heavy chemicals).

It was IG Farben's aim to establish a new order in Europe by changing the rules of the game among the main chemical firms. In competition with the steel and coal industries the chemical industry was producing a multitude of products which were all subjected to patents and different tax systems. Close ties existed between IG Farben and Solvay because the Belgian chemical firm was the second largest shareholder in IG Farben (Gillingham 1977: 52). IG Farben and the Nazi administration in Berlin became more interested in organizing the European textile industry under the command of rayon producers who were to provide the Wehrmacht with uniforms. But these extremist ideas proved to be impractical and therefore were cancelled.

More serious was the strategy of the German banks promoting interpenetration (*Verflechtung*) of Belgian and German capital. Here the Deutsche Bank and the Dresdner Bank proved to be competitors (Hofmans 1992: *passim*). The Dresdner Bank held a strong position in Southeastern Europe, while the Deutsche Bank represented by Hermann Josef Abs specialized in affairs concerning Western Europe. Because the Dresdner Bank had acquired the Zivnostenka Bank in Prague with its large interests in heavy industry, it was logical that the Dresdner Bank would try to control the SGB, Société de Bruxelles pour la Finance et l'Industrie (BRU-FINA) and Solvay, while the Deutsche Bank got the pre-eminence in the Netherlands. But all the attempts of the Dresdner Bank to control the SGB by promising watered-down shares as compensation failed because the SGB preferred to collaborate with the Deutsche Bank. The latter succeeded in taking over the shares the SGB held in Eastern European banks (Böhmische Union-Bank (BUB) in Prague, the Allgemeiner Jugoslawischer Bankverein (Belgrade), the Jugoslawische Union-Bank (Zagreb), Creditanstalt-Bankverein (CABV) (Vienna), Banca Comerciala Romana (Bucharest), Istituto Nazionale di Credito per il Lavoro al Estero, the Eisenbahnverkehrsanstalt (Vienna), the Banca Nazionale d'Albania, the Landesbank von Bosnien und Herzegowina) and in the Banque Générale de Luxembourg (*OMGUS* 1985: 221–57, 408–29). In Belgium the Deutsche Bank controlled the Banque de Commerce in Antwerp via its subsidiary Firma de Bary & Co. in Amsterdam.

The friendly co-operation between the Deutsche Bank and the SGB culminated in the handing over of 1.5 million shares the SGB held in the coal mine Dahlbusch–Gesellschaft to the Deutsche Bank and an agreement on a joint control exercised by both banks on the steel firm ARBED (*OMGUS* 1985: 422). The two banks co-operated when merging the Schlesische AG für Bergbau und Zinkhütten-betrieb (SAG) with the Schlesische Bergwerke & Hütten AG (SCHLESAG). The Dresdner Bank established a subsidiary in Brussels and Antwerp, the Continentale Bank NV also known as the 'SS Bank' because of its close connections with the Gestapo and the Nazis (*OMGUS* 1986: 155–6). The Dresdner Bank financed military works and Belgian businesses working for the *Wehrmacht*, the pro-Nazi newspaper *Volk en Staat*, the Ford Motor Co. factory in Antwerp (now producing for the *Wehrmacht*), the SA Ateliers de Construction de la Meuse, the Organisation Todt, etc. The Continentale Bank NV became an important broker of stock formerly owned by Jewish shareholders, which was sold on the Brussels stock market with the help of the Flemish Kredietbank (*OMGUS* 1986: 164–5). In Luxembourg the Dresdner Bank acquired control over the Banque Internationale à Luxembourg formerly owned by the Banque de Bruxelles. This policy of merging interests marked the end of the period of plundering the conquered territories and a shift towards a policy of closer industrial collaboration.

THE GALOPIN COMMITTEE

The problems the *Militärverwaltung* met were twofold. First, in order to preserve social and economic order it was necessary to obtain the collaboration of persons in charge of public adminis-tration. Second, an ad hoc solution had to be found for normalizing the commercial relations between the occupied country and Germany. Notwithstanding the fact that hundreds of thousands of Belgian soldiers who had been captured during the May Campaign were transported to Stalags in Germany, mass unemployment was threatening.

The Belgian government in London did not yet play a role of real authority and the members of the Galopin Committee in Brussels were not disposed to recognize the primacy of politics in a situation in which they had to face the direct consequences of the German occupation. Meanwhile the Galopin Committee solved some urgent problems concerning payment of civil servants. Because Governor Janssen and his staff of the National Bank had left Brussels, thus leaving the country without a bank of issue, the Galopin Committee decided to assign the privilege of issue to a new bank, the Banque d'Emission SA (Emission Bank). Together with the group of the Banque de Bruxelles (3,500 out of 15,000 shares) the SGB (6,000 shares) dictated the rules in the Banque d'Emission and the latter received the task of regulating the so-called 'clearing' between Germany and Belgium. When the Governor of the National Bank returned to Belgium, the Galopin Committee attached the Banque d'Emission to the National Bank.

The politics of collaboration were initiated by economic and social necessity and started during the summer of 1940 when the *Wehrmacht* was purchasing goods on the Belgian market on an ever-increasing scale. Payment was assured by an advance of 3 billion Belgian francs paid by the National Bank to the Reich for its occupation costs. This decision by the National Bank was inspired by the private bankers who held a stake in the central bank and who also were the first beneficiaries of that measure. The next stage was that Germany now submitted a monthly bill which the National Bank had to pay out in Belgian francs financed by Treasury notes subscribed by the private banks (Gillingham 1977: 68). The Banque d'Emission held the responsibility of handling payments between Belgium and the Reich. But here the clearing system worked in a one-way direction because at the end of the occupation the Banque d'Emission had accumulated some 64 billion Belgian francs which the National Bank had forwarded to the Banque d'Emission to ensure payment to Belgian firms exporting to Germany (Demany 1946: *passim*). The deficit was mainly the result of restrictions Germany had put on its export of foodstuffs to Belgium and the uncontrolled export policy of Belgian firms to Germany. In that way exports generated an unlimited growth of cash which opened the door to unlimited inflation (soaring prices on the black market). This practice of unlimited export to Germany was stimulated by the captains of industry in search of an outlet for their products. They tried to lower costs in order to underbid the German firms on their domestic market. This was realized by a devaluation of the Belgian franc to the Reichsmark and by lowering wages.

Numerous syndicates were set up in order to organize production and allocate raw materials. The 'success' of the politics of production for the Germans was proved by the fact that industrial exports ran at twice the rate set by the Galopin Committee and that the German purchasers in the Occupied Area could command an equal amount. Galopin and his fellow bankers thought that a peace treaty soon would come about (Gillingham 1977: 74; De Jonghe 1972: 259–300). But in vain. Instead of a general settlement the Germans increased their pressure and in Berlin the German Ministry of Finance now was thinking of a removal of Belgian custom barriers and letting the Reichsmark circulate freely in Belgium. Finally, in March 1941 Galopin travelled to Berlin where he discussed the situation with leading civil servants and where he promised that the 'Belgians would learn to work harder, thereby becoming more productive' (Gillingham 1977: 74). The outcome was that all projects for including Belgium economically into the Reich were cancelled. Meanwhile the bankers and lawyers of the Galopin Committee discussed the political consequences of the 'politics of production'. It was the banker and professor of criminal law Fernand Collin who invented the most appropriate term characterizing the precarious situation: the Belgian industrialists were pressed by a situation of necessity to produce for the enemy (Van den Wijngaert 1990: 39). In reality the Belgian industrialists and bankers were simply violating the principle of non-collaboration with the occupying authority. Nonetheless, the arguments that the 'politics of production' saved the Belgian industrial apparatus from destruction and dismantling, received some credibility because during the First World War the Belgian population had experienced enormous casualties and destruction. An important event occurred on 22 June 1941 with the attack by the *Wehrmacht* on the USSR. The German offensive was successful but failed to destroy the Red Army before the beginning of the Russian winter. The reaction of the German leaders consisted of boosting arms production and imposing a mobilization of all productive forces and raw materials. Thus in December 1941 the Reich banned exports to the occupied territories. This measure explained the decrease in German exports to Belgium. In 1941 the Reich exported 417 million Reichsmarks worth of goods. In 1943 this figure had fallen to 278 million Reichsmarks. This provoked difficulties for the Belgian economy which had become dependent on German imports of raw materials. The mobilization for total war provoked a labour shortage in Germany. Now Berlin opted for massive deportation of workers to Germany and in March 1942 the first compulsory labour draft was published. Drafts started in October 1942 and by April 1943 more than 215,000 Belgian workers had been transferred to Germany. This provoked a wave of popular discontent. Apart from a system of compulsory labour the Germans were now striving for the organization of a war economy which had to devise a policy of saving raw materials. This forced the Belgian economy into a more far-reaching form of collaboration. The Belgian consumers were the victims of this policy, because the Germans now forced the Belgian producers to cut production destined for the domestic market and to produce cheap *ersatz* products. But soon the Germans had to change their economic policy, because increased bombing on German cities, railroad stations and factories had made decentralization of production necessary. Hence it would be better to protect the producing units in the occupied countries.

THE BELGIAN WAR ECONOMY

The Belgian industry was of strategic importance for the German war economy, because of its geographical position near the Ruhr area. Belgium was producing important quantities of coal and steel the German war economy needed in ever larger quantities as the *Wehrmacht* was loosing tanks and heavy equipment on the Russian front. The supply of rolling stock and rails became of strategic importance because of the Allied bombings of railroads, bridges and stations. Coal now was the only substitute for oil, because the supply of Romanian oil was not sufficient to fuel the mechanized war machinery of the *Wehrmacht*. France and Italy were cut off from English coal and both countries turned to the German and Belgian coal mines in order to obtain additional coal (Gillingham 1977: 128).

Although the Germans had put the Belgian mines under control of 'assessors', they failed to boost production. During the first month of the occupation Belgian mines were producing at full capacity, but thereafter production dropped at a steady rate. The monthly average rate for 1941 was 2.3 million tonnes; for 1942 2.1 million tonnes; for 1943 2 million tonnes. But in the last months of 1943 and early 1944 production completely broke down (Baudhuin 1945: 290). In May 1944 production averaged only 1 million tonnes. There were several causes for this. First, there was the exhaustion of the labour force employed in the coal mines. The Germans then sent Russian prisoners of war to work in the mines, but these badly fed and lodged workers were of little value. Second, severe food shortages during the winter of 1940–1 created resistance within the mining population. Third, the Belgian mining firms were experiencing the disastrous effects of German supremacy on the European coal market. Because German coal shipped from the Ruhr area was cheaper than Belgian coal the Belgian state had to subsidize coal exports. These subsidies were paid out of a tax levied on sales to Belgian consumers.

The Galopin Committee tried to appease the situation by assigning quotas of orders from the Stahlwerksverband to each Belgian steel producer. Therefore a cartel was established, SYBELAC, which had the power to control the allocation of German orders to the steel works and the manufacturing industry (Gillingham 1977: 140) and enabled the Belgian steel industry to contribute impressively to the German war effort. From the total Belgian steel production of 4.6 million tonnes from June 1940 to September 1944, only 1.2 million tonnes was destined for the local civilian market. The remaining part served the German war effort (Gillingham 1977: 146). After the Second World War it was estimated that the Belgian steel industry was completely exhausted (Baudhuin 1945: 286), due to the fact that the steel firms were producing at low capacity and at low prices. But all these losses which the book-keepers registered could not hide the simple fact that the earnings of firms listed on the Brussels Stock Exchange did very well during the period 1940–2 (see Table 3.2).

Some Belgian firms boosted their production by obtaining German orders. That was the case with the very specialized manufacturers of heating systems, steel construction, the aeronautical

Table 3.1 Sales of coal by Belgian mines, 1941–3 (in million tonnes)

	1941	1942	1943
Total production	30.056	25.758	25.054
Total sales	25.751	21.614	20.845
Total exports	4.066	2.783	2.182
to Germany	0.910	0.847	0.661
to the *Wehrmacht*	0.331	0.300	0.206
Sales to the steel industry	0.687	0.407	0.350
Sales to the cement works	0.596	0.462	0.435

Source: Baudhuin 1945: 290

Table 3.2 Earnings of firms listed on the stock exchange, excluding amortization and cash balances, 1939–43 (in million Belgian francs)

	1939	1940	1941	1942	1943
Coal (by region)					
Borinage	46	75	59	14	− 15
Centre	74	77	63	17	− 4
Charleroi	134	175	122	12	− 5
Liège	89	103	57	18	− 10
Limburg	186	244	243	147	56
Metallurgy	633	564	334	114	− 11
Tramways	73	62	67	69	67
Chemicals	138	205	79	108	113
Glass	–	11	23	19	13
Breweries	48	46	35	23	22
Paper	45	59	54	35	27

Source: Baudhuin 1945: 268

industry, naval construction, small arms, railroad rolling stock, etc. According to the American historian J. Gillingham, Belgian firms in 1943 alone delivered 155 locomotives. In that year Ford Motor produced 400 trucks a month. At the end of 1940 the Belgian producers of rolling stock agreed to produce 200 locomotives (Baudhuin 1945: 288). Three of the most active industries exporting products to Germany were textiles, metal products and steel. The Groupement Principal des Fabrications Métalliques exported more than 50 per cent of its production to Germany during 1942–3 and the textile industry did even better. Some firms established joint ventures with German enterprises. For example, FABELTA agreed to set up a joint venture with German capital and the SNCI–NMKN in order to build a new factory producing artificial woollen fibres destined for the *Wehrmacht* (Verhoeyen 1993: 181–2).

Collaboration practised by the industrialists and bankers became a controversial subject because article 116 of the Penal Code forbade production of arms destined for the enemy. But only a small minority of the industrial firms specialized in arms production, and the overwhelming majority of the firms produced semi-finished goods. But these goods could be transformed into arms or explosives. For example, the big steel-wire producer Bekaert produced barbed wire for the agrarian sector, but his barbed wire was also used as wire entanglement by the German army. A second argument used by the defenders of the 'politics of production' was that this prevented the deportation of workers to Germany. If this argument had any value, there was the fact that the Germans had already started to select workers for compulsory labour in Germany. A third argument the defenders of the 'politics of production' stressed was the fact that the industrialists were losing money when dealing with the Germans. Unfortunately, the problem here was that little was known about the real situation of the firms working for the Germans. A fourth argument in favour of the 'politics of production' was that the bankers and industrialists as good patriots were generously supporting the Resistance movement. Indeed, several Socialist and Christian Democratic leaders were protected by individual industrialists. Finally there was the argument that the Galopin Committee was acting as the local agent of the Belgian government in exile and reported to the government residing in London.

But the opportunist behaviour of the entrepreneurs during the war was a well-known fact. They were hated by the workers, because the entrepreneurial organization CCI immediately had proposed in a circular sent to its members in September 1940 that a radical change in the relationship with the workers had to be considered. The CCI proposed an overall lowering of the wages of the white-collar members by 10 per cent and those of the blue collars by 20 per cent. But the *Militärverwaltung*, fearing an uproar, reacted by forbidding any reduction of wages (Gérard-Libois and Gotovitch n.d.: 159; Luyten 1990: 104).

The entrepreneurs reacted with enthusiasm to the proposals made by the *Militärverwaltung* to organize the economy. The CCI agreed on 7 June 1940 to the founding of *Warenstellen* which corresponded with the German *Reichsstellen* deciding on the allocation of raw materials. But these *Warenstellen* were not completely new organizations – in reality they integrated the already existing sectoral organizations under a new name. For instance, the *Warenstelle* in the coal sector was presided over by the president of the former Fédération des Associations Charbonnières de Belgique. In the steel industry SYBELAC was nothing more than the continuation of the former cartel COSIBEL. The difference was that SYBELAC was now empowered to regulate the allocation of raw materials.

Several projects aimed at reforming the socio-economic and political structures were discussed in entrepreneurial circles. They all reflected the New Order ideology and received the initial support of

Cardinal Van Roey and Catholic trade unionists (Luyten 1990: 111–17). Well-known in this matter was the 'Centre Lippens' which pleaded for a strong executive. There was also the 'Wodon Group', a group of several influential people who proposed several drafts for a new constitution. None of these proposals and plans to reorganize the state in an authoritarian sense were ever realized because Hitler refused a political settlement for Belgium.

THE SOCIAL PACT

The attitude of the entrepreneurs *vis-à-vis* the working class changed fundamentally in 1942. A general agreement on the base of 'corporatism from below' appeared to the industrialists as the best solution in order to avoid a take-over by the Left. Belgian business had become aware of the fact that the liberal Euro–British system of producing and trading had disintegrated and that new forms were prevailing over classical liberalism. During the German occupation business had been subordinated to wage and price controls and the economic system imposed by the Germans had put high finance in a more powerful position. Industrial organization here meant that the industrialists were in a position to realize high profits in cartelized markets. Gillingham quite rightly noted that big capital 'soon came to realize that the changes introduced by the Nazis, or at their behest, could be used by it regardless of the outcome of the war' (Gillingham 1977: 167).

Big capital espoused the idea of more economic regulation, but excluded state intervention in labour relations by referring to the pre-war system of the *commissions paritaires*. The idea of perpetuating the existence of industrial organizations met favourable comment within the financial bourgeoisie (Gillingham 1977: 169) because the occupation had taught that in many sectors of the economy rationalization and reduction of competition had led to lower costs. The decisive role here was played by Galopin who co-ordinated the activities of the Bekaert and Velge Committees on postwar reconstruction. In the summer of 1943 the Velge Committee submitted a report on economic policy in which there was no place for re-establishing economic liberalism, because the *Warenstellen* and the corporations founded during the war had proved their usefulness. Velge believed that industrial organization had to become the cornerstone of a new economic policy, which had to promise social security and wealth to the workers. Social security had to be founded on the willingness of Capital and Labour to co-operate in parity commissions for each industrial branch and the government had to base its economic policy on preserving full employment. Velge no longer wanted to forbid strikes and he now hoped for social peace as a result of a good working system of collective bargaining and arbitration. A system of social security had to be developed and controlled by a parity-based supervisory board. Not centralization, but decentralization on a sectoral base would constitute the framework of the new social system.

All these basic ideas on the social and economic order after the war were incorporated in the Social Pact which a group of representatives of several entrepreneurial organizations and Socialist and Catholic trade unions had prepared. The Social Pact took the form of an informal agreement on the principle of a system of 'social solidarity' financed by entrepreneurs and workers. The Social Pact did not aim to introduce a comprehensive system of social security as the Beveridge Plan proposed for the UK, but was destined to provide only for wage-earners by introducing a compulsory system of social insurance and pension schemes. Civil servants already had their social security with pension schemes. But peasants and self-employed people still had to rely on themselves. Although the Social Pact proposed the establishment of a compulsory system for the wage-earners, this draft for a system of social security had to be carried out by organizations established on a parity base excluding the State (Slomp and Van Mierlo 1984: (II) 14). The influence of the entrepreneurial organization of the metal industry (Fédération des Constructeurs) and its policy-maker Bekaert was reputed as having been decisive for the compromise reached with the representatives of the trade unions. From now on the transforming industry would surpass heavy industry (steel and coal) in influence and promote the idea of incomes policy and economic growth as the basic ideas for the near future.

Meanwhile a group of Socialist politicians and trade unionists in London was also preparing for power in postwar Belgium, and their plans gained sympathy from the other parties. Among the Socialists in London the opportunist wing led by Spaak was pleading for a two-party system with a powerful Labour Party grouping of Socialists, Communists and Catholic progressives, while the Socialist Left believed that a radicalization of the working classes in Europe would favour the establishment of socialist regimes (Gotovitch 1981: 3–63). However, after the war all Socialists in

London wanted to establish a welfare state for 'all citizens without any exception . . . workers or employers, rich or poor . . .' (Smets and Rens 1976: AI55). In matters of economic development the Socialists asked for a real effort to produce goods for the domestic market, which meant coping with the traditional policy promoted by the financial groups. In order to eliminate cyclical imbalances the government should practise an anti-cyclical economic policy in collaboration with other countries (Smets and Rens 1976: AI82). These proposals clearly exceeded the limits the employers – who as such were not represented in London – would concede in matters of social policy and economic reform. Meanwhile the fathers of the Social Pact in occupied Belgium opted for a corporatist form of interest intermediation.

THE GOVERNMENT IN EXILE

The Belgian government in exile had to face different problems intimately linked with Allied warfare and its return to Brussels in the wake of the Allied Forces. First, there was the problem of its own legitimacy. The government did not form a homogeneous block and had lost a good deal of its political prestige in occupied Belgium where a powerful resistance movement had acquired the support of the population. The exile government supported the war aims of the Allies, but the fact that King Léopold III still resided in Brussels as a prisoner of war, complicated its task in many respects. A second problem was that, as the Day of Liberation approached, the government in London no longer wished to back the economic policy known as the 'politics of production'. A third problem the Belgian government was worrying about concerned the inflationary pressure caused by the way the Belgian administration in collaboration with the National Bank and the Banque d'Emission were financing the costs of the occupation imposed on Belgium and the clearing activities with Germany. Instead of increasing taxes the Belgian administration in Brussels was borrowing from the commercial banks and printing additional amounts of paper money. This policy made the banks rich and exempted wealthy Belgians from paying for the costs of the occupation.

The overall problem the government in exile had to meet was the existence of some kind of dual power. In London the Belgian government had kept the full authority over its colonies in Africa, but was powerless when dealing with the top level of the civil administration working under the Germans. Conflicts with the *Militärverwaltung* had forced several secretary-generals of the ministerial departments to resign and they were replaced by new men representing the factions of the New Order. Another significant conflict was about the National Bank and the Banque d'Emission. The latter could be considered as an illegal institution. The National Bank was also operating under dubious circumstances, because the exiled government had created a London branch of the National Bank.

The problems of the Belgian government in exile were partly due to the difficulties it met by communicating with the centres of power in Belgium. Successively several leading personalities left Belgium and reached London taking with them messages from Galopin concerning the 'politics of production' and the way these policies were carried out in occupied Belgium. At the end of 1942 the Belgian government in exile refused to accept the arguments defended by Galopin (Van den Wijngaert 1990: 100). But this governmental decision did not change Galopin's mind. The 'Prince of Belgian industry' was convinced of the fact that the Belgian government was only empowered to deal with the Allies and not with the Germans.

The Belgian government tried to secure the international position of the country in relation to the other European countries fighting against the Nazis. The idea of forming a free trade association with the Netherlands spontaneously appeared as the war effort brought VE Day nearer. On 21 October 1943 the first step was made by fixing the exchange rate of the Belgian franc and the Dutch guilder and, finally, on 5 September 1944 (a few days before the return of the Belgian government to Brussels), the establishment of the BENELUX was announced (Spaak 1969: (I) 250–3); Gutt 1971: 153–9; De Jong 1979: 378–81). The idea of a free trade association was in conformity with pre-war attempts at establishing a free trade zone of the small industrialized countries in northwest Europe. But other diplomatic aims had also guided the Belgian government. Minister of Foreign Affairs Spaak soon started applying for full diplomatic support of the UK for a postwar peace treaty. Apparently the Belgian government had some kind of pre-war security system in mind when approaching the UK for an alliance.

4

POSTWAR RECONSTRUCTION ON A PRE-WAR BASE (1944–58)

The liberation of Belgium at the beginning of September 1944 occurred without heavy fighting on Belgian territory. The port of Antwerp, which was of strategic importance for the supply of the Allied armies and the Belgian population, was liberated without being destroyed by the withdrawing German army. A problem was that the railway system had suffered from air bombing. The steel factories and power plants lacked coal or had been closed. But generally speaking Belgian industry had been left intact. Reconstruction could be started with the supply of coal and an immediate reorganization of the railways.

POSTWAR INSTABILITY

The government in exile returned on 8 September 1944 from London to the airport of Evere (Brussels), but the Communist Resistance Movement considered the 'Men from London' as the representatives of pre-war disorder. Furthermore there was the problem of a temporary vacancy on the throne. King Léopold III, who had lived in his palace at Laeken during the war, was now in Germany as a prisoner of the Germans. The problem of his absence was solved by installing the King's brother Charles as Prince Regent. Meanwhile the monarchy had lost most of its prestige by the dubious behaviour of King Léopold during the war, and after his liberation in May 1945 Léopold went into exile in Switzerland instead of returning to Brussels. This created a serious political crisis, dividing the population into partisans (the Catholics) and enemies of the King (Communists, Socialists, many Liberals). This lasted until 1950 when Léopold abdicated in favour of his eldest son Baudouin I.

In September 1944 the Pierlot–Spaak government had to compromise by accepting three leading persons of the Communist Party as ministers. This compromise proved to be a bad one, because the Communist-backed Resistance Movement was striving for a new social order. In October 1944 the Allied military authorities and General Dwight Eisenhower were seriously concerned about the imminence of anarchy. Eisenhower urged the Belgians to hand in their arms and by the end of October he assured them that the Belgian government would have his full backing in enforcing disarmament of the Resistance. On 13 November 1944 Prime Minister Hubert Pierlot ordered that all arms be returned by 18 November. The three Communist members of Pierlot's government opposed this proposal and resigned. On 17 November the Communist-influenced Front de l'Indépendance refused to hand in their arms and called for a demonstration on 25 November 1944 in the centre of Brussels. This led to a severe clash with the Belgian gendarmerie near the Parliament. But the Red Revolution did not come (Warner 1978: *passim*; Gotovitch 1983: *passim*).

In February 1945 a broad coalition government including the Communists was formed with the Socialist Achille Van Acker as Prime Minister. But in the summer of 1945 the Catholics, who soon formed a new Christian Popular Party, left the government because they could not agree with the majority of the ministers on the conditions of the return of King Léopold. De facto the Left and the Right were now divided on a question which was not a socio-economic issue. A coalition of Communists, Socialists, Liberals and Catholics of the Left was formed and stayed in power until March 1947, but it did not win a clear political majority during the first postwar elections which were held on 17 February 1946. Because the Liberals defended a socio-economic programme that contradicted that of the Socialists or the Communists, the Left governments could only survive as long as Communists and Liberals supported the Socialists and their programme of economic reconstruction. Although the Communists supported a reformist programme while warning against a conservative take-over and economic sabotage, in March 1947 they resigned from government after having opposed higher prices for coal. This meant the end of the anti-Catholic coalition (Gérard-Libois and Lewin 1992: 54–125; Witte 1989: 13–58).

The Christian Democrats and Socialists formed the 'Great Coalition' led by the Socialist Spaak. This coalition government aimed at modernizing the socio-economic system on the principles of corporatist interest intermediation. The Social Pact, which had been legalized in December 1944, received a comprehensive framework of institutions and corporatist arrangements representing capital and labour as collective bargaining partners and establishing advisory bodies to the government. This coalition only stayed in power until June 1949. Now the 'Royal Question' (the return of King Léopold) moved to the forefront. The Christian Democrats were striving for an absolute majority in Parliament in order to impose the return of the King. In the elections of 1950 the Christian Democrats finally gained an absolute majority in both the Senate and House of Representatives enabling them to form a majority government and to force the return of Léopold. But the Catholics failed to restore Léopold to the throne and his son Baudouin I succeeded him (Gérard-Libois and Gotovitch 1983: *passim*; *Dossier 'Question Royale'* 1974: *passim*).

TOWARDS ECONOMIC NORMALIZATION

When arriving in Brussels in September 1944 the Belgian exile government had to face very urgent economic problems. First, there was the problem of the black market and inflationary pressures. Minister of Finance Gutt immediately wanted to stabilize prices and on 6 October 1944 decreed a monetary reform linked with a freeze of practically all bank deposits. Thus some 179 billion francs were frozen in bank accounts and some 88 billion francs in liquidities were recouped by a forced exchange in new banknotes at a rate of 2,000 francs per individual. The parity between the Belgian franc and the British pound was fixed at 162.62 Belgian francs, which corresponded with the exchange rate of the Congolese franc and tied the Belgian economy to the British price level. Second, there remained the question of the fixing of the price of Belgian coal and steel and the wages paid in industry. Here the Pierlot government had no other choice but to invite entrepreneurs and trade unions to a National Labour Conference which met on 16 September 1944. All wages of industrial workers were raised by 60 per cent (Scholliers 1993: 272–3).

Normalization could only be reached by boosting industrial production and exports, by importing foodstuffs and raw materials, by repairing the destroyed railway system and by imposing working discipline. Thus Prime Minister Van Acker established a Coal

Department in order to win the 'Battle for Coal'. Van Acker started employing 45,000 German prisoners of war as a cheap workforce in the coal mines. But their repatriation, which started in May 1947, caused a severe labour shortage. In Italy official recruiting offices were opened and in the meantime Belgian political prisoners were obliged to work as miners. The Communists and some Socialists dreamt of a state-controlled economy, but without success. The Act of 13 August 1947 establishing the Conseil National des Charbonnages (CNC) was nothing more than an advisory board on which the pit-owners and the unions were represented (Evalenko 1968: 257–91).

In order to finance its activities the Pierlot–Spaak government planned a capital levy, because during the war black marketeers and industrialists had acquired large amounts of stock capital. The real aim of this capital levy of 5 per cent was to absorb some 63 billion Belgian francs frozen in bank accounts. A special tax of 95 per cent was levied on war profits (Baudhuin 1958: 57–8). One can appreciate why this special tax was imposed, because war profits also meant that the beneficiary had been working for the enemy (which was forbidden by Article 115 of the Penal Code) (Huysse and Dhondt 1991: 59–71). The Decree of 25 May 1945 stipulated that industrialists who had not increased their production or enlarged their factories during the war, were considered as exempt from suspicion of collaboration. Thus in 1945 the government accepted the 'Galopin Doctrine' (see Chapter 3).

Although the Communists campaigned for a severe repression of big capitalists who had become wealthy during the war, only a few industrialists were condemned as war profiteers and a limited number of industrial firms was provisionally sequestered (Nestor-Martin, FABELTA, Pétrofina, De Coene). The Decree of 25 May sensibly changed the sense of Article 115 of the Penal Code (Van den Wijngaert 1990: 124–6). Obviously it was with this Decree in mind that Minister of Finance Eyskens prepared a decree imposing a 100 per cent levy on 'exceptional' war profits. Eyskens' proposal was adopted by his successor Franz de Voghel in the second Van Acker government (1945–6) (Huysse and Dhondt 1991: 230). This levy raised 12.7 billion francs, and a levy on profits made when producing or working for the enemy raised some 2.6 billion francs (Van den Wijngaert 1990: 130).

CORPORATISM AT BAY?

During the Occupation the reformist leaders of the Socialist Party and some leading industrialists had defined an outline for the postwar period which constituted a form of close class collaboration within a framework of corporatist interest intermediation, and, when in April 1947 the Socialist Spaak and the Christian Democrat Eyskens formed the first so-called Roman–Red Coalition (Socialists and Catholics), a bipartite form of corporatist interest intermediation completed the welfare state as defined in the Social Pact (see Chapter 3). The Social Pact had been legalized by the Decree of 28 December 1944 establishing a comprehensive national social security system, the Office National de Sécurité Sociale – Rijksdienst voor Maatschappelijke Zekerheid (ONSS–RMZ), to be financed by entrepreneurs and wage-earners. The ONSS–RMZ was administered on a parity basis by representatives of the recognized trade unions and the entrepreneurial organizations; also it made a distinction between blue-collar and white-collar workers. Only wage-earners were admitted, which provoked some dissatisfaction among the representatives of self-employed workers and the petty bourgeoisie; but soon the Christian Democrats extended the ONSS–RMZ to all categories of workers and the self-employed.

Although the etatist view had been defended for a long time by the Socialist Minister of Social Affairs Léon Troclet, who had inspired all social legislation during the period 1946–9, etatism was avoided because entrepreneurs and Catholic trade union leaders preferred a privately organized form of corporatist interest intermediation on a parity base. When in May 1945 the system of Health and Invalidity Insurance was created, the Decree stipulated that the Solidarity Fund should be administered on a parity base. The Decree of 9 June 1945 recognized the setting up of parity committees in all sectors and branches, both on a national as well as on a regional level. Important problems concerning wages and other working conditions had to be discussed and solved by national labour conferences. These conferences met several times after the Second World War and helped the government to reach an agreement on the system of indexation of wages and consumer prices, the 8-hour working day and the 48-hour working week, the wage and incomes policies, etc.

Although the Socialist trade union leaders were always attacking capitalism, they practised class collaboration. At the National

Labour Conference of 13 May 1946 the Socialist trade union leader Paul Finet recognized that his Socialist trade union FGTB–ABVV (Fédération Générale du Travail Belge – Algemeen Belgisch Vakverbond) provisionally would accept capitalism. So a central economic council, the Centrale Economische Raad – Conseil Central d'Economie (CER–CCE), based on a parity representation of the interests of capital and labour was set up on 20 September 1948. The Council was nothing more than an advisory body for the government and a debating club instead of a central corporatist organization with broad powers in matters of economic and social regulation. All the socio-economic interest groups (trade unions, entrepreneurial organizations, consumer co-operatives, farmers and small businessmen) could express in the Council their ideas and make declarations destined for their own rank-and-file. Meanwhile the old parity commissions which had already existed before the Second World War received a new legal status. An outstanding role now was played by the Algemene Paritaire Commissie – Conseil Paritaire Général (Central Parity Commission) where the general agreements on wages and working conditions were concluded. The corporatist interests, not the government, defined the terms of the social policy. In order to regulate social tensions and smooth its social policy the government was always able to mobilize the representatives of labour and capital for a compromise. In a period of social and political crisis the Commission also bargained with the government in order to solve the problems in an open debate. It was only in 1952 that the Commission received its legal base and was named the Nationale Arbeidsraad – Conseil National du Travail (NAR–CNT) (National Labour Council) (Keulemans 1989: 189–223).

All these councils and boards give the impression that the Belgian socio-economic system had a clear-cut corporatist character. This was not the case. The representatives of labour and capital were continually involved in labour conflicts which threatened the very existence of the system. But these open clashes and emergency meetings which had to solve social conflicts could be dampened down by compromises made by a few key persons like the entrepreneur Bekaert or trade union leaders like the Socialist Louis Major (FGTB–ABVV) and the Christian Democrat Auguste Cool. The fact that these leading personalities met each other on other occasions than in the parity commissions gave the collective bargaining system some stability. The weekly meetings of the members of the Board of Regents of the National Bank were very important (Slomp and Van Mierlo 1984: (I) 123).

After the Second World War the Belgian State became a shareholder in the National Bank and installed a Board of Regents in which the leaders of all the socio-economic organizations were represented. Influential policy-makers like Bekaert, who also presided over the destiny of the entrepreneurial organization of the metal industry, Fédération de l'Industrie des Fabrications Métalliques (FABRIMETAL), the trade union leaders André Renard (FGTB–ABVV) and Cool made deals here which afterwards were worked out in the plenary meetings of the parity committees (Vandeputte 1979: 211–14). The main concern of the trade unions was the implementation of an incomes policy based on increased productivity and economic expansion. On 5 May 1954 the representatives of the trade unions and the entrepreneurial organizations signed a Joint Declaration on Productivity pointing out that higher productivity should not be reached by exploitation of the workers or by creating higher unemployment. Increased productivity in industry should finance the creation of more jobs, higher wages, better social conditions and a shorter working week (the 5-day week). This was in a nutshell the philosophy of a Keynesian policy based on economic growth, sustained effective demand and a policy of income redistribution.

In entrepreneurial circles there were still many retrograde opponents of this policy. But they lost much of their influence when in 1952 Bekaert, who was known as a modernizer, took over the presidency of the Fédération de l'Industie Belge (FIB), which was the successor organization of the pre-war CCI (Vanthemsche 1989: 109–66). This facilitated a closer collaboration between industrialists and trade unions on the point of their common interest of increasing productivity and sustained economic growth. This also implied a policy of a lowering of production costs (especially of energy and raw materials and not wages) and acquiring advantages of scale by developing mass production.

The weakest link in this corporatist setting was the Socialist trade union FGTB–ABVV which had been formed in 1945 by merging three distinct trade union movements formed during the Occupation. First, there was the trunk of the pre-war reformist Socialist trade unions. Second, there was the radical syndicalist rank-and-file in Liège which had formed an independent movement during the war striving for a profound reform of society. Their uncontested leader was the former metal-worker Renard. A third component was represented by the Communists and their Committees of Union Action promoting the idea of 'One Big Union'. The Communists held a powerful position among the dockers of the port of Antwerp and the miners of Wallonia and Limburg. Finally, the struggle for power was won in 1948–9 by the Socialists in alliance with the Renardists against the Communists. The Socialists in the FGTB–ABVV were in favour of close co-operation with the Catholic unions and they wanted a coalition government of Socialists and Christian Democrats. But in 1949 the 'Roman–Red Coalition' broke down and was only reconstituted in 1961. Because between 1950 and 1954 the Christian Democrats disposed of an absolute majority in both Houses (Senate and House of Representatives), a coalition government with the Socialists was not discussed. And, when in 1954 the Christian Democrats lost their majority, a Socialist–Liberal coalition government under Van Acker was formed. The programme of this anti-clerical government was rather bleak and aimed to modernize the educational system by breaking up the monopoly of the Catholic schools in Flanders (Mabille 1986: 311–12).

THE INTERNATIONAL SETTING

After the disappearance of the Communists from government in March 1947 Belgium was rapidly integrated in the Western bloc led by the USA. But this choice was an opportunist one, because Belgium held important colonial interests in Africa, although its economy was oriented towards full liberalization of trade. The Cold War had started. Meanwhile the USA's necessity of finding an outlet for its production and assuring the supply of huge quantities of raw materials it was lacking, had inspired an anti-colonialist policy. American policy was rebuffing colonialism because the colonial powers still relied on protected colonial markets providing them with cheap raw materials. These colonial monopolies hindered American enterprises from investing in the colonial countries and forced them to compromise with Euro-pean cartels. In the meantime it was also necessary to finance the economic recovery of Europe and to avoid a Communist take-over there. That was why the Truman Administration now concentrated on stabilizing the political and economic situation in Western Europe. This provoked some changes in the foreign economic aid programmes the USA had already launched.

First, economic aid organized by the United Nations Relief and Rehabilitation Administration (UNRRA) was cancelled, because American enterprises now were looking for an outlet abroad without the intermediary of a central credit office. Thus the Export Import Bank started to finance American exports, but this time under the condition that the American government previously had approved the projects submitted by the governments soliciting direct economic aid. Second, the Marshall Plan (i.e. the European Recovery Programme) went a step further by proposing economic and financial aid to all European countries under the condition supervision would be exercised by a newly formed Economic Co-operation Administration (ECA), which soon would become the Organization for European Economic Co-operation (OEEC), the club of the European countries having received aid from the Marshall Fund (Milward 1984: 168–211).

The Marshall Fund could not avoid the reappearance of the old German–French antagonism. The French government feared that within a few years German heavy industry would regain its pre-eminence in Europe. In order to preserve its political position the French now chose closer economic collaboration with Germany, forcing the Germans to deliver enough cheap coke for the French steel factories in Lorraine. This project was named the Schuman Plan and aimed for a unified market for coal and steel and it rapidly led to the establishment of the European Coal and Steel Community (ECSC) (Hahn 1953: 114–20). The ECSC aimed to reorganize European heavy industry on the principle of free competition among steel firms and coal mines in order to supply the transforming industry with huge quantities of cheap steel of high quality. This meant that the ECSC was breaking with all pre-war models of regulation (i.e. cartels and protectionism). The closing-down of the marginal coal mines was the consequence of the liberation of the coal market and the steel firms were obliged to invest in strip mills and high-capacity blast furnaces. In order to convince the Belgian coal and steel barons the ECSC subsidized the social costs of the retraining of the miners in the coal basins (Gillingham 1991: 281).

This policy aimed at liberating the markets was not induced by the initial desire to abolish all subsidies and tariff barriers. In many European countries the state still played a very important economic role and even controlled large parts of the industry. Price controls and subsidies had become appropriate instruments when supply and demand had to be balanced and foreign competition threatened industrial development. In this case Belgium remained an exception. This liberal stance was the effect of special circumstances: the almighty position of the holding companies controlling heavy industry and the fact that the postwar reconstruction drive favoured the export of raw materials and semi-finished products. Thus liberalization of prices and the suppression of rationing already was realized in 1949. Only for some industrial basic products, such as industrial gas and coal, price controls remained until 1950.

Recovery by Belgian industry was largely due to high prices paid in US dollars for its semi-finished products (i.e. steel), not to early liberalization of prices. Although the Belgian export industry was booming, recovery remained weak. Already in 1949 a slowdown of the international economy forced the Belgian producers to lower their prices and lay off workers. The recession was caused by a payment crisis, because foreign clients of Belgian industry were lacking hard currency and in order to sustain its exports Belgium was now forced to offer export credits. Finally, in 1950 the European Payment Union (EPU) was set up as a clearing house between the Western European countries (Milward 1984: 299–334).

Because of its particular position Belgium only received 68 million US dollars of 'unconditional' Marshall aid and 445 million dollars of 'conditional' aid. Aid given to the Belgian Luxembourg Economic Union (BLEU) amounted to some 556 million US dollars. In the case of 'conditional aid' the Belgian government had to reserve this equivalent in Belgian francs for the other European nations purchasing Belgian products, which allowed the Belgian government to hold a large amount of dollars. The latter could be used for buying raw materials in the dollar zone. But in general the Marshall Fund did not fundamentally change the development of Belgian industry, because practically all aid was destined for the modernization and re-equipment of the steel industry and the marginal coal mines in Wallonia.

In the middle of the slump of 1949 the British Labour government decided to devalue the British pound by 30.5 per cent, bringing the exchange rate of the pound sterling back from 4.30 to 2.80 US dollars. This decision, which had been taken by the British government on 18 September 1949 without consulting the other nations immediately provoked a wave of stupor and disarray and obliged the weaker European countries (the Netherlands, the Scandinavian countries, France, Western Germany) to devalue at once their national currencies at the same rate (Milward 1984: 282–98). In Belgium some panic broke out. Prime Minister Eyskens decided to devalue the Belgian franc by 12.345 per cent. This meant a real revaluation of some 14 per cent compared with the major hard currencies. In fact, the devaluation of the Belgian franc only concerned the US dollar. This devaluation was criticized from many sides. It increased the inflationary pressure, because Belgium was paying for the import of its raw materials in US dollars and an important share of Belgian exports was paid for in US dollars. The devaluations of 1949 also showed that the leading role of the US dollar was not accepted by all participants of the International Monetary Fund (IMF) and that postwar economic recovery needed a new impetus.

The slump of 1948–9 was rapidly absorbed when the Korean War (1950–3) imposed a massive re-armament programme on the USA and its allies. Demand for semi-finished products and raw materials boomed and hoarding of raw materials provoked an inflationary pressure. The Belgian economy did very well in this period, although unemployment remained very high with an unemployment rate of some 10 per cent of the total of employed people. Once again the Belgian steel firms could export at high prices and make huge profits. With the end of the Korean War a minor crisis occurred when the hoarded stocks had to be liquidated, but this gave birth to a new boom in the USA where consumers now were buying new automobiles and TV sets. Belgian exports were booming again. This time demand on the domestic market considerably increased because of higher investment and the increased purchasing power of the middle classes. The end of prosperity came at the end of 1957 when the slump in the USA provoked a sudden slowdown of economic activity in Belgium.

Meanwhile Belgium was exporting large quantities of goods with a low degree of added value and products which were reputed to be old-fashioned and requiring a low degree of technological input. The postwar reconstruction brought a rapid economic recovery and a higher average degree of welfare when compared with neighbouring countries, but the situation of the Belgian economy was too dependent on the fluctuation of the prices of raw materials and semi-finished products on the world market. Belgian wealth proved to be ephemeral.

Table 4.1 Registered unemployed, 1948–58 (daily averages)

Year	Permanent unemployed	Short-time working	Total	%
1948	80,959	48,244	129,203	6.5
1949	173,988	60,908	234,896	11.7
1950	169,972	53,565	223,537	10.9
1951	153,452	53,068	206,520	10.0
1952	173,570	72,968	246,538	11.8
1953	183,614	62,193	245,807	11.8
1954	166,926	57,826	224,752	10.9
1955	116,469	55,909	172,378	8.4
1956	91,034	53,742	144,776	7.0
1957	77,860	38,950	116,810	5.5
1958	109,747	71,146	180,893	8.6

Source: Buitengewoon Congres 1959: 14

The labour movement which had pleaded for a more balanced economic growth, higher wages and a shorter working week, was confronted with a high degree of unemployment, even during the Korean boom of 1950–3 and during the boom period of 1955–7 (see Table 4.1). This situation, combined with high profits distributed by the firms, fuelled anti-capitalist sentiments in the working classes. In Wallonia the working class felt insecure because of the big rationalization programmes imposed and financed by the ECSC, and in Flanders mass unemployment combined with migratory labour (Declercq and Vanneste 1954: 165–98) caused discontent in the Catholic trade unions.

After the Second World War Belgian industry was restructured on the pre-war pattern of privately organized cartels and marketing organizations in practically all basic sectors. The Belgian government tried to design an industrial policy, but in general the idea was that financing industrial development had to be implemented by private initiatives and eased by cheap credit granted by the State. All proposals for a nationalization of the basic industries were defeated, and, except for the petroleum industry, all attempts to modernize the industrial structure failed.

SUBSIDIZING THE COAL MINES

The 'heroic' campaign launched by Prime Minister Van Acker in 1945 in order to win the 'Battle for Coal' was a campaign inspired by shortages. When planning subsidies and credit to the industry, the Spaak–Eyskens government (1947–9) seriously reconsidered the strategic position of the coal mines, because coal was a primary product constituting an important basic cost for the making of electricity (40 per cent), coke (50 per cent), steel (30 per cent), cement (20–50 per cent), fertilizers (15 per cent), paper (15 per cent), etc. (*Troisième rapport* 1948: 90). Thus the authorities started subsidizing investment on the advice of the CNC and calculated an annual investment of 2.1 billion Belgian francs over the period 1948–52 (i.e. a total investment of 10.5 billion Belgian francs) and 1.5 billion Belgian francs over the period 1953–7 (i.e. 7.5 billion Belgian francs). Mechanization of the production and integration of the many old pits in the South Basin were planned. But the government did not enter into discussion with the pit-owners about closing the marginal mines in Wallonia. Instead, it discussed the further exploitation of the known reserves in the North and a better utilization of the seams in the Borinage (South Basin) (*Troisième rapport* 1948: 96). For the period 1948–57 the authorities had envisaged a total increase of electricity output of some 1,600,000 kWh, which necessitated an investment of some 3 billion Belgian francs to be made in high-tension networks. The modernization of the low-tension networks required an additional investment of 3.2 billion Belgian francs. Investment in the extension of the electricity network and new power stations required in total about 19.6 billion francs. The Spaak–Eyskens government pointed out that 'the price of electrical energy had to remain as low as possible', which implied the installation of high-quality power stations and combustion of low-quality coal (*Troisième rapport* 1948: 99). A third important investment programme touched the coke industry. The coke ovens produced coke for the blast furnaces of the steel industry, but they also provided urban gas. The idea of acquiring larger quantities of Dutch gas coal inspired the Belgian government to plead for a full integration of the Belgian and Dutch coal markets.

When considering the whole investment programme defined by the Spaak–Eyskens government it appears that the overwhelming majority (88 per cent) of the funds allocated to the modernization programme were destined for the traditional sectors of the economy

Table 4.2 Industrial investment programme of the Belgian government, 1948–57 (in billion Belgian francs)

Coal mines	19.60
Coke ovens, gas, derivatives	4.66
Steel	7.20
Metallurgical industry	12.50
Textile industry	16.10
Non-ferrous metals	5.00
Oil	1.00
Chemical industry	7.70
Cement and construction industries	6.30
Food and tobacco industries	5.50
Consumer products	3.55
Others	0.35
Total investment programme	89.46

Source: Troisième rapport 1948: 127

(textiles, steel, coal, heavy chemicals, etc.), while credits for new industrial activities, such as pharmaceuticals, light industries and oil were practically absent.

Meanwhile the Decree of the Regent of 27 December 1947 granted credits to those foreign enterprises which would establish themselves in Belgium and produce new products or favour further industrial growth (Troisième rapport 1948: 127). But industrial development and state intervention were primarily seen as bringing together the sectoral interests in 'industrial research centres' in each sector. Many of them, founded during the postwar years, were also directly linked with the traditional sectors of the industry, which hindered them from developing research and development programmes. The only exceptions were the burgeoning electronics and nuclear sectors (the government was forecasting investment in a cyclotron). The implementation of this investment programme was soon distorted by the mighty coal lobby, here represented by the pit-owners and the miners' unions which represented at that time some 153,000 miners.

Although the government abrogated all subsidies to the mines on 1 March 1947, a compensation programme in favour of the marginal mines to be funded out of the profits of the other mines was introduced. This system was cancelled on 1 October 1949 and in May 1951 all subsidies were eliminated.

On 10 February 1953 the ECSC came into existence. The Belgian coal mines received preferential treatment. During the next five years the better performing Dutch and German coal mines provided the funds needed for a gradual closure of the marginal mines and investment in the other mines. Only in 1956 was a plan for a closing-down of marginal coal mines formulated. During the previous decade (1945–55) the State had paid some 33 billion francs to the coal sector. In many cases the actual allocation of the subsidies destined for the modernization of the coal mines was beset by cash problems. In August 1956 a mining disaster in Marcinelle killed 261 miners – many of whom were Italian workers – and criticism arose; the idea prevailed that some pit-owners were distributing the subsidies they had obtained in the form of dividends and that the ECSC was in reality subsidizing the steel industry.

Table 4.3 Belgian coal production, 1938–57 (in '000 tonnes)

Year	South	%	Campine	%	Total
1938	23,049	77.9	6,536	22.1	29,585
1949	19,900	71.5	7,954	28.5	27,854
1950	19,199	70.3	8,122	29.7	27,321
1951	20,387	68.8	9,264	31.2	29,651
1952	20,672	68.0	9,712	32.0	30,384
1953	20,577	68.5	9,483	31.5	30,060
1954	19,991	68.4	9,258	31.6	29,249
1955	19,833	66.2	10,145	33.8	29,978
1956	19,087	64.6	10,468	35.4	29,555
1957	18,670	64.4	10,331	35.6	29,001

Source: Evalenko 1968: 261

The structural crisis of the Belgian coal industry was characterized by a general labour shortage. A huge number of foreign workers was recruited in Italy and Spain. In 1957 out of a total of 117,017 miners, 70,943 (or 60.6 per cent) were immigrants. Resistance to the work in the mines was also transformed into absenteeism (25 per cent of the miners and 16 per cent of the surface workers) (Evalenko 1968: 270).

Despite all efforts made to increase productivity the overall result remained rather poor. In the South Basin productivity rose from 1,004 kilos per miner in 1938 to only 1,027 kilos per miner in 1957. In the North Basin productivity even decreased from 1,521 kilos in 1938 to 1,430 kilos in 1957, which was largely due to the introduction of a shorter working week (Moons 1957).

MODERNIZING THE STEEL INDUSTRY

The modernization programme of the steel industry affected three aspects of steel-making. First, amelioration of the quality of the steel produced. Second, improvement of the technical performance of the blast furnaces. Third, increased productivity of the installations (Baudhuin 1958: 269). Because the expanding sector of consumer durables (automobiles, home appliances) required the supply of high-quality steel a modernization of the traditional Thomas blast furnaces producing lower-quality steels became necessary. Apart from the steel factories owned by Boël employing an electrical Siemens–Martin arc, only the Fabrique de Fer de Charleroi decided to install a high-capacity Siemens–Martin oven of some 30,000 kWh. The latter was the largest oven ever built in Europe.

The expansion in the steel industry was enhanced by demand coming from the transforming industry, especially the automobile industry and the shipyards and the policy of the ECSC. This required long-term investment in rolling mills and blast furnaces and a further integration of the dispersed steel factories in Wallonia. But the investment policy of the steel firms was also influenced by the interests of the holding companies dominating the steel industry. Thus the steel industry in the Liège Basin specialized in the production of so-called 'wide products' (strips, sheets and plates), while the Charleroi Basin continued to produce the so-called 'long products' (i.e. merchant bars, rails, joints, angles, etc.). In the early 1950s one could classify the Belgian steel industry into four large categories. First, enterprises producing cast iron (Société Minière et Métallurgique de Musson et Halanzy). Second, nine large integrated enterprises owning coke ovens, blast furnaces, steel and rolling mills and exercising activities in the metallurgical sector and/or possessing coal mines (SA Métallurgique d'Espérance–Longdoz with divisions in Seraing, Jemeppe and Flémalle; SA d'Ougrée–Marihaye; SA John Cockerill; Usines et Forges de la Providence; Société Métallurgique de Sambre et Moselle; Aciéries et Minières de la Sambre; Usines Gustave Boël; SA des Forges de Clabecq; SA des Hauts Fourneaux, Forges et Aciéries de Thy-le-Château et Marcinelle). Third, four steel factories with rolling mills of which three had important metallurgical divisions (Société des

Usines Gilson; Fabrique de Fer de Charleroi; SA des Forges et Laminoirs; SA des Usines Emile Henricot). Finally, there were some fifteen firms established as independent steel-rolling companies (the so-called re-rollers) making sheets or different kinds of 'long products' (Phénix Works and the Usines à Tubes de la Meuse (UTM) in Flémalle-Haute, Usines et Laminoirs du Ruau in Monceau-sur-Sambre, Laminoirs d'Anvers in Schoten, etc.) (Evalenko 1968: 391–2).

The steel industry employed 45,000 people in the period 1946–52, producing 5,170,000 tons of crude steel in 1952. Productivity was certainly boosted by investment and by mergers that occurred in the steel industry that gave Cockerill–Ougrée in the Liège Basin and the Forges de la Providence in the Charleroi Basin a dominant position. Cockerill had absorbed Angleur–Athus in 1945. In June 1955 Cockerill (controlled by the SGB) merged with Ougrée–Marihaye (Banque de Bruxelles/BRUFINA/Compagnie Financière et Industrielle – COFININDUS) and Laminoirs à Froid de Fer-blanc à Tilleur (FERBLATIL), to form an integrated steel company and a new central selling organization Union Commerciale de la Sidérurgie Belge (UCOSIDER) representing apart from Cockerill–Ougrée also the Forges de la Providence, the Aciéries et Minières de la Sambre, the Minière et Métallurgique de Rodange, the Laminoirs d'Anvers and the Aciéries et Laminoirs de Beautor. In 1955 the Métallurgique du Hainaut-Sambre was formed by the Usines Métallurgiques du Hainaut and the Métallurgique de Sambre et Moselle (Evalenko 1968: 406–9).

STAGNATING SECTORS

Development in the cement industry was characterized by a process of further concentration of the production in ever-larger units with new high-capacity ovens. Profitability of the cement sector increased in a considerable way now that the firms were producing cement of better quality at full capacity than in the pre-war period. Portland cement remained the most popular type of cement produced in Belgium, but export now was of minor importance because of high transportation costs and cartelization (Phlips 1962, 189–239). After the Second World War the pre-war cartels were re-established. They were at the origins of the huge profits the sector was generating in a period when the building industry was booming. In 1950 the Agreement of Paris (a gentleman's agreement signed by the main producers) reorganized the German, Belgian and Dutch markets by eliminating all forms of competition between the producers. Meanwhile the big cement companies closed down their small factories while CBR built a modern factory in Lixhe (Liège) (Phlips 1962: 229). The relative decline (see Table 4.4) of the Belgian cement industry has to be considered in connection with the investment policy of the holding companies abroad.

Table 4.4 Cement production and consumption, 1913–60 (in '000 tonnes)

Year	Output	Import	Export	Consumption
1913	1,385	26	887	524
1929	3,719	11	1,909	1,821
1938	3,054	4	992	2,066
1950	3,550	5	1,223	2,332
1960	4,388	12	1,324	3,076

Source: Evalenko 1968: 429

Many other sectors and branches of the heavy industries were also stagnating. In the sector of fertilizers the producers had cartelized the Belgian market, but they failed to make progress on foreign markets. In Belgium COBELAZ organized all producers of fertilizers and imposed fixed prices and set up storage facilities.

As before the Second World War the textile industry was still dominated by medium-sized family owned enterprises. In 1955 some 3,779 enterprises employed 164,778 people, especially women. The textile industry was concentrated in Flanders with 95,328 registered workers. A good half of the total output was exported, especially to France, Germany and the Netherlands. At that time a multitude of small firms existed in the garment industry. In 1955 7,573 enterprises employed 83,804 people. The difference between the textile industry and the garment industry was that the latter was producing for the domestic market, while the former was exporting half of its produce.

NEW INDUSTRIES

The petroleum sector was one of the most innovative and fast-growing sectors of the postwar period. This was due to several factors. First, there was the fast-growing demand for petroleum products caused by the democratization of car ownership. In the postwar period automobiles became available in ever larger quantities. In 1938 there were 233,000 automobiles on the road; in 1956 there were 700,000 (of these some 500,000 were privately owned). The increase in the number of cars forced the government to face the problem of supplying the country with enough petroleum. Oil had become an extremely important strategic raw material. During the Second World War the American chemical industry had started to use oil as a raw material for the production of plastic, a new basic material that could be used for a wide range of products.

Before the Second World War the Belgian petroleum industry had been poorly equipped. Belgian Shell, in which Belgian capitalists held a stake, owned a small refinery near Ghent and four refineries existed in Antwerp (Redevenza, Atlas, Radiant, Raffinerie Belge de Pétroles (RBP)) all producing special products. Their production capacity was limited and they were set up as refining units for Romanian oil.

The big oil companies were not really interested in building large refineries in Belgium because of the narrowness of the market. They all preferred refining their crude in the oil fields far from their markets in Western Europe, especially in the Middle East and in the Caribbean. But after the Second World War the oil companies had to reconsider their industrial and commercial strategy. First, growing oil production in the Middle East where new refineries had been built became the subject of international conflicts generated by tensions between Arabs and Israelis. Second, there were growing transportation problems. Transporting crude was less expensive than shipping refined products in small quantities. Thus the oil companies decided to build supertankers destined to carry crude oil, which required more storage facilities.

In 1947 the Ministry of Re-equipment asked four Belgian chemical firms (Solvay, Union Chimique, Carbochimique, Société Belge de l'Azote) to study the possibilities of the setting up of an integrated petrochemical complex for the production of plastics. Finally, the Ministry of Economic Co-ordination invited the small Belgian oil firm Pétrofina to carry out the project. But Pétrofina had known many problems. Immediately after the war the firm had been prosecuted because of its economic collaboration with the Germans. Moreover, Pétrofina was a trading firm owned by the Compagnie d'Anvers (a subsidiary of the holding company, Compagnie Belge et Continentale de Gaz et d'Electricité (CONTIBEL) which belonged to Imperial Continental Gas). Therefore investing in a petrochemical complex would be hazardous without the backing of a major oil company. Fortunately for Pétrofina, in this period British Petroleum (BP) (formerly the Anglo–Iranian Petroleum Co.) had to withdraw its refining activities from the Middle East. This facilitated the setting up of the joint venture Société Industrielle Belge des Pétroles (SIBP), a refinery with a capacity of some 3 million tonnes of crude oil. This enabled Pétrofina to set up the Pétrochim factory in Antwerp producing ethylene and glycol. Meanwhile Solvay had set up a joint venture with ICI SA pour l'Industrie des Matières Plastiques (SOLVIC) producing plastics (Baudhuin 1958: 301–5).

The development of the Belgian oil industry was boosted by financial aid given by the Belgian government. First, the government provided the funds necessary to modernize and equip the port of Antwerp. Investment in the new refineries was largely financed by the SNCI–NMKN. On a total investment of 1,300 million Belgian francs allocated by the SIBP in 1951 the SNCI–NMKN financed a credit worth 500 million Belgian francs. Meanwhile Esso (Standard Oil Co.) invested 1,250 million Belgian francs in its new refinery. Here the SNCI–NMKN provided a credit worth 900 million Belgian francs. RBP, which had been created in 1934 by the British Lianosoff White Oil Company, modernized its installations by using a credit worth 125 million Belgian francs granted by the SNCI–NMKN. Initially RBP specialized in producing bitumen and pitch, but now started refining lighter products. Redevenza, which had been destroyed during the war, operated under a new company name (Albatros) (Baudhuin 1958: 306–12).

The automobile industry was dominated by foreign firms which had established plants in Belgium. Before the Second World War the government levied heavy taxes on imported automobiles, which obliged some major automotive firms (General Motors, Ford Motor Co., Renault and Citroën) to assemble their vehicles in Belgium. After the Second World War the Belgian government increased the administrative restrictions on the import of automobiles. In theory the import of foreign automobiles was prohibited after 1 January 1954. All foreign automobile firms had to assemble their cars in Belgium and to incorporate in them a given percentage of components made in Belgium (Baudhuin 1958: 314–16).

The automobile components industry was progressing and many Belgian firms started subcontracting. Especially the glass industry specialized in producing safety glass. FABELTA produced synthetic fibres and Bekaert set up a special factory producing steel-cord, both products were indispensable for the production of tyres. But the more sophisticated components were produced by foreign companies now starting up in Belgium (Monroe, Bosal, Uniroyal, Michelin, etc.). Until the mid-1950s the automobile firms only produced for the local Belgian market, but then General Motors started assembling vehicles which were re-exported to other European countries.

After the Second World War a complete modernization and reorganization of the electricity supply industry became an urgent question in terms of investment in, control over, and adaptation of the electricity networks. Although some concentration already had occurred, too many independent producers still existed.

Many industrial firms operating in the coal, steel and chemical sectors were so-called self-suppliers, consuming a large part of the electric power they generated in their own electricity power stations and selling their surplus to the networks. All these self-suppliers were federated in the Association des Centrales Electriques Industrielles de Belgique which founded the Comité Permanent de Coordination de l'Autoproduction (CPCA) in 1956. The other electricity-supplying firms belonged to two distinct categories (i.e. the privately owned supplying firms and a small group of municipal electricity companies owned co-operatively by the cities of Ghent and Liège). The supply of electricity to the public was regulated by a multitude of municipal firms in which private companies could also hold a stake. This anarchical situation was the result of a very liberal policy in the early 1920s allowing city councils to set up municipal services and electricity networks. In July 1947 a study group was established in order to prepare a report on the reorganization of the sector, but it was only in 1951 that the report became available. The report did not propose a thoroughgoing reform of the whole sector and the government hesitated to submit its own conclusions to Parliament. Finally, in October 1954 the trade union congress of the Socialist FGTB–ABVV asked for a complete nationalization of the energy sector. Because the Socialist–Liberal coalition government led by Van Acker (1954–8) could no longer avoid the question, a Round Table Conference met in order to re-align all participants (industry, consumers, trade unions and suppliers of electricity) in a compromise.

The conclusions formulated by the Round Table on Electricity went in the direction of a form of self-regulating control exercised by suppliers and consumers of electricity, but did not adhere to the idea of a complete nationalization of the sector. Two conventions were signed at the end of the Round Table Conference. First, a convention organizing a management committee deciding on production and distribution of electricity leading to co-ordination of investment, transport and tariffs. Second, a convention giving birth to a controlling committee comprising representatives of trade unions, entrepreneurial organizations and a management committee which had to advise on all matters concerning the sector (Evalenko 1968: 309–36).

Table 4.5 The cost of electricity, 1953–6
(average price of low and high tension in Belgian francs/kWh –
Index established in relation to Belgian prices)

	1953		1954		1955		1956	
	BF	Index	BF	Index	BF	Index	BF	Index
Belgium	1.58	100	1.54	100	1.49	100	1.45	100
Germany	1.28	81	1.21	79	1.20	81	1.16	80
France	1.09	69	1.09	71	1.08	72	1.10	76
Netherlands	1.12	71	1.08	70	1.07	72	1.10	76
Italy	0.83	53	0.85	55	0.85	57	0.86	59
UK	0.79	50	0.80	52	0.81	54	0.85	59
Switzerland	0.72	46	0.73	47	0.72	48	0.73	50

Source: Trappeniers 1967: 192

Investment in the electricity sector became a priority, because of increased consumption by the transforming industry and the high prices paid (see Table 4.5). Investment in the sector progressed on an annual basis from 1,900 million Belgian francs in 1948 to 2,088 million Belgian francs in 1950 and reached 2,432 million Belgian francs in 1955 and 3,500 million Belgian francs in 1956. The electricity-generating stations were burning coal, but combustion of gas and oil made some progress because of the falling prices of crude oil and the availability of petroleum, gas and pitch. But in 1956 coal was still providing some 78 per cent of all fuels. Investment in new installations strengthened the role of the private electricity suppliers and weakened the position of the once powerful self-supplying industrial firms. In 1957 the commercial electricity suppliers held a market share of 61.9 per cent.

Because the Union Minière du Haut-Katanga possessed the rich uranium mine of Shinkolobwe in the Belgian Congo the idea of investing in nuclear power stations and nuclear technology for the chemical industry was actively debated. During the Second World War the Union Minière had sold its uranium ore to the USA. The Belgian government signed an agreement on the acquisition through the Atomic Energy Commission of specialist know-how about the development and use of atomic energy. After the war the Belgian Institut Inter-universitaire des Sciences Nucléaires (IISN) was set up in order to promote research in this field and in 1950 the government decided to establish the Commissariat à l'Energie Atomique. But these initiatives sponsored by the Belgian government were soon taken up by private interest groups organized in the Association Belge pour le Développement Pacifique de l'Energie Atomique (BELGICATOM). In 1957 they appeared as partners in the Centre d'Etude Nucléaire (CEN) which had been set up in 1952 by the Belgian government. The private interest groups also associated their firms active in the nuclear sector (Syndicat d'Etude de l'Energie Nucléaire – SEEN) and co-ordinated the efforts made by the holding companies and their engineering departments (i.e. Compagnie Générale d'Entreprises Electriques et Industrielles – ELECTROBEL and Société de Traction et d'Electricité – TRACTIONEL). The most important were the Société Belge pour l'Industrie Nucléaire (BELGONUCLEAIRE) (1957), Electronucléaire (1956), Bureau d'Etudes Nucléaires (1956), SA Métallurgique et Mécanique Nucléaires (MMN) and SA Belge de Chimie Nucléaire (BELCHIM) (1956) (Evalenko 1968: 353–68).

In 1952 the Centre d'Etude des Applications de l'Energie Nucléaire (CEAN) started up in Mol with the building of experimental reactors developed by Belgian engineering firms. The partners of BELGONUCLEAIRE (i.e. practically all the Belgian engineering, mining and steel firms) now hoped for a breakthrough of the Belgian nuclear industry in connection with the colonial mineral mining and metal refining companies (Union Minière du Haut-Katanga, Métallurgie Hoboken). The electrical equipment industry was the main beneficiary of this investment boom in the sector of the electricity-generating industry. Thus ACEC could expand its activities in other countries. But ACEC was at that time jointly owned by the Empain family and the SGB. Both shareholders had conflicting interests. After the war the Empain Group lost ground because of nationalizations in several countries of Eastern Europe and in the Third World.

Many firms still operated in the sector of railway equipment and heavy construction. Here the Brugeoise et Nivelles (BN) became the most important firm, employing some 4,000 workers. Because the market for railway equipment was stagnating, BN had to operate as a subcontractor of Swedish and American firms.

The situation of the many firms producing railway equipment was even worse because their poorly equipped workplaces were not able to participate in the modernization programme (including 349 electrical locomotive engines and 95 diesels) the Belgian government had launched for the Belgian railway system and that was evaluated at some 10.5 billion Belgian francs.

CONCLUSIONS

The Belgian economy recovered within a few years and prospered because of high demand of steel, non-ferrous metals and heavy equipment Belgian industry was selling at high prices in the developing countries. But this recovery hid a fundamental weakness which would become apparent only after a decade. Unemployment remained high, even during the boom years of the Korean War and economic growth was low when compared with many other countries of Western Europe. Belgium was producing semi-finished industrial products at high costs with a low degree of added value. Investment in new products and activities was carried out by foreign companies building their production units near the port of Antwerp. The alliance of coal and steel still existed during the 1950s, but would be broken by the ECSC, which had imposed its policy of free competition on the coal and steel producers. The Belgian steel industry reacted by investing in modern technology and high-capacity blast furnaces. Meanwhile many coal mines in Wallonia postponed the moment of their closure.

5

THE RECESSION OF 1958-60

During the winter of 1957–8 the Belgian economy was hit by a recession caused by falling exports and a general slowdown in the steel and coal industry. The weakness of the Belgian economy now became obvious in its crudest form and provoked some panic in leading political circles and within the working classes. At the same time the call for a structural reform of the economy became louder and now was expressed by the trade union movement and the modernizing factions of the bourgeoisie. Finally, during the winter of 1960–1 a general strike led by the most radical faction of the Walloon trade union movement swept away the last political and economic factions still resisting a new economic policy.

THE ANATOMY OF THE CRISIS

The Belgian economist Alexandre Lamfalussy has argued that the Belgian economy was suffering from a low degree of investment leading itself to a slow economic growth. Belgian exports were not sufficiently diversified and therefore heavily dependent upon cyclical price movements which were induced by the world market and especially by the American trade cycle. Investment was defensive and oriented towards rationalization, deliberately neglecting the sector of consumer goods. In comparison to the other European countries the Belgian economy was growing at a very slow rate, 2.9 per cent over the period 1953–60; meanwhile the economy of the ECSC was growing at a rate of 5.7 per cent. Lamfalussy explained this slow growth as being caused by the low level of capital expenditure (Lamfalussy 1961: 25) and the slowly growing domestic market could not provide any effective stimulus for investment. In the period 1948–58 the domestic market increased by only 27 per cent and if services and expenditure on food are excluded, the rise in domestic expenditure on industrial products was no more than 25 per cent. At the same time, the protection of the domestic market against foreign competitors was among the weakest in Europe in terms both of tariffs and import restrictions (which were negligible) (Lamfalussy 1961: 25). Sales abroad rather than on the domestic market acted as a powerful incentive to capital expenditure. But as the wage level rose and the pattern of Belgian exports (concentrated on traditional products of standard quality) remained unchanged, profits had the tendency to fall. In 1957 labour costs in Belgium were the highest in Western Europe (see Table 5.1). Other costs were also higher in Belgium, especially energy costs.

Table 5.1 Labour costs per unit of output in manufacturing in 1957 (1948=100) in US $

Belgium	102
UK	101
Germany	68
France	83
Italy	65
Netherlands	83
USA	123

Source: Lamfalussy 1961: 26

Lamfalussy's explanation had two main features. First, the Belgian overspecialization in semi-finished products produced goods in a capital-intensive fashion by standard processes and with low or even zero rates of technological progress (soda ash, cement, fertilizers, Thomas steel, glass). Second, Belgian 'defensive investment' (i.e. investment preventing a firm in a highly competitive industry like textiles from running losses but from which the average rate of profit is very low (about 2 per cent)) had induced slow growth and consequently high unemployment. Although postwar recovery had been faster in Belgium than in many other European countries, the Belgian economy was growing more slowly than elsewhere (see Table 5.2).

In order to analyse the inducement to invest in Belgian industry Lamfalussy studied the type and the volume of investment over a longer period in thirteen Belgian industries (coal, electricity and gas, textiles, steel, food and beverages, chemicals, electrical engineering and electronics, cement, rolling stock and railway equipment),

Table 5.2 Growth of industrial production, 1948–57

	1948 (1937=100)	1957 (1948=100)	1957 (1937=100)
Belgium	109	141	154
OEEC	99	190	191
France	100	182	182
Italy	101	222	221
Germany	56	335	188
Netherlands	125	178	222
UK	119	142	169

Source: Lamfalussy 1961: 6

covering about 60 per cent of Belgian industrial output, and all factors affecting investment decisions. These factors common to all industry were the abundance of labour and of finance in the postwar period. Labour was not fully employed and capital was abundantly available to industrialists. Another common factor was the relative price fall of capital goods (in terms of labour costs) and rising fuel prices. This stimulated the industrialists to invest in energy-saving technology and to substitute petroleum for coal, because the fuel-oil price was decreasing (a price fall of 40 per cent between 1947–57).

In the 1950s the 'costs of finance' remained relatively low and did not exceed 4.8 per cent. Industrialists could obtain discount of commercial paper from the banks and bank charges for overdrafts varied between 5 and 6.5 per cent. During this period (1948–57) all Belgian industries invested in order to substitute capital for labour and many were encouraged to substitute petroleum products for coal. The rate of increase of profitability was unequal. Net profits were rising in the electrical engineering, electricity, gas, and cement industries. The situation in the steel industry was characterized by peaks and a fluctuation of profits, which was due to the cyclical nature of the sector. Performance in the food and beverages industries, rolling-stock manufacturing, the textile industry and especially coal mining were poor. Lamfalussy noticed that in steel, textiles, rolling stock and coal mining the average rate of profit had been lower than the normal profit rate. In the rolling-stock, textile and coal mining industries profits were so low that there were good reasons to disinvest or to carry out defensive investment. Here the food and the steel industries were in an intermediate position.

Because of the cyclical nature of the steel industry, the low level of profits here pointed towards the likelihood of defensive investment. The choice between disinvestment or defensive investment in four out of thirteen of the industrial sectors (coal mining, rolling stock, textiles and steel) suggests equal investment conditions. But in the case of the steel industry the incentive to choose defensive investment was much stronger, because extension of output capacity, if carried out by improvement of existing capital stock, could increase profitability. This policy was encouraged by the ECSC and reinforced by the fact the Belgian steel factories were exporting 70 per cent of their output. In the textile industry defensive investment boosted falling prices on the world market and competition on the domestic market, a situation which forced many textile manufacturers to invest in high-quality products in order to escape from bankruptcy. But in general this tendency was reversed by the fact that many textile firms had a short planning horizon, lacked mobility and were dominated by small firms. Only 4 per cent of textile companies had net assets (in 1951) of more than 50 million Belgian francs; 34 per cent of them had net assets of between 5 and 50 million Belgian francs; while 62 per cent had net assets of less than 5 million Belgian francs. Many textile firms were even smaller, because these figures refer to joint stock companies, not to small family concerns. In the coal and the rolling-stock industries disinvestment appeared as a rational choice because of the permanent losses.

During the 1950s the rate of growth of the capital stock correlated with the rate of development of real profits. The cement industry and the electrical engineering industry were the two sectors where profits were high and where the capital stock was growing most rapidly (Lamfalussy 1961: 140). In chemicals, electricity and gas the formation of capital stock was also important, because stronger protection played an important role. Lamfalussy pointed out that capital stock in ailing sectors like rolling stock, railway equipment and coal mining also increased in the 1950s, but this did not occur because of increased profitability. Investment in coal mining and railway equipment was the result of subsidies granted by the government for a variety of reasons. The Belgian government granted direct subsidies of 12,409 million Belgian francs in ten years to the coal mines. The rolling-stock firms had been earning large profits during the immediate postwar period when the government was carrying out reconstruction works and the neighbouring countries were ordering rolling stock for their own railways. But after 1948 the rolling-stock producers had to rely solely on orders coming from the SNCB–NMBS, which provoked a slowdown in the sector leading to heavy losses for the many companies still operating in this sector. According to Lamfalussy 'both coal mining and the rolling stock industry have been encouraged to invest defensively. In contrast to the steel and textile industries, their defensive investment has had a deepening (rather than an expansion) bias' (Lamfalussy 1961: 142) (see Table 5.3).

Table 5.3 Real gross fixed assets in Belgian industry (1957 as a percentage of 1948)*

Electrical engineering	170	
Chemicals	167	
Electricity and gas	154	
Cement	160	(142)
Food and beverages	154	
Steel	141	
Textiles	170	(150)
Coal	136	(142)
Rolling stock	n.a.	

* These are output indices, except for steel, textiles and cement where the indices refer to output capacity, the output indices for these three industries is given in parentheses.

Source: Lamfalussy 1961: 140

As a result of investment, output and output capacity grew in the period 1948–57. Especially in the electrical engineering industries, cement, electricity and gas, chemicals and food the capital–output ratio had increased. In the steel and textile industries the capital–output ratio fell because of defensive investment with an expansion bias (Lamfalussy 1961: 143). The reason for the low marginal capital–output ratio in Belgian steel firms, according to Lamfalussy, was that all Belgian steel firms grew through departmental expansion, through the replacement of old capital goods by new ones and through the improvement of existing capital assets. In Belgium there was no new integrated steel plant built in this period, so the 3.1 million tonne increase of capacity was obtained by spreading it over a large number of steel plants. The reason for this strategy has to be found in the fact that the holding companies controlling more than two-thirds of total Belgian steel production found it easier to merge the single steelworks into the new steel giant Cockerill–Ougrée instead of building an entirely new integrated steel factory. Thus increase in capital intensity also led to a substantial increase of employment in the Belgian steel industry (+7 per cent over the period). Belgian steel firms did their best by trying to sell abroad as much as possible, but they could do no long-term planning on this basis and there were no development plans in Belgium comparable to those which had been worked out in the UK or in France. According to Lamfalussy 'the result was a policy of improvements, of refurbishing and of cost-reduction which resulted, as a sort of by-product, in a considerable expansion of output capacity. But the primary aim of capital expenditure was not the extension of productive capacity. Nobody was prepared to set up an entirely new plant, for nobody expected that there would be scope for such an expansion in the export markets' (Lamfalussy 1961: 148–9). Hence Belgian steel firms increased capital intensity less than in the neighbouring countries. High elasticity of demand on the export markets pushed them simultaneously towards enlarging their capacities. But with the ECSC this policy changed and during the 1950s a project aimed at building a new integrated steel plant near the North Sea was put forward by the financial groups and the Belgian government.

Although there was a clear investment growth in petroleum refining and in the automobile assembly factories, more than 50 per cent of Belgian output came from industries relying on defensive investment (Lamfalussy 1961: 153). According to Lamfalussy defensive investment played an unusually great part in Belgian investment policies and total fixed capital formation was markedly lower in Belgium than in Western Europe or the USA. Defensive investment was linked with delayed scrapping of machinery and equipment. Thus many capital goods in existence in 1952–4 included a vast proportion of assets acquired prior to 1929 (Lamfalussy 1961: 155). This explains why Belgium invested a smaller part of its income than the other countries and a much greater part of it was directed towards declining industries (coal mines, textiles, rolling stock). Lamfalussy criticized this strategy with the remark that defensive investment in these declining industries had been a failure and that sooner or later a number of these firms would have to go out of business (Lamfalussy 1961: 156).

Lamfalussy's overall conclusion was that capital expenditure would have to be increased in those industries where defensive investment had been successful and that the share of capital formation in the country's national product would have to be raised. But other economists, like Jacques Drèze, have argued that the relative decline of the Belgian economy was largely due to its inability to attain advantages of scale (Kindleberger 1967: 75).

The complaint that Belgium was overspecialized in the wrong products – having such a large short-run comparative advantage in goods with poor long-run growth prospects owing to both income-inelastic demand and inherently limited external economies in technical change – echoed the arguments of Raúl Prebisch and Hla Myint concerning the limited growth possibilities which foreign trade offers the less developed countries (Kindleberger 1967: 74). (Prebisch stated that the less-developed countries which export primary products cannot depend on export-led growth because of the low income elasticity of demand for their exports.)

The fact that the Belgian economy grew at faster rates after 1959 can cast some doubt on long-run explanations and makes it useful to look for proximate factors. Kindleberger found these factors in the behaviour of wages and prices of raw materials. Wages grew too rapidly in the immediate postwar period, far outstripping productivity and holding down profits. This was partly the result of the Korean boom in raw-material prices, in which Belgian exports did not share, so that the terms-of-trade change from 1948–50 to 1953–5 adversely affected real national income by 11.5 per cent. This was more than made up, but wage rates rose by 49 per cent between 1948 and 1952, and labour costs (wages adjusted for productivity) climbed by 28 per cent over the same period. In addition to this cost-push inflation, there was insufficient demand, both in the domestic market until 1956 and from 1951 to 1955 in exports. Until about 1959, therefore, Belgium conformed more or less perfectly to the diagnosis which the British economists had made of their own economy: insufficient demand combined with cost-push inflation. Demand only picked up in 1954 but ran into balance-of-payments difficulties and a relapse of employment until 1959. After 1959 recovery appeared and unemployment dwindled rapidly for four successive years, so that foreign labour was recruited by the Belgian authorities (Kindleberger 1967: 74–6).

ANTI-CAPITALIST STRUCTURAL REFORMS

The decline of Belgian industry was also debated during the postwar period in political and trade union circles. In Flanders unemployment had always been much higher than in Wallonia. Here the Catholic trade union movement stressed the necessity of industrial investment in order to develop the distressed areas (West Flanders, the Campine). In Wallonia the influential Socialist trade union movement now became aware of the relative decline of heavy industry and analysed the problem of slow growth in terms of the unadapted capitalist power structures: the decline of Walloon industrial competitiveness on the world market was to a large extent caused by the policy of defensive investment by the Belgian holding companies and the growing importance of industry in Flanders. Figures illustrate this presumed growing preponderance of the Flemish economy. In 1920 53.5 per cent of all Belgian industrial workers were employed in Wallonia. In 1947 only 49.5 per cent of the Belgian industrial workers were still working in Wallonia (Quévit 1978: 82). The Depression of the 1930s had accelerated this tendency, because concentration of industrial activities combined with rationalization had favoured the relative decline of Wallonia's industrial employment.

When analysing this phenomenon Michel Quévit argued that Wallonia's decline was due to the inability of the local industrialists to innovate and the passivity of the holding companies in a period when the Flemish entrepreneurs were showing more dynamism. Here Quévit broadened a thesis Walloon syndicalists like Renard had already formulated during the 1950s (Quévit 1978: *passim*).

In 1954 a report presented by Renard to the extraordinary congress of the Socialist union FGTB–ABVV contained a comprehensive analysis of the problems the Belgian economy was then suffering from. The FGTB–ABVV report asked for structural reforms (i.e. a form of compulsory planning by the State with the help of the trade union movement). A second report issued by the FGTB–ABVV in 1956 under the title *Holdings et Démocratie économique* gave an overall picture of the financial structure of the Belgian economy, so making clear that all economic power was concentrated in the hands of 212 families controlling practically all important industrial firms and banks. The guiding idea of this report defended by Renard was that the labour movement had to choose for a planned economy, because 'the people who are controlling the economy, i.e. the 200 men of the holding companies, are doing their job in a bad way. They are doing it in a bad way because they are acting in their personal interest, not in the interest of the common people' (Moreau 1984: 51; tr. A.M.). Although the FGTB–ABVV leadership could agree with Renard's theoretical critique of capitalism, the reformist trade union leaders and Socialist members of Parliament were interpreting the so-called 'structural reforms' as Keynesian proposals aiming at allocating cheap investment credit and loans to innovating firms. Finally, Renard stood alone with his radical appeal for anti-capitalist structural reforms, because even a majority of the technocrats (Roland Beauvois, Henri Neuman, Herman Biron, Albert Deridder, Robert Evalenko, Georges Rogissart, William Fraeys, Albert De Smaele, Henri Janne and Ernest Mandel) who had written the FGTB–ABVV report, were won over to neo-capitalist planning.

NEO-CAPITALIST PLANNING

It was not the Socialist Party and the FGTB–ABVV who played a dominant role in Belgian politics, but the Christian Democrats. After having formed a minority government in 1958 the Christian Democrats allied with the Liberals; meanwhile they were striving for economic and social reforms. In 1958 Christian Democratic reformers had campaigned for the creation of 100,000 new jobs and the modernization of the agricultural sector. These reforms appealed to the Flemish working class suffering from high unemployment rates and to the Flemish smallholders. The crisis in the agrarian sector was largely due to rising costs (machinery, fertilizers, etc.) and falling agrarian prices (in 1960 a decrease of 8 per cent when compared to 1950), both leading to declining agrarian income and investment capacity. Notwithstanding some agrarian regulations, average income in the agrarian sector reached only 60 per cent of wages earned in the industrial sector. Although Belgian agriculture had been protected by a preferential BENELUX tariff of 20 per cent and higher tariffs existed for the other countries, peasants suffered from increased competition on the domestic market. Thus the Belgian authorities established an intervention price based on production costs, but which by no means constituted a guaranteed price. Several governmental offices also regulated the agrarian market (Office National des Débouchés Agricoles et Horticoles, Office National du Lait et de ses Dérivés, Office Commercial de Ravitaillement) and cared about quality, output and prices (Krul 1964: 76–8). Because the European Economic Community (EEC) announced increased competition and a dismantling of national protectionism all agrarian

107

interest groups now stressed the necessity for an active agrarian policy.

The EEC also threatened the Belgian economy which suffered from inefficiencies (Loeb 1965: *passim*). On 24 September 1958, when speaking to an audience of entrepreneurs and bankers, Minister of Economic Affairs Raymond Scheyven developed the idea that the recently founded EEC would impose a lowering of all production costs and this would necessitate investment in large-scale production. Scheyven stated that the risks of investing in large-scale production were high and certainly could only become successful in the event if all entrepreneurs could agree on the idea of a central co-ordinating economy. Here Scheyven pleaded for structural economic orientations defined by the State easing the programming of private investment (*La Décision* 1965: 253). Scheyven also announced the foundation of the Bureau de Programmation Economique (BPE), which finally was set up on 14 October 1959. When on 11 May 1960 the government, the trade unions and the entrepreneurial organizations agreed on the principle of programming economic and social development, the idea of an incomes policy had imposed itself. The 'social partners' immediately signed a general agreement on an increase of all salaries by 2 per cent and later on, by a Royal Decree of 10 November 1960, a national committee for economic expansion, the Comité National d'Expansion Economique – Nationaal Comité voor Economische Expansie (CNEE–NCEE), was formed. This committee ordered the BPE to formulate a first five-year plan starting from the assumption that an average economic growth of 4 per cent a year could be reached (Krul 1964: 36–7; Quévit 1978: 138).

Meanwhile two important acts stimulating investment were passed in the summer of 1959. The General Act of 17 July 1959 defined the possibility of governmental help to private industrial investment aimed at the creation, reconversion or modernization of industrial enterprises (Quévit 1978: 165–6). Governmental aid was given in the form of low-interest loans granted by the State and private banks or in the form of an exemption of paying taxes for at least five years. The Specific Act on Regional Development passed on 18 July 1959 defined specific measures for those regions suffering from high unemployment, migratory labour and industrial decline. These areas were now clearly defined and grouped 322 communes in 15 regions, representing 18.2 per cent of the total population (Quévit 1978: 166).

THE COAL MINING CRISIS

In 1957–8 the coal industry still occupied 175,000 workers or 10 per cent of all industrial workers and produced 12 per cent of the Belgian industrial product. The future of the coal mining sector had become extremely uncertain because of its high production costs and the low-priced American coal arriving at Antwerp. In 1958 stocks of unsold Belgian coal kept by the coal mines were some 8 million tonnes. Although over the period 1953–8 many coal mines were closed, the reduction of the total production capacity of only 2.727 million tonnes represented no more than 10 per cent of total Belgian coal output. On 10 February 1958 all subsidies coming from the ECSC for the marginal mines had been exhausted. Now the Belgian government decided to accelerate the closure of other marginal mines, especially in the Borinage.

Meanwhile the big consumers of Belgian coal federated in the Union des Utilisateurs et Négociants Belges de Charbon (UNEBECE) and led by the electricity-supplying companies had openly blamed the central selling organization COBECHAR for obtaining a permanent rent in favour of the more efficient coal mining companies while assuring the survival of the marginal mines (*La Décision* 1965: 273). COBECHAR broke up shortly thereafter because some minor Walloon coal mining companies and three important mines of the North Basin (which the SGB did not control) decided to market their own coal, which weakened the bargaining position of all coal mining companies. Now a complete restructuring of the sector was imposing itself.

But the planned closing of many mines in Wallonia provoked a social upheaval in the Borinage in February 1959, forcing the Eyskens government to prepare an emergency programme for the distressed areas.

The coal mining crisis of 1958–9 forced the government to neutralize the still resisting coal mining interest groups. On 23 February 1959, at the height of the coal mining crisis, the central entrepreneurial organization FIB, the Socialist FGTB–ABVV and the Catholic trade union Confédération des Syndicats Chrétiens – Algemeen Christelijk Vakverbond (CSC–ACV) signed a protocol pleading for a non-corporatist solution to the coal mining crisis with the central entrepreneurial organization of the coal industry, Fédération Charbonnière Belge (FEDECHAR) and the miners' unions. The setting up of a national coal board controlling the whole coal industry was decided. Meanwhile the government prepared a new package of subsidies for the coal industry and a new compromise was worked out with the ECSC on a gradual closing-down of all remaining marginal mines within a five-year period. On 31 July 1959 a provisional programme concerning the elimination of some 5.5 million tonnes of production capacity was signed and in December 1959 an additional plan aiming at the suppressing of 9.5 million tonnes of production capacity was launched. The costs of the whole operation were paid out of a solidarity fund financed by the French, German and Dutch mines. Sales of coal coming from the other ECSC members remained strictly limited on the Belgian market.

THE WINTER OF DISCONTENT (1960–1)

During the Summer of 1960 the Eyskens government was weakened by two important political problems. First, there was the aftermath of a disastrous policy of decolonization (see Chapter 6). Second, due to the economic crisis, the government had to face serious financial problems. Although the business cycle was moving up-ward and the deficit on the balance of trade was decreasing, unem-ployment remained high. The spectre of paying higher taxes and the loss of many social benefits provoked some discontent among civil servants, teachers and workers. In the meantime the international bankers were pressing the Belgian government to decrease the deficit on its current budget (see Table 5.4).

At the end of July 1960 Prime Minister Eyskens announced an 'austerity programme', but Conservative Catholics and Liberals immediately objected to the proposal of levying new taxes. In order

Table 5.4 The Treasury problems of the Belgian state, 1956–60 (in million Belgian francs)

Year	Fiscal revenues	Expenditures	Deficit
1956	90,801	96,606	− 5,805
1957	100,758	111,765	− 11,007
1958	95,655	118,528	− 22,873
1959	105,392	135,293	− 29,901
1960	110,238	145,392	− 35,154

Source: La Décision 1965: 214

to avoid an open conflict in his own Catholic Party, Eyskens started to include several fiscal, administrative and social reforms within the so-called 'Loi Unique'. The labour movement discovered many discriminating measures against the unemployed and the pensioned civil servants. Increased indirect taxation also meant a heavier burden for the wage-earners and pensioners, while nothing was proposed against tax evasion practised by stockholders and professionals. Unfortunately for Eyskens, protest demonstrations and sectoral strikes against the 'Loi Unique' gained the support of the masses in the industrial areas. Thus the anarcho-syndicalists led by Renard increased their following among the workers. They decided to go ahead. On 20 December 1960 the strike became general throughout the country. Lasting for more than five weeks this strike became known as the 'Strike of the Century' (Deprez 1963: 49–93; Féaux 1963: 67–183; Meynen 1978: 481–513; Buyens *et al.* 1985: 8–26; Neuville and Yerna 1990: 63–95).

Although the General Strike mobilized the entire working class in Wallonia and a significant portion of the Flemish workers, already at the beginning of January 1961 it became evident that the 'Loi Unique' would be passed on 13 January 1961 without defections by the Christian Democrats. In the eyes of Renard the General Strike had been lost because the Flemish Socialist politicians and trade union leaders had refused to strike until the 'finish'. After the strike Renard launched a new mass movement, the Mouvement Populaire Wallon (MPW), which had to carry out his project of anti-capitalist reforms and Walloon autonomy (Neuville and Yerna 1990: *passim*). The General Strike also led to the fall of the Eyskens government. The Liberals and several Catholic politicians had hoped that parliamentary elections would bring electoral gains for the governmental parties. Instead the Catholic Party lost many seats. This incited the Christian Democrats to conclude a coalition with the Socialists (a 'Roman–Red' government).

CONCLUSIONS

The end of the 1950s was marked by a dramatic economic breakdown and clumsy behaviour by all social and political actors when managing the economic crisis. The conservative investment policy practised by the major holding companies in combination with the relative decline of Belgian industry and exports brought the country near to the abyss of rapid economic decline.

6

PARADISE LOST
The decolonization of the Congo

On 30 June 1960 the Belgian Congo acquired the status of an independent country. In the eyes of the Belgian interest groups independence meant a political construction without major changes in the economic and social structures. Although a parliament elected by black voters had been established and a government composed of a broad spectrum of politicians representing a coalition of several political parties had been instituted, all economic and administrative powers remained in the hands of the Belgian colonialists (Bouvier 1965: 284–343; Vanderlinden 1985: 79–125). Unfortunately for the big colonial firms this construction collapsed within a few days, making the Congo a centre of political and military instability in Africa.

THE END OF BELGIAN COLONIALISM

The first blow against colonialism came from some critical members of the Belgian administration in the Congo and from intellectuals criticizing the way the government was administering the colony. But this criticism remained within the realms of goodwill proposals aimed at reforming the administrative and schooling system, and reforms which aimed at eventual decolonization 'still betrayed their authors' complete lack of political acumen' (Willame 1972: 20), because nobody was thinking about the possibility of an independent Congo State ruled by a black majority government. Thus when in 1955 professor Joseph Van Bilsen proposed a 30-year plan for the political emancipation of the Congo, he only received enthusiastic responses on behalf of some Congolese intellectuals, while his proposals were fiercely opposed by the colonial lobby and the bourgeois parties in Belgium.

112

The Belgian government discovered the problem of decolonization on 4 January 1959 when in Léopoldville, the capital of the Belgian Congo, riots occurred and black urban masses started plundering the shopping centre. In reaction to these troublesome events the Belgian government immediately announced that an acceleration of the process of decolonization had to be taken into consideration (*Congo 1885–1960* n.d.: 79–116; Demany 1959: *passim*; Bouvier 1965: 201–83). This proposal was not opposed by the colonial companies, apparently because they had no alternative policy and the spectre of large-scale upheavals was so deterring that the spokesmen of colonial capital now tried to adapt to the tempestuous pace of events (Young 1965: 151–2).

But a few days after the proclamation of the independence of the Belgian colony riots and panic spread among the Belgian settlers as a process of territorial and political disintegration of the Congolese State began to take place. Immediately, the Belgian government decided to send in air-borne troops in order to protect and evacuate the white population and to defend Belgian property. This armed intervention revealed the weakness of the Congolese State and its dependence on the former colonial power. Finally, the Congolese political élite decided to appeal to world opinion and the United Nations in order to restore its lost prestige (Maurel 1992: 299–352).

After a period of indecision Washington opposed the policy of the Belgian colonial firms favouring the subdivision of the Congolese territory into independent states (Kalb 1982: 46–196) and under American pressure the dissenting mining province of Katanga had to reintegrate into the Republic of the Congo. Meanwhile revolts in the other Congolese provinces still undermined the authority of the central government until in November 1965 general Joseph Mobutu took full power.

THE BELGIAN MINING INTERESTS

Until 1960 the importance of the Belgian Congo for the Belgian economy had been largely overestimated. Baudhuin asserted that the withdrawal from empire liberated Belgium from a heavy investment burden it was no longer able to sustain (Baudhuin 1970: 231). Because the Belgians had not created a large white community in the Congo, a withdrawal from Africa did not provoke a massive reflux of Belgian citizens. In 1960 only 87,000 Belgians lived in the Belgian Congo and the overwhelming majority of them worked in the rich mining province of Katanga. Many of them were not permanent residents in the colony and usually they preferred to return to Belgium after having retired.

Because investment in the Congo remained highly profitable, financial revenues coming from the colony guaranteed the survival of the Belgian bourgeoisie. By 1920 revenues from financial and industrial investment largely exceeded profits from metropolitan industries (see Table 6.1).

Table 6.1 Net income of industrial enterprises in Belgium and in the Congo, 1936–57 (percentages earned on investments)

Year	Enterprises in Belgium	Enterprises in the Congo
1936–9	7.00	10.10
1947–50	6.88	15.07
1951–4	8.20	21.48
1955	8.19	18.47
1956	9.40	20.16
1957	9.49	21.00

Source: Willame 1972: 11

There were also the revenues obtained from colonial trade which enriched the bourgeoisie in Antwerp. But the overall impact of the Congo on the Belgian economy was rather limited and did not exceed 3 per cent of GDP. Only 2.7 per cent of Belgian exports went in the direction of Central Africa and only 5.7 per cent of all imports came from the colony.

Because the colonial firms raised funds from all levels of the bourgeoisie and provided huge profits to their shareholders, the Congo appeared as some kind of El Dorado. Total private investment in Congolese industry, mining activities and real estate was estimated at some 60 billion Belgian francs, which mainly comprised shares issued by the Union Minière du Haut-Katanga and a few other colonial firms which were in the overwhelming majority controlled by the SGB. It was generally admitted that the SGB controlled directly or indirectly 70 per cent of the Congolese economy and that its influence was practically total in certain mining areas (copper, cobalt, diamonds) and in maritime and rail transportation. Its mining activities were concentrated in the provinces of Katanga and Kasai. Furthermore the SGB was equally interested in Tanganyika Concessions Ltd (TANKS) and the Diamond Company of Angola (DIAMANG). The jewel in the SGB's crown was the Union Minière du Haut-Katanga, which had exclusive mining rights over a large area of Katanga and controlled the refineries established in Belgium.

The Union Minière du Haut-Katanga was founded in 1906 by the SGB. In that year two other important firms – Société Internationale Forestière et Minière du Congo (the FORMINIERE) and the BCK – were launched. The BCK railway linking the port of Matadi to the mining areas was undercapitalized and, finally, in 1936, in the middle of the Depression, the Colony bought the BCK. Meanwhile the BCK developed mining activities in Kasai and founded the Minière du Bécéka which specialized in mining industrial diamonds and which developed as an independent company. The FORMINIERE produced jewelry diamonds and in 1959 produced 400,000 carats of jewelry diamonds. In that year the Minière du Bécéka produced 14 million carats (Stengers 1989: 214) or 60 per cent of the total world production of industrial diamonds.

The mining companies constituted a state within the Belgian Congo because they produced 22 per cent of the colony's GDP and 60 per cent of its export. Of this production, 75 per cent came from Katanga. More than half of the total mining output, and 70 per cent of Katanga's, consisted of copper – in which Union Minière had a monopoly. It was estimated that half of the Congo's budgetary receipts and the majority of its foreign exchange came from Katanga (Weissman 1974: 24).

The start of the Union Minière had been difficult. In 1920 the firm only produced 19,000 tonnes of copper, but soon advantages of scale were obtained. In 1929 total output of copper amounted to 137,000 tons. Subsequently the Union Minière became one of the leading mining companies in the world. In 1959 production of Katangese copper amounted to 280,000 tons and profits made by the Union Minière attained the sum of 3.5 billion Belgian francs (Chomé 1960: 35). This success was largely due to the SGB's commercial strategy. In 1921 it established the SGM in order to break the power of the non-ferrous metals cartels controlled by the British Metal Corporation, the German Metallgesellschaft and the French company Minerais et Métaux (*Union Minière* 1956: 136–54). This strategy was successful because after the First World War the SGB acquired several sequestered non-ferrous metals refining factories previously owned by German companies: the refineries in Olen, Reppel and Hoboken.

After 1923 the Union Minière developed the Shinkolobwe mine. Here uranium ore was produced and then shipped to Belgium. On the eve of the Second World War uranium became a metal of strategic importance. That was probably the reason why in 1940 the Union Minière shipped its uranium reserves to New York, where this precious metal could be used to develop the first atomic bombs (Groueff 1967: 54–6; Lekime 1992: 120–1). Although uranium was a strategic metal the Union Minière never published production statistics. This secrecy and the fact that the Shinkolobwe mine was one of the best protected places in the world created the myth that the Union Minière was making fabulous profits out of its uranium business. However, in 1956 the Union Minière admitted that its uranium trade accounted for only 1.5 per cent of the company's total profits and in 1960 the Shikolobwe mine was closed down because of its very low profitability (Lekime 1992: 196).

Apart from the SGB, other Belgian holding companies were operating in the Belgian Congo. BRUFINA controlled all tin mines via Symétain. The railroad king Baron Empain owned the Chemin de Fer des Grands Lacs and the Compagnie Lambert was involved in plantations. As early as 1911 William Lever had founded the Huileries du Congo, which possessed large palm plantations in the Central Congo. They provided Unilever's Union Margarinière in Antwerp with palm oil. But Unilever was not the sole British investor to have interests in the Belgian Congo. It was well-known that British capital held a significant minority stake in the Union Minière (for instance in 1906 the British company TANKS was present among the founders of the Union Minière du Haut-Katanga).

Although the SGB exercised control over the Union Minière, this only occurred through direct and indirect stakes of two Congolese holding companies: the Compagnie du Congo pour le Commerce et l'Industrie (CCCI) and the Compagnie du Katanga. Furthermore, the Congolese administration held in portfolio a two-thirds stake in the Comité Spécial du Katanga (CSK), whose main investment was a stake in the Union Minière. Nonetheless it was the Board of Directors of the SGB who nominated the President of the Board of the Union Minière. This also applied to the FORMINIERE in which the Congolese authorities held a 55 per cent stake, while the SGB only owned a 5 per cent stake.

The Union Minière du Haut-Katanga was known as a very rich mining company with a diversified output. In 1953 the company produced 7 per cent of all copper, 80 per cent of all cobalt and 5 per cent of all zinc in the world. Large quantities of cadmium, silver, platinum, columbium, and tungsten were refined by the non-ferrous metals factories of the group. By 1959 production of copper had risen to 300,000 tonnes and profits exceeded 3,535 million Belgian francs (US dollars 70.7 million). Net profits made between 1950 and 1959 totalled 31,000 million Belgian francs (US dollars 620 million). In 1959 the Belgian Congo produced 9 per cent of all copper, 49 per cent of all cobalt, 69 per cent of all industrial diamonds, and 6.5 per cent of all tin in the world.

CONTROLLING CONGOLESE COPPER

Although the USA had no vested interests in the Katanga–Rhodesia Copperbelt, American capitalism became increasingly involved in the Congo. Katanga provided approximately three-quarters of the cobalt imported into the USA and one-half of the tantalum (Weissman 1974: 29). The Katanga–Rhodesia Copperbelt accounted for nearly 10 per cent of American copper imports. During the Korean War American foreign diplomacy had become extremely interested in Central Africa and the American government provided the Rhodesian copper industry with loans repayable by deliveries of copper and cobalt to American stockpiles. The industrial diamonds coming from the mining area of South Kasai provided 80 per cent of American supply. Thus a closing down of the copper and diamond mines in the Congo would certainly have affected the American economy and threatened Europe's industrial vitality.

American interests in the Congo totalled less than 20 million US dollars in the early 1960s and were heavily concentrated in the Rhodesian Selection Trust (owned by American Metal Climax – AMAX) which along with the Anglo-American Co. controlled the Rhodesian Copperbelt. Both companies purchased hydro-electric power from a subsidiary of the Union Minière in Katanga. Furthermore, Lazard Frères (New York) remained a traditional stockholder in the Union Minière and the Paris branch was one of the largest stockholders in TANKS, whose major asset was a 14.5 per cent holding in the Union Minière and the right to a special annual royalty. But the Anglo-American Co. also held a large block of stock in TANKS. FORMINIERE owned the jewel diamond mines of South Kasai and had a stake in DIAMANG (also a subsidiary of the SGB). The American group Ryan–Guggenheim held one-quarter of the shares in FORMINIERE and Guggenheim still played a major role in the Kennecott Copper Co. and held shares in the Belgian–American Banking Corp., a subsidiary of the SGB established in New York.

The Morgan Guaranty Trust had always had a good relationship with the Belgian government and the Congolese administration. Many times Morgan was the syndicate manager participant in loans to the Congo and sometimes Morgan acted as banker to the Belgian government. Because the Morgan Guaranty Trust was very close as principal banker to Newmont Mining and Kennecott Copper, Morgan's position was by far the most influential in the Congo.

During the pre-independence negotiations the SGB tried to tighten its control over the Union Minière. The problem worrying the SGB directors was that the Union Minière was controlled by six directors of the CSK and that four of CSK's directors were appointed by the Congolese government. In the event that the Congolese government which came to power after independence was willing to implement changes in the Union Minière's policy, the SGB would become powerless. But in May 1960 just before the declaration of independence the SGB obtained the dissolution of the CSK from the Belgian government. Because the SGB, the Compagnie du Katanga and TANKS together now had an absolute majority on the board of the Union Minière, the authorities of the Republic of the Congo were relegated to the position of a powerless minority shareholder (Lanning and Mueller 1979: 229–33).

The crisis of decolonization had a negative effect on the credit rating of all colonial firms now facing significant losses on their investment. Many colonial firms had transferred their holdings to Belgium well before independence day. For instance, the Union Minière possessed some 15 billion Belgian francs outside of the Congolese territory. Large stocks of non-ferrous metals had been built up in order to protect the company's market position in case the Katangese mines stopped delivering copper to the Belgian refineries. But this did not protect them from raiders. When in November 1965 Mobutu took over political power, he could unite all political factions only by promising economic nationalism and a policy of 'authentification'. Zaïre was the new name of the country governed by dictator Mobutu-Sese-Seko. Mobutu immediately launched a campaign against the Union Minière by decreeing that all companies legally constituted in the Congo had to move their headquarters to Congolese territory before 1 January 1967. The Union Minière resisted. Then Mobutu nationalized the company's Congolese assets and established a new company, the Société Générale Congolaise des Minerais (GECOMIN). Although he offered a 40 per cent stake in it to a consortium constituted by American banks and led by the Compagnie Lambert (Lekime 1992: 283), no agreement could be reached with the Newmont Mining Corp., the Rhodesian Selection Trust, the Anglo-American or the Pennarroya Co. who all had been invited to participate in the project. After some hesitation they all withdrew because without the production capacity of the refineries of the Métallurgie in Hoboken (Belgium) wire bars (copper) coming from the Katangese mines could not be refined. So the government in Washington compelled Mobutu to resolve his differences with the Union Minière and the SGB. Finally the Union Minière agreed that the SGM, a subsidiary of the SGB, would execute all service agreements with GECOMIN and look after the marketing of Congolese minerals. In September 1969 Mobutu conceded a share in the profits obtained by the export of Congolese copper to the SGM. Simultaneously the Union Minière victoriously resisted an attack launched by 'Tiny' Rowland's Lonrho and Martin Thèves' COMINIERE (Société Commerciale et Minière du Congo) (Lanning and Mueller 1979: 248–51).

CONCLUSIONS

The decolonization of Africa had many victims among Belgian stockholders. Colonial revenues dried up, while investment opportunities elsewhere in the Third World were rather limited now the former colonies were enticed by a policy of import substitution and economic nationalism. In particular the SGB had to write off a significant part of its colonial assets and to prospect for new investment opportunities abroad. For a while Canada, where Sogémines Ltd (in 1968 Genstar Corp.) acquired more weight (Laureyssens 1984: 97–142), appeared as a 'second Congo', but all these fabulous promises were never fulfilled. Meanwhile the Belgian taxpayer endorsed an important part of the Congolese public debt inherited from the Belgian colonial administration. In 1959 total colonial debt was estimated at more than 43 billion Belgian francs of which the Belgian government had guaranteed some 10.5 billion Belgian francs of total outstanding debt. Because the Congo was unable to guarantee the service of this huge debt, the banks forced the Belgian government to convert the guaranteed part of the Congolese debt into Belgian State bonds.

7

THE GOLDEN 1960s

The 1960s were characterized by rapid economic growth and increased mass consumption. The social and political changes Belgium was experiencing were the results of an overall modernization process of the economy imposed by the irruption of foreign multinational investment. Governmental attempts aimed at rationalizing the traditional industrial sectors (coal, steel, textiles) and agriculture were less successful. Opening up of the Belgian economy for imports not only stimulated economic growth, but also accelerated the decline of the traditional industrial sectors and the disappearance of many smallholders.

THE POLITICS OF MODERNIZATION

On the political level, the neo-capitalist predicament was legitimated by the victory of coalition governments built on alliance between modernizing entrepreneurship and the trade unions, with economic growth and social welfare as basic issues. Although the process of decolonization in Africa for a while obscured the guidelines of this policy, the decline of the traditional industries controlled by the Belgian holding companies in Wallonia had started well before 1960. The politics of economic modernization had been prepared by the reformist wing of the Christian Democrats when they formed a minority government in 1958. A compromise on the so-called 'School Question' was necessary to restore political stability and avoid polarization. But meanwhile the Liberals joined the government, making a Centre–Left coalition government impossible. Notwithstanding the presence of the Liberals, the government implemented important reforms making State planning a key concept. This resulted in the foundation of the BPE (*La Décision* 1965:

121

247–67) and two decrees defining a policy of national and regional economic expansion (17 and 18 July 1959).

Regions suffering from unemployment and economic backwardness were stimulated by fiscal, financial and infrastructural measures favouring private investment. After 1953 the State banks were empowered to provide small and medium-sized firms with loans on soft conditions and fiscal incentives had made investment attractive to industrial firms. But these reforms were insufficient. The reforms of 1959 conferred governmental guarantees to loans provided by commercial banks to companies when they decided to invest in the so-called distressed areas. The latter reform made Belgium attractive to multinational companies looking for investment opportunities in Europe and started from the assumption that a peaceful co-existence between entrepreneurs and trade unions was possible. Indeed, in May 1960 leading entrepreneurs and trade union leaders signed a new Social Pact completing the previous Declaration on Productivity of 5 May 1954. The new Social Pact stipulated that social conflicts could be avoided. Mutual trust had to guide the 'social partners' (i.e. entrepreneurs and trade unions) to successful collective bargaining and to a policy of income distribution based on productivity gains (Slomp and Van Mierlo 1984: (II) 84–6).

After the general strike of 1960–1 parliamentary elections were held on 26 March 1961 and enabled the Labour wing of the Christian Democrats to make overtures to the Socialists. A Centre–Left coalition government of Socialists and Christian Democrats led by Théo Lefèvre (Hoflack 1989: 66–89) came into power and promised to enhance economic reforms. Belgium entered into the era of Keynesianism. On 2 April 1962 the National Investment Company (Société Nationale d'Investissement – Nationale Investeringsmaatschappij (SNI–NIM)) was founded. Although leading financial circles opposed this initiative by the Socialist Party, private capital was used in its funding (Vandeputte 1985: 84). In June 1961 the government set up a commission headed by the banker De Voghel in order to study the problems of the Belgian economy and finances. A report published by the commission confirmed the thesis that high interest rates were responsible for difficulties enterprises had when issuing shares (Mommen 1982: 125). Many firms remained undercapitalized and investment rates lagged behind those in neighbouring countries. Multinational firms in Belgium did not suffer from high real interest rates because their profits were substantial and they could always contract cheap loans on the international capital market. They could also obtain subsidies and fiscal advantages from the Belgian government when contracting loans from the commercial banks. Meanwhile the Belgian banks extended their financial activities. They opened individual savings accounts and promoted the contracting of personal loans for private use. Meanwhile the total number of bank accounts increased from 1,300,000 accounts in 1960 to 2,600,000 in 1965. The number of local branches increased from 1,700 branches in l960 to 3,000 in 1965. In 1965 some 80 Belgian and foreign banks employed about 30,000 employees. Their total balance account amounted to 330 billion Belgian francs. Mortgage banks and specialist savings banks opened local branches in order to compete with the public savings bank, the Caisse Générale d'Epargne et de Retraite – Algemene Spaar- en Lijfrentekas (CGER–ASLK). The latter remained by far the largest savings bank with a total balance account of 136 billion Belgian francs, while the balance account of the Bank of Belgian Cities (Crédit Communal – Gemeentekrediet) totalled some 36 billion Belgian francs. As a result of the Act of 1 July 1956 making automobile insurance compulsory, the insurance sector boomed. Additional pensions schemes were contracted by big employers making 'extra-legal pensions' popular. In matters of banking and insurance activities Belgium remained a very liberal country, with branches of foreign banks and insurance companies gaining important market shares in the life insurance sector (Vandeputte 1985: 88).

The government of Théo Lefèvre had to face serious budgetary problems inherited from the past (see Table 7.1) and therefore studied a comprehensive tax reform. The Tax Act of 20 November 1962 standardized all personal revenues and made them assessable. Professionals had to pay their income tax in advance. Finally, the government imposed taxes on dividends and interest paid to individuals (*précompte*) (*La Décision* 1965: 232–46; *Régime fiscal* 1963: *passim*).

In the 1960s economic growth averaged 4 to 5 per cent a year, while private consumption increased by only 3.2 per cent a year. Economic progress was due to heavy investment in new industrial sectors (petrochemicals, automobiles, electronics) and in services. The traditional industrial sectors (coal, heavy industries, textiles) were in decline, but the weight of these traditional products on the trade balance remained relatively high at the end of the 1960s (see Table 7.2). Meanwhile exports were increasing in the direction of the neighbouring countries which was both the effect of the EEC

Table 7.1 The evolution of Belgian public debt in current prices,
1955–70 (in billion Belgian francs)

Year	GDP	Public debt	% of GDP
1955	456.5	312	68.3
1956	487.3	318	65.3
1957	516.7	324	62.7
1958	520.7	346	66.4
1959	536.6	374	69.7
1960	571.5	396	69.3
1961	606.4	411	67.8
1962	648.1	423	65.3
1963	696.0	446	64.1
1964	778.3	462	59.4
1965	848.9	485	57.1
1966	912.7	504	55.2
1967	978.0	525	54.1
1968	1,045.0	567	54.3
1969	1,160.0	598	51.6
1970	1,293.6	622	48.1

Sources: De nationale rekeningen van België 1963–1971: 3; Baudhuin 1970: 426;
België. Basisstatistieken 1965–1974: 73

and multinational investment in automobile assembly and petro-chemicals (see Table 7.3).

Foreign trade progressed at 6 per cent a year (see Table 7.4) opening up the Belgian economy to international economic and financial influences.

By 1970 the era of mass consumption had become a fact. Wage increases paid out of productivity gains in all sectors enabled the financing of growing welfare expenditures (see Table 7.5).

During the slowdown of 1965–6 average economic growth did not exceed 2 per cent per year, but at the end of 1967 an upswing occurred and in 1968 annual average growth attained 8 per cent. With a utilization rate of 94 per cent in industry, overheating of the economy was becoming evident. In 1969 industrial output increased by 16 per cent and the export volume of industrial products grew by some 23 per cent (Vandeputte 1985: 91–2). Credit expansion and high investment rates in combination with growing exports created full employment, but also wage inflation. Costs of living increased because prices paid for services incorporating higher labour costs rose faster than prices of industrial and agricultural products. This situation was called 'stagflation' now that prices were rising faster

Table 7.2 Structure of the export balance, 1965–70
(in percentages)

	1965	1966	1967	1968	1969	1970
Iron and steel	17.9	16.1	16.4	16.1	16.2	16.9
Metal products	23.1	22.4	22.8	22.1	23.0	23.5
Non-ferrous metals	7.7	9.2	8.4	8.6	7.8	7.9
Textiles	14.4	14.8	13.2	12.9	12.6	11.5
Chemicals	6.2	6.2	6.8	7.8	8.0	8.5
Foodstuffs	6.7	6.8	7.9	7.8	7.8	8.1
Diamonds	3.9	4.5	4.4	4.4	4.0	3.3
Coal and coke	0.7	0.4	0.5	0.3	0.3	0.3
Oil products	2.5	2.3	2.3	2.8	3.0	2.5
Other industrial products	7.0	7.1	7.4	7.5	7.5	7.4
Other sectors	9.9	10.2	9.9	9.7	9.8	10.1

Source: België. Basisstatistieken 1965–1974: 65

Table 7.3 Geographical spread of Belgian exports, 1958–68
(in percentages of total exports in US$, fob)

	1958	1963	1965	1966	1967	1968
Europe	66.1	79.2	79.1	79.4	80.0	79.5
EEC	45.1	60.8	61.9	62.8	63.0	64.3
France	10.6	14.5	14.5	16.2	17.7	18.6
Italy	2.3	5.2	3.4	3.3	4.0	3.8
Netherlands	20.7	22.6	22.1	22.2	21.5	21.0
Germany	11.5	18.5	21.8	21.1	19.8	20.9
UK	5.7	5.7	4.8	4.7	4.7	4.4
USA	9.2	8.5	8.3	8.7	8.4	9.4
Canada	1.1	0.9	1.0	0.9	0.7	0.6
Congo	3.8	0.9	1.0	1.0	0.7	0.9

Source: Based on Vandenabeele et al. 1969: 37

Table 7.4 Evolution of the Belgian trade balance, 1955–70
(in billion Belgian francs)

Year	Export				Import			
	Current prices		Growth rates		Current prices		Growth rates	
	(1)	(2)	(3)	(4)	(1)	(2)	(3)	(4)
1955	155.3	34.0	20.3	14.3	143.2	32.0	10.9	10.0
1956	179.7	36.9	15.7	8.5	170.1	34.9	16.3	13.0
1957	184.6	35.7	2.7	2.0	178.5	34.5	4.9	1.8
1958	177.3	34.0	−4.0	0.9	160.1	30.7	−10.3	−3.5
1959	176.3	32.8	−0.6	6.5	176.1	32.8	10.0	0.2
1960	200.1	35.0	13.5	9.9	198.7	34.8	12.0	1.4
1961	216.7	35.7	8.3	8.8	217.1	35.8	9.3	6.7
1962	233.6	36.0	7.8	7.7	230.2	35.5	6.0	4.6
1963	254.2	36.5	8.8	7.0	258.1	37.1	12.1	7.8
1964	295.0	37.9	16.1	11.1	295.0	37.9	14.3	10.7
1965	325.7	38.4	10.4	7.7	317.6	37.4	7.7	6.6
1966	350.1	38.4	7.5	4.0	352.5	38.7	11.0	8.1
1967	376.8	38.5	7.6	6.7	368.0	37.6	4.4	3.5
1968	430.1	41.2	14.2	13.8	420.5	40.3	14.3	13.6
1969	520.9	44.9	21.1	15.9	503.4	43.4	19.7	15.9
1970	616.0	47.6	18.3	11.5	576.0	44.5	14.4	8.6

(1) In billion Belgian francs
(2) In % of GDP
(3) In real prices
(4) At 1963 prices

Source: De nationale rekeningen van België 1963–1971: 7

Table 7.5 Average growth of added value per worker/year in some economic activities, 1965–70 (in constant prices)

	Added value		Agriculture		Industry		Services	
	1960–1965	1965–1970	1960–1965	1965–1970	1960–1965	1965–1970	1960–1965	1965–1970
Belgium	4.0	4.3	3.7	7.6	4.8	6.2	3.1	2.3
EEC	4.3	4.6	6.4	7.0	4.7	5.3	3.1	2.8

Source: Belgique: pays en voie 1978: 54

than productivity gains in industry. In Belgium wage increases of 10 per cent a year were not unusual, but in the meantime profits made by industrial firms decreased, making investment out of their cash flow less attractive (Vandeputte 1985: 92).

THE REGIONAL DIVIDE

The 1960s brought a higher standard of living for many workers on the assembly-line factories, but in basic industries many workers suffered from job insecurity and temporary unemployment. Especially in Wallonia, the decline of the steel and coal industry provoked structural unemployment. That was not the case in Flanders where young workers were recruited by multinationals whose factories were established in the 'green fields'. Here the automobile and chemical industries were employing a 'new working class'. The authorities tried to protect workers in the declining industries on behalf of the trade unions. Although mass lay-offs of workers could not be entirely avoided, the government agreed to the principle that a special fund had to be established in order to pay compensation to workers losing their jobs because of bankruptcies. During the period 1950–9 bankruptcies of industrial firms had caused 26,930 dismissals. The Act of 27 June 1960 established a special indemnity fund paying a premium to victims of bankruptcies (*L'Année sociale* 1960: 31). The decline of heavy industry in Wallonia was considered an acute political problem, because here the radical rank-and-file of the Walloon trade union movement was now organized outside of the Socialist Party in the MPW. In Flanders in 1961 the Flemish Popular Union (Volksunie – VU) had already gained five seats in the House of Deputies while the Walloon nationalists had to wait until 1965 before winning two seats in Parliament. The acceleration of the break-up of the old Jacobin Belgian State caused a reaction in the French-speaking middle classes in Brussels which formed a linguist party of their own (Front Démocratique des Francophones – FDF) against Flemish claims on Brussels.

Against these centrifugal forces a 'Belgicist' reaction headed by the old Liberal Party representing the francophone Belgian bourgeoisie tried to mobilize all conservative forces against federalism and the 'almighty' trade unions. In 1961 the Liberals transformed themselves into the Parti de la Liberté et du Progrès (PLP). In 1965 the new party doubled its parliamentary strength at the expense of the Christian Democrats and the Socialists. The latter parties reconstituted their Centre–Left coalition government but because of the severe electoral defeat of 1965, the coalition fell apart in January 1966. Fearing an electoral confrontation the conservative Christian Democratic leader Paul Vanden Boeynants immediately established a coalition government with the Liberals and promised to freeze the 'linguistic' problem.

Vanden Boeynants did not break with the economic strategy of the Centre–Left governments. He only stressed the necessity of a tighter budget control in order to lower the accumulated deficit. But the Vanden Boeynants government was also known for its pro-business character. When the chemical firm Solvay wanted to change its capital structure, the Act of 15 July 1966 established a favourable fiscal system not punishing such an operation. Furthermore he intervened actively in saving the 'Belgian character' of Pétrofina when in 1966 a non-identified raider started buying shares in this Belgian oil company. In 1967 the Vanden Boeynants government allowed the coal mines of the Northern Basin to arrange an advantageous integration of their mining activities into the newly founded NV Kempense Steenkolenmijnen (KS) without bringing in their non-mining properties. But Vanden Boeynant's autocratic style of governing created aversion against his government. How could one reconcile Walloons and Flemings without giving them more control over their own regional affairs? That was the problem the 'Belgicist' Vanden Boeynants was not able to solve. In the spring of 1968 a general uprising by the Flemish students against francophone domination at the Catholic University of Louvain caused the fall of the Vanden Boeynants government. Parliamentary elections held in 1968 resulted in a victory for the regionalist/linguistic parties. Then the Flemish Christian Democrat Eyskens formed a coalition government with the Socialists and his Centre–Left government and proposed a revision of the Constitution and a decentralization of the unitarian Belgian State.

In the mind of many Flemings regional decentralization would establish their cultural autonomy within the Belgian State, but meanwhile the Walloon nationalists were pleading for economic regionalization. The Walloons imputed the economic decline of Wallonia to the Belgian State which had become colonized by Flemish pressure groups. Although it was widely admitted that the decline of Walloon industry was due to the defensive investment policy of the big holding companies (Quévit 1978: 109–25), the

128

industrial workers in Wallonia felt themselves threatened by an ever-growing Flemish majority imposing its own will on the Walloon minority. The fact that multinational enterprises preferred Flanders to Wallonia when locating their new factories was interpreted as conspiracy by the Flemish politicians against the Walloon working classes (see Table 7.6).

Table 7.6 Regional distribution of foreign investment during the period 1959–73 (in percentages)

Total = 155.606 billion Belgian francs			
Flemish provinces		*Walloon provinces*	
Antwerp	30.9	Hainaut	15.1
West Flanders	2.6	Liège	9.4
East Flanders	9.1	Luxembourg	1.0
Limburg	13.8	Namur	1.9
	Brabant	16.2	

Source: Quévit 1978: 177

Multinational investment was particularly interested in building new plants in the 'green fields' of Flanders near the of port of Antwerp, not in Wallonia where demographic and environmental conditions were less-favourable than in Flanders. When taking over existing small Belgian firms, multinational companies preferred to acquire producers of quality products (for instance biscuits and chocolates). Many of these firms were established in Flemish towns, not in Wallonia. In fact, multinationals were not interested in investing in the regressive steel and coal industries of Wallonia.

In order to avoid a general social crisis, economic reconversion of Wallonia became an urgent problem. But initiatives in that direction failed because they were curing the symptoms. For instance, when in 1967 the SA Ateliers Germain–Anglo in La Croyère went bankrupt, the Vanden Boeynants government implemented a large-scale investment programme aimed at the modernization of the rolling stock of the State railway company SNCB–NMBS and by doing so permitted the survival of the remaining rolling-stock plants in Wallonia (*L'Année sociale* 1967: 246–61). But these measures were inappropriate for enhancing the industrial reconversion of the area. Thus structural unemployment (see Table 7.7) remained higher in Wallonia than in Flanders (Nova 1970: *passim*), creating a favourable ground for anti-Flemish sentiments and a strengthening of the

Walloon regionalist party (Rassemblement Wallon) and syndicalist opposition, who both stressed the necessity of creating additional jobs in Wallonia by using the levies of regional state power (Delbovier et al. 1969: 217–58; Nova 1970: 222–8; *Quelle Wallonie?* 1971: 69–109; *Priorité 100,000 emplois* 1975: 55–126; Carton et al. 1976: 115–17).

Although the authorities recognized that selectivity was necessary when favouring regional economic development, industrial reconversion of the distressed areas did not accelerate. In July 1966 an additional act on regional development was passed, but without adequate effects on employment in the coal mining areas of Wallonia and Limburg. Thus growing differences in income and wealth between Flanders and Wallonia did not cease (see Table 7.8).

In order to solve this problem the Act of 15 July 1970 reformed the BPE into a Planning Bureau and instituted regional economic councils for Flanders, Brussels and Wallonia which had to co-ordinate regional economic development. The government also created societies for regional development studying regional and local economic problems. The act of 30 December 1970 worked out the principles of a new regional economic policy in the function of job creation, while a system of 'contractual planning' enabled the authorities to set up the conditions for industrial reconversion when giving financial support to private investors or when purchasing industrial equipment (Quévit 1978: 166–7; Mommen 1982: 131). Thus the government hoped to influence investment decisions when purchasing new telephone equipment from multinational firms (ITT, General Telephone and Electronics Corp. – GTE, Philips, Siemens) who had production facilities in Belgium.

THE SECTORAL DIVIDE

Though economic growth was rapid during the 1960s, industrial development was uneven, because decline or stagnation in several industrial sectors (textiles, footwear, coal mining) was not halted while growth in the 'modern' sectors was remarkable (see Table 7.9).

After the Second World War the Belgian government started to modernize all infrastructures, especially railroads, ports and roads. Choices had to be made regarding the development of the ports of Antwerp, Ghent and Zeebrugge. The decision to build a new steel factory (Sidérurgie Maritime – SIDMAR) near Ghent forced the Belgian government to enlarge the sea canal from this town to

Table 7.7 Distribution of regional unemployment, 1949–70

Year	Flanders		Wallonia		Brussels	
	(1)	(2)	(1)	(2)	(1)	(2)
1949	129,258	13.6	21,432	12.3	23,298	13.4	7.1
1953	127,983	13.4	29,990	16.3	25,641	14.0	7.8
1957	52,018	5.2	14,739	18.9	11,103	14.3	3.3
1959	82,428	8.1	25,713	20.6	16,834	13.5	5.0
1964	28,382	2.6	15,589	30.9	6,392	12.7	1.8
1968	49,814	4.5	42,574	41.4	10,342	10.1	2.6
1970	30,520	2.7	33,648	47.2	7,093	10.0	1.8

(1) Percentages of total unemployment
(2) Regional unemployment rates

Source: Carton et al. 1976: 45

Table 7.8 Regional distribution of GDP, 1960–70 (in percentages)

Year	Wallonia	Flanders	Brussels	Belgium
1960	32.1	45.1	22.8	100
1966	30.0	51.6	16.4	100
1970	29.1	53.8	17.1	100

Source: Belgique: pays en voie 1978: 64

Table 7.9 Added value realized in some sectoral activities, 1963–70 (in 1963 market prices)

	1963	1964	1965	1966	1967	1968	1969	1970
Agriculture/ fisheries	100	102	95	90	104	106	107	108
Coal mining	100	93	85	78	69	60	55	50
Foodstuffs	100	103	105	111	115	120	127	134
Textiles	100	107	100	110	100	104	113	114
Clothing/ footwear	100	103	101	104	96	91	99	100
Wood and furniture	100	116	123	142	148	151	166	170
Paper	100	106	109	113	117	124	136	142
Chemicals, rubber	100	111	119	124	131	148	185	198
Cement, glass, bricks	100	118	114	115	122	123	139	155
Iron and steel	100	126	131	136	151	176	210	213
Non-ferrous metals	100	108	110	108	116	122	135	140
Metal construction	100	111	119	125	121	132	152	163
Diamonds, others	100	104	112	136	153	171	200	209
All industries	100	110	113	120	122	131	148	156
Electricity	100	111	120	131	139	158	184	202
Municipal services	100	102	113	120	130	155	193	238

Source: De nationale rekeningen van België 1963–1971: 24–5

Terneuzen in Holland. The modernization of Antwerp was still the backbone of all governmental plans. Although Zeebrugge was destined to take over some traffic, the harbour interest groups of Antwerp were able to postpone the decision to make Zeebrugge a major port receiving oil and gas tankers and ore carriers.

Because Antwerp could attract investment in the petroleum sector and possessed an extensive network of railroads and canals, Zeebrugge never could become a serious competitor for Antwerp. The Act of 1956 establishing a 10-year investment programme estimated the costs of the modernization of Antwerp at some 5 billion Belgian francs. New sea locks and docks were built in order to receive super tankers from Arabia and container ships from North America.

Chemical firms – Union Carbide Belgium, Amoco Fina (a joint venture of Amoco Chemical Corp. and Pétrofina), Pétrochim (a joint venture of Pétrofina and Phillips Petroleum), Polyolefins (a joint venture of Rhône Poulenc, Phillips Petroleum and Pétrofina), Polysar Belgium (a subsidiary of Polymer Corp. of Canada), USI–Europe (formerly Atlantic Polymers), Bayer, Bayer–Shell, BASF (Badische Anilin- und Sodafabrik AG Ludwigshafen), Air Liquide, Badiphill (a joint venture of Phillips Petroleum and BASF), Monsanto Europe, Distrigaz, Quaker Furans, Solvay–UCB, Deutsche Gold- und Silberscheideanstalt AG (DEGUSSA) – established large processing units in Antwerp during this period. In 1970 annual production capacity of the petrochemical industry reached some 5 billion tons and the sector employed about 5,220 workers (*Haven van Antwerpen* n.d.).

Although Solvay remained the largest Belgian firm active in the chemical industry, it was surpassed in size and turnover by many other European firms (Aszkenazy 1971: 22). Meanwhile Solvay had moved into the market of polyvinyls and in collaboration with UCB the production of polyphosphates was developed. SOLVIC established a joint venture with ICI for the production of vinyl chloride. In 1969 UCB sold the FABELTA division (synthetic fibres) to the Algemene Kunstzijde Unie – Koninklijke Zout-Organon (AKZO) and reinforced its position in the branch of cling film after acquiring the NV Papierindustrie Van Straten & Boon and Transparent Paper Ltd (Aszkenazy 1971: 57–8). Pétrofina acquired more importance after forming joint ventures with Phillips Petroleum and BP. In 1969 the French firm Entreprise Minière et Chimique, owning the Produits de Tessenderloo and the Produits Chimiques du Limbourg joined the Dutch firm De Staatsmijnen (DSM) in the Société Limbourgeoise du Vinyle. Gevaert, an important producer of photographic paper, merged with Agfa (a subsidiary of Bayer).

Notwithstanding, Antwerp had become a major petrochemical centre, and in 1968 Texaco opened up a new petroleum refinery in Ghent, hoping that a pipeline coming from the new port of Zeebrugge would provide its processing units with imported crude from Arabia and Libya. Meanwhile the sea canal from Ghent to Terneuzen was enlarged and deepened, permitting access of medium-sized tankers of 60,000 tons to the port of Ghent. Other processing and chemical industries (Bowater–Philips, Papeteries de Belgique, Gulf Oil, Anglo–Belge des Pétroles, Air Liquide, Electrochimie, Distillerie Bruggeman, Kuhlmann, Oléochim, Palmafina, Purfina) established themselves in the area of Ghent-Terneuzen.

Table 7.10 Total output of the processing industries, 1958–68 (in '000 tonnes)

	1958	1961	1962	1963	1964	1965	1966	1967	1968
Fertilizers	241	372	412	535	595	622	651	709	790
Coke	6,906	7,210	7,195	7,204	7,398	7,334	6,961	6,857	7,243
Paper	363	436	441	469	503	515	548	564	655
Plastics	1,113	2,106	2,514	2,888	3,556	4,085	4,671	5,308	6,462
Rubber	–	–	–	–	15	21	21	21	25

Sources: Bairoch *et al.* 1966: 29; Vandenabeele *et al.* 1969: 29

The other processing industries (paper, fertilizers, rubber) which practically were all controlled by the Belgian holding companies responded to increased demand by expanding their production capacity (see Table 7.10). The big holding companies also backed the modernization of the electricity sector and promoted mergers of the scattered electricity firms. In 1963 Intercommunale Belge de Gaz et d'Electricité (INTERCOM) was formed out of a merger of Gazélec with nine other companies in the Hainaut. In Flanders the Sociétés Réunies d'Energie du Bassin de l'Escaut – Verenigde Energiebedrijven van het Scheldeland (EBES) absorbed the Société Générale Belge de Production d'Electricité (Interescaut) and the Compagnie du Gaz d'Eeckloo et du Nord de la Flandre Occidentale (*Morphologie* 1966: 110). The holding companies controlling these electricity producers now decided to build nuclear power plants near Antwerp, Liège and Chooz (France), because the expanding electricity sector promised a constant flow of high profits. In 1954 the electricity sector produced 10,339 billion kWh and by 1968 had amounted to some 25,027 billion kWh. Investment in nuclear power stations fitted in with the plan aimed at rationalizing the sector. This plan was drafted by the Controlling Committee for Electricity, a committee advising in matters of prices, distribution and investment (Evalenko 1968: 316). Meanwhile the big holding companies were rivals for a closer control over SOFINA, and in 1964 the SGB succeeded in beating the Compagnie Lambert for control over SOFINA. Although the Union Minière was losing ground in the Congo, the SGB held a firm grip on the sector of non-ferrous metals. Due to large investment projects the Belgian factories of the SGB doubled their total output of refined copper (see Table 7.11).

Table 7.11 Total output of Belgian non-ferrous metals industries, 1958–68 (in '000 tonnes)

	1958	1961	1962	1963	1964	1965	1966	1967	1968
Copper	155	222	222	271	286	309	303	318	341
Lead	96	100	93	98	83	111	93	108	110
Zinc	215	246	206	206	223	240	252	227	251

Sources: Bairoch et al. 1966: 29; Vandenabeele et al. 1969: 29

The Walloon steel industry was engaged in a longlasting process of mergers and modernization, which involved building new blast furnaces and high-capacity rolling mills. The introduction of the LD (Linz-Donawitz) system (introduced by Cockerill–Ougrée in 1966) and the oxygen convertor improved the quality of Thomas steel so that a continued cast and rolling of crude steel became possible (*Belgique* 1978: 21). Meanwhile the Usines Henricot in Court-Saint-Etienne and Allegheny–Longdoz in Gent produced special quality steel. Innovations enhanced capital investment in the steel industry (see Table 7.12) and increased output (see Table 7.13).

Pressed by the holding companies mergers occurred in the steel industry. In 1966 Cockerill–Ougrée in Liège merged with the crude steel producer Forges de la Providence and Tolmatil in Charleroi. Then the Usines de Thy-le-Château et Marcinelle merged with the Aciéries et Minières de la Sambre, forming the Forges de Thy-Marcinelle et Monceau (TMM).

Espérance-Longdoz (controlled by Evence Coppée) built a new steel factory in Chertal (Liège) producing 1.6 million tonnes of high-quality LD steel, but the slowdown of 1966–7 forced Coppée to merge Espérance–Longdoz with Cockerill–Ougrée–Providence.

Table 7.12 Investment in the Belgian steel industry, 1954–73
(in million current Belgian francs)

Years	Total	Rolling mills (%)	Steel factories (%)	Investment per worker year
1954–58	12,500	37.38	14.46	43,814
1959–63	31,973	52.44	12.18	108,725
1964–68	28,516	45.06	21.16	99,103
1969–73	45,589	49.48	17.13	153,370

Source: SOS Sidérurgie 1978: 21

Table 7.13 Production of crude steel, 1953–70
(in '000 tonnes)

	1953	1958	1963	1965	1967	1968	1970
Belgium	4,497	6,013	7,528	9,169	9,716	11,577	12,607
France	9,997	14,616	17,557	19,604	19,655	20,394	23,774
Italy	3,500	6,271	10,157	12,681	15,890	16,951	17,277
Luxembourg	2,659	3,379	4,032	4,585	4,481	4,833	5,462
Netherlands	867	1,438	2,342	3,138	3,407	3,707	5,042
Germany	18,103	26,265	31,597	36,821	36,744	41,151	45,041
			1953 = 100				
Belgium	100	134	167	204	216	257	280
France	100	146	176	196	197	204	238
Italy	100	179	290	362	454	484	494
Luxembourg	100	127	152	172	169	182	205
Netherlands	100	166	270	362	393	428	582
Germany	100	145	175	203	203	227	249

Sources: Vandenabeele et al. 1969: 73; De Belgische economie in 1975: 120

Finally, as a result of all these mergers, Cockerill acquired a total production capacity of 7 million tonnes and several steel factories in France (in Réhon and Haumont). Because Cockerill also held a stake of 22 per cent in SIDMAR and controlled different steel factories producing tubes and sheets (the Aciéries et Laminoirs de Beautor, Tolmatil, the UTM, the Tubes de la Providence and the Phénix Works) all situated in Wallonia, a giant firm was formed without internal synergies.

In the region of Charleroi the Belgian–French steelmaker Société Métallurgique Hainaut-Sambre was floated by the government. In

1966 this firm took over the French steel firm Aciéries et Tréfileries de Neuves-Maisons Châtillon.

Although these mergers aimed to rationalize the different steel firms, they could not cope with the congenital weakness of the Walloon steel industry and rivalry between the holding companies who deliberately had postponed closures of the weaker performing steel factories. As long as the latter could sell their produce for a good price, their undercapitalization did not hamper their profitability. But as any slowdown of the economy provoked falling steel prices, the viability of the indebted steel firms was not guaranteed.

The integrated steel factory SIDMAR was created in 1962 near the canal from Ghent to Terneuzen. SIDMAR's promotors were the Luxembourg steel firm ARBED, the SGB, Compagnie Belge de Participations (COBEPA), Schneider, COFININDUS and the Walloon steel firms controlled by the SGB (Cockerill and Providence). The project obtained generously accorded loans from the State banks SNCI–NMKN and the CGER–ASLK (*La Décision* 1965: 287–317).

During the 1960s the Walloon rolling-stock and metal construction industries practically disappeared after a series of bankruptcies. Among them were important factories, such as the Ateliers Germain–Anglo (1967), Baume–Marpent (1968) and Usines Gilson (1968). The FN, a subsidiary of the SGB, expanded as a producer of small arms and started participating as a subcontractor while working in the multinational weapons industry. Together with Empain the SGB controlled ACEC, an important producer of heavy electrical equipment, which employed 13,750 workers in 1968. Furthermore Empain controlled several rolling-stock and heavy equipment firms which had been merged in 1959 into the Ateliers Belges Réunis (ABR). Baron Ede-János Empain concentrated all his efforts on the French and Belgian market of nuclear power stations. In France Empain already owned the Forges et Ateliers de Constructions Electriques de Jeumont which he merged in 1964 with Le Matériel Electrique SA of the Schneider group and via the Société Parisienne pour l'Industrie Electrique (SPIE–Batignolles) he took over the whole Schneider group. Because of his alliance with Westinghouse, Empain already controlled the Société Franco–Américaine de Constructions Atomiques (FRAMATOME) and then he forced his competitor, the Compagnie Générale d'Electricité (CGE) (the ally of General Electric in France) into a compromise (Empain 1985: 104–5). Thus Baron Empain became the most powerful French entrepreneur of Belgian nationality who presided over the fate of the French nuclear industry after having merged Creusot with the Loire factories (Marine–Firminy group) (Allard et al. 1978: 136–7; *L'Electronucléaire* 1975: 136–40). In Belgium Empain acquired all nuclear technology previously developed by the firms BELGONUCLEAIRE, BELCHIM and Eurochemic. In 1970 Empain suddenly withdrew from ACEC in favour of Westinghouse in a period when the Walloon firm was suffering from increased competition on the world market and had to stop its activities in the sector of consumer products.

The Coppée group was confronted with analogous difficulties after having withdrawn from heavy industry. In 1968 Coppée allied with Rust Engineering Co. in order to reinforce its position in the engineering industry and in 1972 formed the Compagnie Coppée de Développement Industriel (CDI) (Dubois 1988: 235), which specialized in engineering, biochemicals, aromatics, agribusiness, real estate and energy.

After the coal mining crisis of 1958–9 the Belgian government decided to close down several marginal coal mines in the Southern Basin (Van der Rest 1962: 89–108) and to recruit new contingents of miners from Turkey and Morocco. Thus average productivity increased from 1,146 kilos per miner a day in 1952 to 1,388 kilos in 1959. But average productivity of the Belgian collieries was much lower than in other European countries. Although the government had established a directorate for the coal industry on 16 November 1961, this new body was unable to solve the problem of high production costs (about 60 per cent of all production costs were paid out in the form of wages and pensions). In 1965 the Belgian coal mines lost 1.1 billion Belgian francs and in 1968 losses amounted to 4.7 billion Belgian francs. Although the government discussed a further reduction of coal production in 1964, closures of marginal coal mines in Wallonia were postponed until the end of 1965. In the Northern Basin the Cockerill mine of Zwartberg employing 4,000 miners was to be closed. But in January 1966 a violent strike of Zwartberg miners obliged the authorities to lend special assistance to all miners victim of closures and a programme aimed at the 'social reconversion' of jobless miners was launched (*L'Année sociale* 1966: 158–96). Finally, in 1967 the coal mines of the Northern Basin were merged into the KS. The former mining companies obtained generously accorded financial compensation. They were allowed to keep their non-mining activities out of KS and were allowed to sit on the Board of Directors of KS. The survival of the remaining coal mines in Wallonia and KS in Limburg was granted by long-standing coal supply contracts imposed by the authorities on the coke and electricity producers.

Table 7.14 Belgian coal production, 1957–69 (in '000 tonnes)

Year	Campine	%	Wallonia	%	Total
1957	10,331	35.5	18,755	64.5	29,086
1958	9,973	36.9	17,089	63.1	27,062
1960	9,385	41.8	13,080	58.2	22,465
1965	9,706	49.1	10,080	50.9	19,786
1967	8,846	53.8	7,589	46.2	16,435
1969	8,015	60.7	5,185	39.3	13,200

Source: De Smet et al. 1971: 98

In the early 1960s the Belgian government decided to import natural gas from the Netherlands. Therefore the State acquired a minority stake in the SA Distrigaz and financed the adaptation of home appliances from town gas to natural gas (Baudhuin 1970: 122–3). Meanwhile coal consumption decreased from 69.2 per cent of total energy consumption in 1960 to 44.4 per cent in 1968, provoking an increased dependency vis-à-vis foreign suppliers of primary energy sources. In 1950 Belgium imported only 15 per cent of its total energy supply, but in 1970 85 per cent had to be imported (Vandeputte 1985: 95).

The decline of the Belgian textile industry was caused by competition from developing countries. Employment in the industry rapidly declined from 185,000 jobs in 1948 to 60,000 jobs in 1968. Although productivity increased, profitability was lagging behind other sectors. Progress was made in the woollen industry, especially in the branch of carpet-weaving. In the cotton industry small firms closed their doors and total production of cotton fibres declined from 99,800 tonnes in 1953 to 72,500 tonnes in 1968 (Bairoch and Vandenabeele 1968: 72). Only the producers of nylon and other synthetic fibres increased their output.

In Wallonia, where commercial farming always had been dominant, agriculture was based on growing wheat and sugar beet. In Flanders many smallholders specialized in animal farming (pigs, poultry) and dairy products (milk, butter). The Belgian government tried to stabilize agricultural prices, but subsidies combined with protectionism soon led to productivity gains resulting in over-production. In the meantime agriculture became a capital-intensive sector after smallholders started to invest in modern machinery and more adequate buildings. The number of tractors increased from 41,000 in 1959 to 81,000 in 1968 and the number of combine harvesters from 2,600 to 7,700 units. In 1967 capital engaged in agricultural activities was estimated at some 569 billion Belgian francs, while total working capital amounted to 97 billion Belgian francs. Between 1962 and 1967 agricultural debt rose from 21 to 43 billion Belgian francs. Because after 1958 agricultural prices stagnated and costs increased, the average peasant's income lagged behind that of workers. For instance, between 1958 and 1967 agrarian costs increased by 27 per cent while agricultural prices only rose by 18 per cent (Baudhuin 1970: 98), which provoked a sharp decline of the number of farms (from 174,163 in 1959 to 132,400 in 1967). But meanwhile the average size of the agricultural holdings increased steadily (from 8.74 hectares to 11.08 hectares), while the number of people employed in farming declined from 308,600 to 184,800. Farmers' protests against their low standard of living culminated in 1962 in blockades of motorways. But these protests were far less important than in France, because the Boerenbond could justify all structural reforms the authorities were striving for. In order to facilitate them in 1961 the Belgian government created an Agricultural Fund and in 1965 a special fund sponsoring a programme of early retirement for elderly peasants wanting to leave the sector.

All these reforms occurred prior to the establishment of the European Agricultural Guidance and Guarantee Fund (EAGGF), by the EEC in 1962 which subsequently helped to finance the modernization and improvement of farms and facilities and to finance a guaranteed price system (as well as storage costs, marketing subsidies and export rebates). The EEC set up the Common Agricultural Policy (CAP) which came into existence on 29 July 1968. For a long time the common market for agricultural products was virtually the only common policy that the Community was able to implement. The CAP was based on three main principles. First, a single market for agricultural produce (free movement throughout the Community and common prices). Second, community preference (a common tariff barrier against imports from outside the EEC). Third, a common financial responsibility (costs are paid from a common fund to which all members contributed).

Under the CAP agricultural production and productivity increased greatly, making the EEC virtually self-sufficient in all but tropical foods and a number of animal feeding stuffs. The average standard of living of those living off the land rose sharply, thanks to a two-thirds reduction in their number. Belgium received more financial compensation from the EEC than it contributed to the Common Fund, and was thus a beneficiary of the CAP. Compared to the period between the two world wars productivity of Belgian agriculture increased by 40 per cent. Wheat, barley and sugar beet became by far the most important crops, while total output of potatoes decreased (see Table 7.15). Enhanced productivity was also due to the increased use of fertilizers, insecticides, pesticides and herbicides which the Belgian chemical industry produced in ever-increasing quantities at low prices.

Table 7.15 Agricultural production, 1934–68 (in '000 tonnes)

	1934–8	1948–52	1962	1964	1966	1968
Wheat	4,504	5,133	8,345	8,999	6,501	8,394
Barley	906	2,444	4,993	5,156	4,860	5,744
Sugar beet	14,588	21,345	20,190	31,135	25,857	41,076
Potatoes	31,685	21,235	18,720	17,547	14,748	15,662

Source: Vandenabeele et al. 1969: 28

Table 7.16 Production of food and beverages, 1948–68
(in '000 tons unless otherwise indicated)

	1948	1953	1958	1963	1965	1968
Flour	720.0	755.0	794.0	772.0	761.0	707.0
Sugar	244.0	383.0	434.0	340.0	610.0	830.0
Butter	62.0	87.5	89.9	84.4	82.9	91.5
Margarine	69.7	75.2	101.2	120.4	130.0	130.9
Cheese	8.6	12.4	15.6	30.2	34.9	43.2
Beer*	11.3	10.2	10.1	10.7	11.1	11.9
Mineral water*	1.3	2.0	3.0	4.3	4.8	5.8

* In billion hectolitres

Source: Vandenabeele et al. 1969: 29

MULTINATIONAL CAPITAL

During the 1960s multinational capital became predominant in several sectors of the Belgian economy (Michel 1971: 75–117). The oil and petrochemical industries, electronics, the automobile and food processing industries were largely multinationalized. Although the exact number of subsidiaries of multinational companies in Belgium cannot be established, research done by the University of Ghent ascertained in 1968 the existence of 624 foreign firms, at least 240 of which were owned by American companies (Van den Bulcke et al. 1971: 7). These subsidiaries of multinational firms occupied about 20 per cent of the Belgian labour force and belonged to the category of large employers. On a list of the five hundred largest industrial companies in Belgium ninety-five belonged to the category of subsidiaries owned by multinationals. Compared to total industrial employment the multinational subsidiaries had become extremely important in metal products, rubber and chemicals (see Table 7.17).

Table 7.17 Employment in foreign multinational companies (June 1968)

	(1)	(2)	(3)
Foodstuffs	113.8	15.0	13.2
Textiles	211.3	19.4	9.2
Wood, paper, leather	120.4	10.1	8.4
Rubber	8.4	3.6	42.9
Chemicals	63.5	29.3	46.1
Petroleum	10.8	4.6	42.6
Non-metal minerals	67.6	9.9	14.6
Iron and steel	116.0	3.9	3.4
Metal products	60.7	13.9	22.9
Machinery and vehicles	245.3	77.8	31.7
Others	30.3	4.5	14.9
Total	1,051.4	192.1	18.3

(1) Total industrial employment in '000s.
(2) Employment in multinational subsidiaries in '000s.
(3) Employment in multinational subsidiaries as a percentage of total industrial employment

Source: Van den Bulcke et al. 1971: 22

Practically all of these firms established their factories in Flanders. The Ford Motor Co. built a new plant in Genk and General Motors Continental expanded its assembly capacity in Antwerp ('Plant II'). Volvo–Europe established a new factory in the area of Ghent. Thus within a decade Belgium became an important automobile assembling and exporting country. In 1970 total output attained 840,000 vehicles (Vandeputte 1985: 98). The expansion of the automobile industry in Belgium had a major impact on firms manufacturing vehicle components. Most of them were of American origin (Monroe, Champion Spark Plug Co., Don International, Gould National Batteries, Borg Warner, Uniroyal), but Belgian firms specializing in security glass (SA Splintex Belge), steel cord (Bekaert), plastics (Solvay) and fibres (American Celanese) and textiles expanded their activities.

Table 7.18 Production of cement and tar, 1948–68 (in '000 tonnes)

	1948	1958	1963	1965	1968
Cement	3,331	4,057	4,709	5,905	5,740
Tar	189	247	276	282	263

Source: Vandenabeele et al., 1969: 29

Investment in infrastructural works (motorways, ports, industrial areas) necessitated large quantities of steel, cement, tar (see Table 7.18) and heavy machinery. In the glass manufacturing industry GLAVER merged in 1961 with the Union des Verreries Mécaniques Belges (MECANIVER) which gave birth to GLAVERBEL. The Glaceries de Saint-Roch absorbed the Glaceries de la Sambre in 1964 and in 1969 the Verreries Bennert–Bivort et Courcelles Réunies and Sopaverre. Under the aegis of the SGB the Syndicat Belge des Travaux (SYBETRA) emerged as a leading engineering firm selling industrial installations in developing countries. Mechanization of agriculture attracted American firms to Belgium (Ford Tractor in Antwerp, International Harvester in Vilvorde and Clayson [acquired in 1968 by Sperry Rand Corporation] in Zedelgem, Caterpillar Belgium in Gosselies) (Baudhuin 1970: 245–6). Siemens, Philips, and ATEA (taken over by GTE in 1962) built new factories in provincial towns or villages where industrial areas had been established by local authorities and where cheap labour (women) was available. Several multinational computer firms established their headquarters in Belgium, but only Burroughs founded a plant (in Seneffe in Wallonia).

Until the early 1950s Unilever was the only multinational food processing firm having important factories in Belgium. But the EEC encouraged Belgian firms to acquire advantages of scale. In 1965 the Biscuits Parein merged with the Biscuits et Chocolats De Beukelaer and formed General Biscuit Company (GBC). GBC acquired Victoria and the Chocolaterie Meurisse and allied with the French firm Céraliment when acquiring a majority stake in the Alsacienne des Biscuits (Aszkenazy 1971: 224–5; Joye 1984: 9). In 1969 ITT tried to take over GBC, but failed. Finally in 1977 Jean and Marcel Thèves (the owners of Céraliment) acquired full control over GBC (Joye 1984: 9). In 1961 Biscuits Delacre and in 1972 Godiva were taken over by Campbell. In order to escape from foreign control Imperial Products and Devos–Lemmens merged and formed Continental Foods in 1968. As long as consumers preferred local products Belgian producers of chocolates (Côte d'Or, Callebaut, Chocolaterie Jacques) could still survive as independent firms. In the tobacco industry Belgian labels were bought by Rothmans International (De Bock et al. 1978: 65). In the sugar industry the Raffinerie Tirlemontoise, which was jointly controlled by the Wittouck and Kronacker families, established a virtual sugar monopoly.

High profits made by Unilever and Nestlé in Europe attracted American food processing firms to Belgium. Thus Beatrice Foods bought Lacsoons (dairy firm) and Artic (ice cream), National Dairy Product Corp. acquired Franco–Suisse (cheese) and Grace took over Materne (preserves) (Michel 1971: 103).

In the distribution sector wholesale shops (in 1969 some of them merged into SA Innovation–Bon–Marché) and retail chains (Delhaize) opted for investment in supermarkets and shopping centres situated in the expanding suburbs, while multinational companies acquired department stores in the cities. In 1968 Penney took over SA pour la Revente d'Articles en Masse (SARMA) and Sears Roebuck bought the Galeries Anspach. The clothing industry with its sweatshops in the towns had to face competition coming from multinational companies (Blue Bell, Macintosh, etc.) establishing their factories in the 'green fields' of Flanders. The subsidized health services created a booming market for pharmaceuticals and medical appliances. Because research and development costs increased, many Belgian laboratories disappeared or were taken over by multinationals. Only UCB with its Dipha division could withstand foreign competition, but the independent firm Janssen Pharmaceutica was acquired by Johnson & Johnson.

Mergers and large-scale investment projects eliminated many breweries. Artois in Louvain became by far the biggest Belgian brewer. In 1969 Artois acquired a stake in Spa Monopole. British breweries started taking over smaller Belgian breweries (Whatney's acquired Lamot, Delbruyère and Vandenheuvel; Whitbread bought Dendria). In 1969 Schlitz (USA) took over the Brasserie de Ghlin (formerly Caulier). Growing output in the food and beverages industries caused concentration in the packaging industry. In 1960, after having taken over the Verreries du Pays de Liège et de Campine and built a new factory in Ghlin, the SA Bouteilleries Belges Réunies (a subsidiary of Verlica–Momignies) acquired a near monopoly in the Belgian bottle industry. In the meantime foreign companies (Owens Corning de Belgique, SA Pittsburgh Corning de Belgique, SA Osram Belgium (EMGO), SA Sylvania Benelux, SA Ballotini Europe) established factories in Belgium for the production of 'technical glass'.

CONCLUSIONS

Within a decade multinational companies had contributed to a rapid recovery of the Belgian economy. The automobile industry and the petrochemical industry were the biggest investors in Belgium in a period when traditional industrial activities were suffering from a dramatic set-back. The neo-corporatist system of interest intermediation smoothed this transformation, while generously accorded subsidies and tax facilities attracted multinational investors. But structural problems in heavy industry (coal and steel) still hampered a thoroughgoing modernization of the Belgian economy. Thus industrial decline in Wallonia was not reversed, because the multinational companies preferred to invest in the 'green fields' of Flanders instead of in the distressed coal mining areas in Wallonia.

8

THE POLITICS OF
INFLEXIBLE ADJUSTMENT
(1971–81)

In the early 1970s businessmen and politicians were still dreaming of a never-ending period of prosperity. All political parties were convinced of the fact that the golden 1960s had laid the base for a very high standard of welfare which had to be subsidized by the government and paid out of productivity gains in industry. Especially Socialists and Christian Democrats were striving for a welfare state sponsoring free education and promoting social mobility. The first oil crisis (1973–4) did not annihilate this dream, but incited the authorities to reconsider the opportunity of a further increase in collective expenditures. Finally, the authorities had to face a general slowdown of the economy and a painful process of industrial adjustment combined with growing unemployment rates and high inflation.

THE POLITICAL SETTING

After an ill-fated governmental coalition with the Liberals in 1966–8 the Christian Democrats opted for a durable coalition with the Socialists. This Centre–Left government promised a further decentralization and regionalization of the Belgian political institutions. The representatives of the Flemish bourgeoisie within the Christian Democratic Party agreed on the principle that the political authorities had to intervene in order to smooth economic growth, to maintain full employment, to create a surplus on the balance of trade and to combat inflation, but they refused etatism. The influx of multinational capital convinced the Flemish entrepreneurs that rapid economic growth was obtained by giving fiscal incentives to private companies. In their view a Keynesian policy had to transfer savings (in the form of cheap loans) to firms desiring to invest in

146

new products and production facilities, while social benefits had to be financed out of social transfers and taxes. Planning activities initiated by the government had to be confined to ailing industries (coal mining) and regional economic development initiatives. But notwithstanding this overall consensus a break-up of the coalition of Christian Democrats and Socialists occurred in the early weeks of 1974.

After the elections of March 1974 the Flemish Christian Democrat Léon Tindemans formed a coalition government with the Liberals, and, soliciting the favours of the Walloon nationalist Rassemblement Wallon, he promised a further regionalization of the State and a return to economic 'normalcy'. This manoeuvre caused surprise because the oil crisis necessitated an important price and wage adjustment in order to hold down inflation. It was widely known that an alliance with the Liberals would alienate the support of the powerful trade unions and could provoke a broad working-class resistance movement against the Tindemans government. But the bourgeois wing of the Christian Democrats fearing a further etatist advance now clearly preferred an alliance with the Liberals in a period when the Socialists were trying to impose the establishment of a State oil refinery, Iranian Belgian Refining and Marketing Co. (IBRAMCO) without having previously obtained the consent of the Belgische Petroleum Federatie – Fédération Pétrolière Belge.

The Tindemans government did not present a concrete economic programme, but only stressed the necessity of holding down inflation rates (12 per cent in 1974). Tindemans tried to prevent cost inflation and proposed controlling wage increases. Although he wanted to freeze all incomes (including distributed profits, fees and royalties) the trade unions refused to discuss the principle of the suppression of the wage indexation system. Meanwhile social discontent among some categories of workers and civil servants increased during a period when many of them were longing for better living conditions. Although mass consumption of durable consumer goods had spread among all social classes (see Table 8.1), some households still were excluded from the pastures of plenty.

Tindemans' stop-and-go policy soon eroded his social base and diminished his political credibility and his 'Programming Bills' aimed at reducing public spending and holding down inflation met increased resistance. In order to prevent a general social conflict Tindemans convened a national employment conference on 24 May 1976, where the authorities discussed with representatives of the

Table 8.1 Durable consumer goods owned by Belgian households, 1974–7 (in percentages)

	1974	1975	1976	1977
Automobiles	58.5	64.6	67.7	68.0
Refrigerators	82.0	86.5	87.9	89.6
Washing machines	62.5	66.6	69.5	73.0
Black and white TV sets	73.3	68.1	61.9	52.0
Colour TV sets	14.7	23.0	31.6	41.6
Dishwashers	6.3	10.0	10.9	11.2

Source: De Belgische economie in 1979: 341

trade unions, the entrepreneurial organizations and the Belgian holding companies the disastrous economic and financial situation. But no agreement could be reached. In the eyes of the trade unions a Keynesian deficit spending policy had to absorb unemployment, while the entrepreneurs preferred to lower production costs, especially wages, in order to solve their cash problems.

Meanwhile Tindemans became a prisoner of his own 'soft' budgetary policy. The banks warned him that deficit spending would open up a financial crisis of the State. Finally, in February 1976 Tindemans proposed severe budgetary cuts which the trade unions immediately opposed as being anti-social attacks on the standard of living of the workers and the unemployed. Within a few weeks the unions succeeded in defeating the Tindemans government. After the parliamentary elections of 17 April 1977 Tindemans established a coalition government with Socialists and Christian Democrats. For more than four years (1977–81) coalition governments of Socialists and Christian Democrats remained in power. In the autumn of 1978 Tindemans resigned when the Belgian Socialist Party split up into a French-speaking and a Flemish-speaking party. Then Wilfried Martens (Martens 1985: 59–117; De Ridder 1991: 115), leader of a younger generation of Christian Democratic politicians, formed a new coalition government of Socialists and Christian Democrats. Martens resigned in April 1981 after having led four different coalition governments of Socialists and Christian Democrats.

Although the Centre–Left governments recognized inflation as a serious enemy, they paid attention also to unemployment and industrial restructuring. Minister of Economic Affairs Willy Claes (Socialist) launched a plan destined to rescue the ailing industrial sectors. Five industrial sectors (steel, textiles, coal, glass and shipbuilding) were labelled as 'national sectors' receiving support from the national authorities. Minister of Social Affairs Guy Spitaels (Socialist) launched a plan (1978) aiming at the creation of 'temporary jobs' in public services and costing 23.7 billion Belgian francs. He extended the system of early retirement (*pré-pensions*) to all enterprises in difficulties. The De Wulf Plan (1979) subsidized enterprises when shortening the working week to thirty-eight hours and hiring an additional number of young workers. Finally the Humblet Plan (1977) provided a premium to small and medium-sized enterprises when they created additional jobs. In 1980 fiscal advantages and subsidies amounting to 1.5 billion Belgian francs were allocated for job creation projects (Mommen 1987: 24), while other proposals favouring the creation of part-time jobs, schooling and training of the unemployed, industrial apprenticeship, etc. were implemented.

Table 8.2 The effects of the unemployment programmes on employment, 1977–81 (in individuals)

Year	Totals	(1)	(2)	(3)	(4)	(5)
1977	56,386	24,201	–	16,832	15,353	–
1978	120,146	31,005	22,119	31,471	22,176	13,375
1979	140,705	36,252	27,426	30,778	29,072	17,177
1980	150,898	36,591	26,984	28,289	38,083	20,951
1981	158,287	35,138	24,107	27,539	45,092	26,411

(1) Unemployed employed in general services
(2) Temporary civil servants
(3) Trainees
(4) Employment created after early retirement of the elderly
(5) Special benefit programmes for early retired workers
Sources: *L'Année sociale* 1980: 207; *L'Année sociale* 1981: 282

Costs of all employment programmes increased from 32.7 billion Belgian francs in 1979 to 42.7 billion Belgian francs in 1981. Meanwhile the system financing unemployment benefits was running into a large deficit. This yearly deficit increased from 46.3 billion Belgian francs in 1979 to 76.2 billion francs in 1981 (Mommen 1987: 33). As the economic crisis endured the government was forced to regulate wages and other earnings and to freeze the level of public spending. Indirect taxes on luxury goods were increased, while those on higher incomes had to pay higher direct taxes. Although these measures fitted in well within the framework of the

Socialist programme, they could not prevent the fiscal crisis of the State. In 1981 the deficit on current expenditures was estimated at 160 billion Belgian francs, while the total expenditure deficit reached 595 billion Belgian francs or 12.6 per cent of GDP. Total public debt amounted to 2,439.1 billion Belgian francs or 67.3 per cent of GDP giving birth to an increasing financial burden (the so-called 'interest snowball').

THE ANATOMY OF THE CRISIS

The Belgian economy showed a pronounced disequilibrium in three areas: employment, public finance and the balance of payments. After the first oil crisis inflation accelerated sharply, largely due to higher wage and energy costs. This weakened external competitiveness and had an adverse effect on the trade balance and employment. After 1978 a pick-up in economic activity occurred and, together with the effects of the governmental employment policy, the unemployment rate stabilized. But at the end of 1980 unemployment rose again. A new oil crisis pushed the foreign trade account further out of balance and for 1980 the BLEU current payments deficit reached 170 billion Belgian francs or about 5 per cent of GNP. Rising unemployment and slow growth caused higher public spending and an increased government borrowing requirement. At the end of the 1970s government borrowing was attaining the equivalent of 9.5 per cent of GNP.

Rising unemployment (see Table 8.3) was felt as a major social problem the government had to combat. Since 1977 the government aimed at bringing down unemployment by means of employment support measures, improving firms' competitiveness by fostering investment and trying to compress real wage growth, and by reducing the budget deficit through spending cuts. These policies were unable to hold the growing disequilibrium in check, except in the area of inflation. But price and wage growth remained relatively moderate after the second oil crisis.

During the recession of the second half of the 1970s one of the major problems was unemployment. Unemployment rates rose faster in Belgium than in the other European countries, due to the difficulties Belgian industry was having in adjusting to the changes in the pattern of demand and the new conditions of international competition. Loss of external competitiveness was apparently the major cause of all evil. The rise in unemployment was a

Table 8.3 Evolution of total unemployment, 1968–81

Year	Total full-time unemployed*			Part unemployed†		
	Men	Women	Total	Men	Women	Total
1968	68,664	34,066	102,730	31,854	9,478	41,332
1969	53,115	32,228	85,343	30,645	7,072	37,717
1970	42,387	28,874	71,261	24,997	8,715	33,712
1971	42,368	28,508	70,876	31,830	7,792	39,622
1972	51,855	34,967	86,822	27,405	9,175	36,580
1973	48,608	43,094	91,702	25,511	8,774	34,285
1974	49,841	54,879	104,720	28,790	13,160	41,950
1975	85,158	92,209	177,367	59,536	23,036	82,541
1976	98,304	130,233	228,537	42,934	15,554	58,488
1977	106,286	157,998	264,284	47,875	21,183	69,058
1978	111,239	170,925	282,164	48,447	21,389	69,836
1979	110,006	184,410	294,416	49,754	19,883	69,637
1980	120,719	201,176	321,895	–	–	80,347
1981	166,992	224,794	391,786	–	–	93,588

* Full-time unemployed receiving benefits
† Daily average

Source: De Belgische economie in 1982: 32

trend which had been going on since the early 1970s. The jobless total would have been higher, but this was reversed by several measures taken by the government. For instance, firms with over fifty employees were obliged to take on a number of trainees equivalent to 2 per cent of their workforce and smaller enterprises received a premium for each trainee taken on. Public enterprises and services could recruit jobless persons, who could retain their unemployed status and receive increased benefits or get a short-term contract. In addition, the early retirement system had been developed since 1974 in a number of different ways. These programmes produced their full effects at the end of the 1970s, because in 1979–80 some 160,000 persons (i.e. 4 per cent of the labour force) were affected by these measures. Half of them were elderly persons who took early retirement. Because the number of unemployed women rose dramatically, the gap between male and female unemployment rates widened further. In 1975 the female unemployment rate was twice as high as the rate for males and in 1980 it was three times as high. Unemployment especially among the group of under 25s increased between 1971 and 1979. As a result of special

151

employment programmes the proportion of youth unemployment stabilized at the level of one-third of total unemployment in 1980. The early retirement schemes had the effect of reducing the proportion of unemployed older people (over 45 years of age), so that the group aged between twenty-five and forty accounted for about half the jobless total at a time when the average period of unemployment was lengthening. The proportion of persons out of work for more than six months rose form 60 per cent in 1972 to 75 per cent in 1975. Between 1975 and 1979 prolonged unemployment declined, but this was largely due to a cyclical trend and early retirement facilities accorded to elderly people (OECD 1981: 10–15).

Table 8.4 Sectoral employment, 1974–8

	1974	1978	Difference
Private sector	2,295,050	2,147,536	−147,514
Public sector	723,837	816,208	+ 92,371
Total	3,018,887	2,963,744	− 55,143
White collar workers	1,603,648	1,419,068	−184,580
Blue collar workers	1,415,239	1,544,676	+129,437

Source: De Belgische economie in 1979: 12

Although between 1960 and 1968 the labour force hardly grew at all, between 1969 and 1975 it increased by 1 per cent a year. The fast rise in female participation rates, more than offsetting the fall in male participation rates, was the main factor of labour force growth and of unemployment. Employment climbed steadily until 1974 and declined until 1978 and then in 1979 regained the 1974 level. This was due to an expansion of the tertiary sector (about 220,000 new jobs created between 1974 and 1979) which compensated for the loss of industrial jobs. After the first oil crisis activities in the industrial sector slowed down. In those sectors where employment had been falling prior to 1974 (i.e. mining and textiles) the downward trend became steeper. But the loss of jobs in industry had been twice as rapid as in the other EEC countries. Shortening of hours worked in industry by 2 per cent curbed the downward trend in employment somewhat, but at the end of the 1970s this practice had slowed down and therefore the government introduced subsidies to encourage enterprises to shorten hours and increase their workforce (OECD: 1981: 13).

But the industrial sector was too exposed to foreign competition, so that shortening of the working week was not accompanied by additional recruitment. Gains in apparent labour productivity remained very high in industry because of the sharp workforce cutbacks in some industries. Increased productivity was due to wage growth making staff cuts necessary, while the remaining workforce was incited to produce more in a shorter working week. In industry capital/labour substitution increased, because investment was mainly rationalization-oriented, thus helping productivity to rise (*Het verlies* 1981: 263–73; OECD 1981–2: 10).

Because of the economy's high foreign trade ratio (55 per cent of GNP in 1980), Belgium was particularly vulnerable to cyclical fluctuations in the economies of its trading partners and to foreign competition. The neighbouring industrial countries in Europe had provided the main outlet for Belgian exports, but after the first oil crisis these markets were affected by a recession; while the newly industrializing countries were reducing the outlets for certain industries (textiles, basic chemicals, steel, civil engineering) Belgium was still exporting to the non-industrialized developing countries and to some industrialized countries (see Table 8.6). This explains why the Belgian economy was harder hit than the other OECD countries as a whole since the products in question accounted for a large share of its exports. Belgium's economy partly suffered from the pattern of production (textiles, steel and heavy industry) inherited from the past and from production processes requiring high energy costs (non-ferrous metals, heavy chemicals).

The difficulties in the steel and iron industries were due to the chaotic investment policy of the holding companies in the Walloon heavy industry. The steel sector had grown rapidly before 1974 and now was particularly hard-hit by the change in the pattern of demand and by international competition. After 1974 Belgium's steel sector experienced a particularly sharp fall in activity. The weakness of the Belgian economy in this period was also caused by too high labour and production costs. The nominal rise in hourly earnings was 16.5 per cent a year in the period 1970–5 and then 8.5 per cent a year on average in the period 1975–80. Apart from the effects of indexation of wages, there still was a steep rise in real earnings (8.5 per cent per annum in industry) up until 1975 followed by a slowdown until 1980 (2 per cent per annum). As productivity

Table 8.5 Comparison between Belgium and some other OECD countries

	GDP growth	Unemployment rate		Goverment net lending/GDP		Current balance/ GDP	
	1973/ 1980	1973	1980	1973	1979	1973	1980
Belgium	2.3	2.2	7.8	−3.3	−7.0	2.8	−5.1
Germany	2.3	1.0	3.9	1.2	−3.0	1.3	−2.1
Austria	3.0	1.6	1.9	0.1	−3.4	−1.3	−5.6
Denmark	1.8	1.1	6.7	0.8	−8.1	−1.6	−4.4
France	2.8	2.6	6.8	0.9	−0.8	−0.3	−1.2
Netherlands	2.1	2.9	6.3	1.1	−3.1	3.9	−1.8
Sweden	1.9	2.4	2.0	4.2	−2.7	2.4	−4.1
Switzerland	0.0	0.0	0.2	–	–	0.7	−0.8

Source: OECD 1981, 10

Table 8.6 Pattern of Belgian exports, 1965–78
(in percentages)

	1965	1970	1973	1978
Metals	29.5	28.1	24.9	17.8
Textiles	14.1	11.2	11.2	8.5
Vehicles	10.2	11.0	11.4	12.8
Machinery, electrical appliances	9.9	10.1	9.9	11.0
Chemicals	6.6	7.8	8.8	10.4
Others	25.0	26.3	29.2	32.5
Total	75.0	72.7	70.8	67.5

Source: Verlaeten 1979: 45

gains remained insufficient to digest this rise in real wages, a shift in the pattern of national income distribution away from profits towards wages occurred. Because there was also a sharp deterioration in the terms of trade between 1974–80 national income grew less rapidly than real output. Thus the productivity gains to be distributed to the national factors were reduced commensurately. Consequently, the real wage gap in Belgium widened appreciably more than in the majority of competitor countries, where the real wage gap narrowed between 1976 and 1979. The second oil crisis did not bring such a marked change in the pattern of income distribution as the first, but Belgium's relative position continued to deteriorate rapidly.

While the share of wages in national income increased during the 1970s from 62 per cent in 1970 to 72 per cent in 1979 net real wages grew less rapidly than total wages because of the more than proportional rise in social security contributions. The deterioration of the terms of trade caused higher domestic prices and provoked a widening of the divergence between real labour costs of entrepreneurs and real wage incomes. Although labour costs were rising, average inflation (5.5 per cent) remained rather low after 1978. This was due to competition from imports which narrowed profit margins of industrial and commercial firms working for the local market. Moderate inflation rates and increased productivity meant that unit labour costs in manufacturing measured in Belgian francs only rose by 4 per cent on average after 1975, which was far lower than the average of 6 per cent in the boom period between 1970 and 1973. Belgian exporters were forced to hold their prices in line with those of their foreign competitors which caused declining profitability and investment cutbacks after 1973 at a time when the general slowdown in activity was sharpening competition and making the adaptation of the productive sector more necessary (OECD 1981: 15–19).

Although the first oil crisis had caused a worsening of the terms of trade and had had a damaging effect on the balance of trade, the widening of the deficit after 1975 was also due to the structure of Belgian industry, which was unable to adapt to world demand. The volume growth of BLEU exports lagged behind the growth of the world market, causing a loss in market shares. Of course, export results varied according to product categories. For some products (machinery for specialist industries, mechanical and electrical engineering products) the share of exports in world trade changed very little. Chemicals and automobiles, whose share in Belgian exports had risen during the 1960s, did not suffer from losses of market shares. Steel and textiles were the victims of the crisis. Meanwhile the BLEU specialized in exporting manufactured goods to the OECD countries, leaving the expanding markets such as the OPEC aside. The worsening of the trade balance after 1973 was largely due to the increased weight of household consumption of GNP, while at the same time imports of capital goods had fallen (OECD 1981: 19–21; OECD 1981–2: 33–7).

In the period 1966–73 the trade surplus rose steadily, but began to decline after the first oil crisis. Import prices rose faster than domestic prices and only stabilized after 1978. Meanwhile the deficit on the trade balance became permanent reaching some 4.75 billion US dollars by 1980. A surplus on services, due in particular to expenditures by international organizations based in Belgium, still procured substantial inflows of hard currencies. But remittances by foreign workers began to weaken the balance on private transfers. Thus in 1977 a deficit appeared on the service balance which widened substantially in 1979 and 1980 when it reached approximately the equivalent of 5 per cent of GNP. Falling growth rates and rising unemployment had a negative impact on public finance, because the government tried simultaneously to provide direct support to the private sector and to lighten the social costs of the slump.

Increasing public demand and public aid and structural reorganization with adjustment in the production capacity of the industrial sector had to smooth industrial conversion and to uphold employment. But as a result of this policy, public expenditure rose and in 1980 reached more than 50 per cent of GNP. Although direct taxation had increased very rapidly, the borrowing requirement of the central government grew and in 1980 attained 9.5 per cent of GNP. The increased weight of public sector expenditure was the combined result of the consequences of the economic crisis and the policies introduced in order to alleviate its effects. Automatic stabilizing mechanisms and propping-up of economic activities by granting tax reductions on investment and aid for restructuring enterprises or sectors in difficulty created a growing public sector deficit. Furthermore, the government favoured an employment policy which aimed at creating jobs in the civil service. All these measures laid a heavy burden on the central budget, representing 1.75 per cent of GNP in 1980.

Unemployment benefits were equivalent to 2 per cent of GNP, to which shortfalls on both tax revenues and social security contributions had to be added. Meanwhile the number of people employed by the local authorities increased at a consistently higher rate (60 per cent) than those employed by the central government. In 1974 civil service employment accounted for 24 per cent of the dependent working population, and in 1979 28.5 per cent. Increased deficit spending and rising interest rates threatened this government welfare policy because of soaring costs of debt servicing. In 1980

Table 8.7 Net borrowing requirements and public debt, 1973–80
(in billion Belgian francs)

	1973	1974	1975	1976	1977	1978	1979	1980
I Central government net borrowing requirement								
Total	−95	−91	−158	−202	−219	−248	−305	−409
Central government	−71	−78	−133	−154	−186	−193	−241	−319
Local authorities	−16	−20	−23	−29	−19	−27	−29	−45
Social security	17	18	20	12	16	3	−6	−16
II Financing of treasury net borrowing requirement								
Direct/indirect financing by NBB	−7	3	1	16	15	25	79	119
of which:								
liabilities in foreign currencies	−4	−2	−1	−1	−1	12	42	92
Other financing in Belgian francs	58	54	109	117	153	158	133	180
of which:								
short term	−4	3	14	35	18	14	7	110
III Public debt								
Outstanding debt	1,069	1,162	1,314	1,495	1,709	1,933	2,214	2,700
Interest payments	59	73	83	98	118	139	167	212
GNP at current prices	1,791	2,104	2,326	2,642	2,854	3,064	3,254	3,473

Sources: OECD 1981: 27; Nationale Bank van België 1981: 52–60

interest payments amounted to more than 12 per cent of total public expenditure. Meanwhile total social insurance expenditure rose by 17.5 per cent per annum in value from 1973 to 1978, as compared to 13.5 per cent from 1960 to 1973. In 1978 income guarantee expenditure represented almost 23 per cent of GNP. Rapid growth of unemployment benefits which were indexed to wages increased the nominal amount sevenfold from 1973 to 1978.

The growth of public expenditure forced the government to raise direct taxes because raising indirect taxes (VAT) would have affected the level of consumer prices. The indexation of wages and salaries made the latter method of financing increased government expenditures unattractive. Especially serious was the fact that receipts did not keep pace with expenditure and that the level of the public deficit was among the highest in Europe. Because the proportion of social security expenditures covered by receipts had declined rapidly (from 84 per cent in 1974 to 63 per cent in 1979), the central government had to finance the shortfall. Meanwhile the Treasury had to cover the deficit by issuing bonds on the domestic market, mainly medium- and long-term maturities. From 1977 a proportion of the deficit was covered by the National Bank and then by increased external borrowing (in 1980 about 30 per cent of the total debt).

Foreign borrowing caused a growing current balance of payments deficit and weakened the position of the national currency. At the end of the 1970s it became clear that the authorities' net financial deficit had exceeded individuals' lending capacity and this increased borrowing was already exercising an excessive pressure on the internal capital market. Because of the outstanding debt and high interest payments the Belgian government now faced serious problems. At the end of 1980 direct debt amounted to 1,900 billion Belgian francs – almost 55 per cent of GNP and total public debt (including local authorities) amounted to 2,700 billion Belgian francs.

The rapid increase in public expenditure and the widening deficit had no substantial effect on the economy. Apart from the direct impact of the rise in the number of civil servants in the labour force, the social transfers did not create additional jobs. Leakages limited the effect of public expenditure. But meanwhile direct taxation had an important redistribution effect. Transfers received from individuals that had accounted for less than 4 per cent in 1960 amounted to 9.5 per cent in 1980, while the net resources (taxes minus subsidies) drawn from firms by the public sector fell between 1973 and 1979 as a percentage of GNP.

BLAME IT ON THE MULTINATIONALS

During the 1970s the reputation of the multinational companies operating in Belgium was shaken by several scandals implicating politicians and managers. Especially ITT with its Belgian subsidiary Bell Telephone had been criticised for bribery and corruption practised in many countries. Bell Telephone was known for its special contacts with bureaucrats and politicians in the Belgian Socialist Party, which for many years controlled the Ministry of Communications. But ITT was also known for the role it played in Chile against the Allende regime (De Haes 1978: 71-99). Thus multinational capital could easily be identified with illegal activities and undermining of the national state. But there were other reasons to blame the influence of multinational capital. During the early 1960s the influx of multinational capital created many jobs in expanding industrial activities. In general these multinational firms paid higher wages and offered better security conditions than Belgian firms. But in the 1970s some multinationals were hit by the economic crisis, forcing some of them to withdraw from Belgium. In many cases they did so without consulting the trade unions. Some of them preferred to disappear to the so-called low-wage countries. Subsequently the volume of foreign investment in Belgium decreased abruptly (see Table 8.8). Investment no longer appeared to induce additional employment. In 1979 total investment made by foreign companies reached some 10 billion Belgian francs, but created only 630 new jobs.

American multinationals especially were suffering from the recession, the oil crisis and the fall of the US dollar. Saturation of the newly developed and conquered markets incited multinational companies active in the petrochemical industry to consolidate their position or to close their old refineries (for example RBP) (Geerts 1979: 12-17). In the rubber industry American firms were not able to break the hegemony exercised by the major European producers (Dunlop–Pirelli, Continental Gummi, Michelin) and in the automobile industry Ford and General Motors failed to conquer the French and Italian markets.

Because the trade union movement was not able to formulate a strategy against the withdrawal of multinational firms from

Table 8.8 Foreign or mixed investment projects, 1959–79

Years	Total number of projects	Planned investment in employment projects (in Belgian francs)		Additional employment
		in real prices	in constant prices 1970	
1959–68	3,445	80,214	–	51,543
1969–73	3,717	67,533	39,084	30,162
1974	917	24,384	18,840	5,616
1975	698	9,790	6,887	2,138
1976	745	10,560	7,153	1,764
1977	1,001	9,196	5,850	1,863
1978	1,083	12,156	7,378	1,213
1979	553	10,701	6,242	630
Totals	12,159	224,534	91,434	94,929

Source: Buitenlandse investeringen 1979: (I) 8

Belgium, workers occupied the buildings of these firms, forcing the trade unions and the authorities to intervene. Notwithstanding governmental intervention many jobs were lost. Famous was the case of FABELTA (a producer of synthetic fibres). In 1969 AKZO had acquired FABELTA from UCB, but already in 1976 AKZO decided to withdraw because of overcapacity problems in the synthetic fibres sector and FABELTA was handed over to the Belgian authorities immediately, forcing them to invest 1,600 million Belgian francs in the viable Zwijnaarde plant. The two other plants (Ninove and Tubize) went bankrupt. The bankruptcy of the paper producer Intermills in 1977 was the result of a sudden withdrawal of the American owner Champion from Belgium after having disinvested during many years. The regional authorities of Wallonia and Flanders constituted a new holding company SA Financière Intermills in order to float the paper mills in Andenne, Warche, Steinbach, Saint-Gervais, Huizingen and Rhode for which they sought investors willing to take them over for a decent price (Lentzen and Vincent 1981: 29).

Because the Belgian holding companies were not able to sustain increased investment burdens by issuing new shares or bonds, they progressively retreated from several sectors, for example the glass industry. The French conglomerate Boussois – Souchon – Neuvesel (BSN) which had acquired Gervais–Danone in France bought a majority stake in GLAVERBEL in 1972. BSN tried to diversify downstream in the packaging industries by moving into the diary and biscuits industries and into brewing activities (Kronenbourg in France and than Alken in Belgium). Because Saint-Gobain already owned the Glaceries de Saint-Roch, French companies now controlled the Belgian glass industry.

During the 1970s public opinion became aware of the fact that a take-over by a foreign multinational was not a guarantee for job security. In many cases such a take-over implied subordination to the multinational strategy of the foreign firm. Furthermore, the new owner would soon restructure his newly acquired Belgian subsidiary and in the case of overcapacity he would decide to close down some production units or department stores (that was the case with the paper mills of Intermills, the electrical equipment producer ACEC, the department stores Galeries Anspach and Grand-Bazar). Four automobile firms (Peugeot, SAAB, Citroën, British Leyland) closed down weaker production units. In 1980 the Ford Motor Co. closed down the Ford Tractor factory in Antwerp. Some firms had overestimated their growth potentialities (Burroughs in Seneffe, Badger in Antwerp, Prestige Housewares in Tessenderloo) and disappeared from Belgium.

These incidents which mobilized public opinion against multinational capital did not prove that the position of multinational capital had been weakened during the crisis. In reality multinational firms established in Belgium did very well. For instance, in 1976 they were exporting 68 per cent of their produce. The automobile industry exported more than 90 per cent of total output (Van den Bulcke 1981: *passim*). In the middle of the recession (1974–8) multinationals had created 12,576 additional jobs and during the second slump (1979–81) 1,705 additional jobs were created. Compared to Belgian capital, the performance of multinational capital was much better, because during the period 1960–77 out of a total of 107,378 industrial jobs which were lost, only 20 per cent were due to multinational companies. Meanwhile multinational firms created more than 130,000 industrial jobs during the period 1968–75. Most of the jobs lost in industry were attributable to Belgian firms (140,000 in 1968–75; 120,000 in 1975–78) (Van den Bulcke 1981: *passim*; Halsberghe and Van den Bulcke 1981: *passim*).

THE SECTORAL DIVIDE

The oil crisis illuminated the structural difficulties which were latent in a number of sectors. From the mid-1960s a gap opened up between the fast-growing industries (chemicals, metal-working and automobiles) and the low-growth sectors (coal, steel, textiles). The recession and the new conditions of international competition further widened this gap. From 1975 the authorities took a number of measures to bring about a restructuring of Belgian industry, but without complete success. In 1975 an administrative organization was set up for the restructuring of firms in difficulties. The SNI–NIM created a separate Société de Coopération à la Reconversion des Entreprises (SCRE) in July 1977 to manage state participation in ailing firms. On 5 August 1978 the Fonds de Rénovation Industrielle – Fonds voor Industriële Vernieuwing (FRI–FIV) was set up and the SNI–NIM was supplemented in 1980 by the Sociétés Régionales d'Investissement – Gewestelijke Investeringsmaatschappijen (SRIs–GIMs) operating in Wallonia, Flanders and Brussels, but each having different powers. These regional investment corporations soon became involved in rescue operations destined to float ailing industrial firms in their region (Société de Prayon, Sodemeca, SA De Coene, Claeys–Flandria, Gregg Europe, Jumatt, Potteau) (Lentzen and Vincent 1981: 27).

In addition to aid to firms in difficulty, a policy of industrial renovation gradually evolved. In 1975 a national energy committee Nationaal Comité voor de Energie – Comité National pour l'Energie (NCE–CNE) was set up and in 1976–80 priority was given by the plan to certain sectors: mechanical and electrical engineering, pharmaceuticals and chemicals. Diversification plans had to adjust industrial production to domestic and world demand. These options guided the measures announced in a new industrial policy (February 1978). Much attention was paid to textiles and clothing, and iron and steel-making, which were suffering from the general slowdown of the economy and foreign competition. In 1978 the government announced a 5-year plan for the textile sector, but the report written by McKinsey and Bekaert-Stanwick was only discussed in August 1980. The authorities hoped that financial aid given to the textile sector would save many enterprises from bankruptcy. With that purpose in mind in 1981 the SNI–NIM created a specialized holding company, the Société Nationale pour la Textile et la Confection – Nationale Maatschappij voor Textiel en

Confectie (SNT–NMT) for the textile sector. In 1978 the SA Financière de l'Industrie Textile (FIT) was founded as a holding company destined to float the bankrupt textile empire of the Motte family and some minor textile firms in Wallonia (Lentzen and Vincent 1981: 27), while the Institut pour la Textile et la Confection – Instituut voor Textiel en Confectie (ITCB–ITECO0) promoted a more up-to-date commercial strategy. The total cost of this plan was estimated at some 35 billion Belgian francs, which the government had to find on the capital market.

Nonetheless, the Belgian authorities had some good reasons to finance this extremely expensive rescue project, because the textile and clothing industries employed many low-skilled industrial workers in Flanders for whom there would be no employment in their region. But in the textiles and clothing sectors, which accounted for 14.5 per cent of dependent employment in manufacturing and 7.6 per cent of value added and 9 per cent of exports, decline dated back to the 1950s. From 1970 there was a steep fall in employment and production. The decline in employment was mainly due to reductions in the numbers of workers employed by firms still in existence and by shutdowns. The number of firms varied little, because in this sector firms were rather small and new firms could easily continue in the production of goods of bankrupt ones. The textile industry was exporting 75 per cent of its output to neighbouring countries, which made these firms vulnerable to the state of activity in those countries. From 1977 the textile industry applied for employment credits granted by the banks with interest paid by the State. But the decline in output of textile products could not be halted and employment declined from 121,500 jobs in 1971 to 79,600 in 1978. In the clothing industry employment decreased between 1971 and 1978 from 79,600 jobs to 56,800.

In the other sectors the crisis was also acutely felt. For instance, after 1975 all building activities suffered from a general slowdown. In 1975 the number of buildings put out to contract totalled 77,000 units, but in 1979 this number had decreased to 62,000 units. High interest rates (in 1979 11 per cent) had a negative impact on all building activities. Production of cement stagnated as did the production of window glass and other building materials (bricks, tiles, chalk). But in other sectors the crisis was rather benign. That was the case in the coal industry, metal products, food and tobacco, chemicals and rubber, electricity and gas (see Table 8.9).

The non-ferrous metals sector, still dominated by firms (Métal-

Table 8.9 Industrial production, 1971–9 (1970 = 100)

	1971	1972	1973	1974	1975	1976	1977	1978	1979
Industrial production	103	109	116	120	109	118	118	120	126
Mining	99	95	80	75	69	68	64	58	53
Manufacturing	103	110	118	123	111	121	121	124	130
Basic metals	97	107	116	122	90	100	97	106	114
Metal products	98	102	110	118	113	123	124	127	133
Non-electrical machinery	95	100	112	123	121	122	121	121	–
Transport equipment	110	118	124	115	123	140	152	165	183
Food, drink and tobacco	104	107	117	121	119	122	125	126	130
Textiles, clothing, leather	106	110	108	105	93	99	88	86	90
Chemicals, rubber	109	122	137	142	121	138	146	150	163
Electricity, gas	109	121	132	137	133	151	151	162	167
Construction	100	99	93	99	97	95	93	87	70

Source: OECD March 1981: 74

lurgie Hoboken–Overpelt, Prayon, Vieille–Montagne, Union Minière) controlled by the SGB, was also confronted by stagnating markets, higher energy and labour costs and low prices. Meanwhile copper production was progressing while the zinc industry was suffering from a significant malaise. Nonetheless, total output of the non-ferrous metal industry made progress (see Table 8.10).

At the end of the 1960s a consensus existed among all policy-makers that Belgian coal production had to contract and that finally all mines would be shut down. But no clear programme was launched because the Belgian authorities feared the reaction of the Limburg miners who still constituted a local pressure group of some importance. The oil crisis gave the advocates of a rational energy policy based on Belgian coal a broader audience now the spectre of an increased dependence on expensive imported oil was haunting the Belgian authorities. Meanwhile the government subsidized the coal mining sector because the traditional coal consumers (especially the cokeries) preferred imported coal to Belgian coal. In 1979 60 per cent of total coal consumption originated from foreign countries. The amount of subsidies increased. In 1977 total subsidies going to the coal mines reached 8.6 billion francs and in 1979 they accounted for 11.8 billion francs. In 1979 the average price of coal paid by consumers on the Belgian market was 1,725 Belgian francs per tonne, but real costs of the Belgian mines were 3,633 Belgian francs per tonne. In 1979 the Belgian government paid a subsidy of 1,900 francs per tonne of coal, and direct subsidies for coal production amounted to 11.8 billion francs, or 1 per cent of current government expenditure.

The crisis of the Belgian coal mines was largely due to high production costs and a stagnating demand for coal. In the period 1960–75 the annual coal consumption by Belgian cokeries stagnated at some 10 million tonnes and later stabilized at some 7.5 million tonnes per annum. The crisis in the steel industry and technological progress in iron and steel-making led to a decreased demand for coke. The overall effect of the economic crisis was a stagnating energy consumption, but after 1977 consumption of electrical power increased again (see Table 8.11). The Belgian coal mines invested heavily in new machinery and co-operation among the five pits especially in the Northern Basin allowed a substantial increase of their productivity. But during the 1970s productivity per miner had declined from a daily production per miner of 2,643 kilos in 1972 to 2,207 kilos in 1981. In the Southern Basin the process of

Table 8.10 Output of non-ferrous metals, 1972–80 ('000 tonnes)

	1972	1973	1974	1975	1976	1977	1978	1979	1980
Zinc	259.7	281.1	293.6	225.0	241.2	258.2	240.5	261.7	249.2
Copper	325.8	378.0	388.3	357.0	481.8	563.3	504.9	519.9	526.3
Lead	106.6	113.7	109.6	114.9	121.5	122.8	125.0	113.4	127.9
Tin	5.8	5.4	4.2	5.5	6.1	5.0	5.2	4.7	5.0
Cadmium	1.2	1.1	1.0	1.0	1.2	1.4	1.2	1.4	1.5
Aluminium	5.9	11.8	11.1	8.2	8.6	7.0	3.6	4.6	4.1
Zinc powder	44.6	44.8	54.0	46.3	42.4	43.6	32.9	27.4	30.1
Total	749.6	835.9	861.9	757.9	902.8	1,001.3	913.3	933.1	944.1

Sources: De Belgische economie in 1974: 112; De Belgische economie in 1981: 80

closing down the marginal mines had practically reached its final stage, because the total number of registered miners had declined from 13,400 in 1972 to 1,500 in 1981. In 1983 the last Walloon coal mine (Roton) was closed. Meanwhile the Northern Basin still employed 18,300 miners.

The policy pursued by the Belgian authorities was to pass on supply cost increases to domestic prices. Belgian coal, which cost more to produce than imported coal, was an exception and its selling price was subsidized by the government. The prices of electricity and coal to industry were among the highest in the OECD area, as was the price of electricity to households. In the 1970s the price of industrial kWh was about 20 per cent higher than in neighbouring countries. Apparently the energy-intensive Belgian industry rapidly recovered from the slowdown and was working at full capacity and consuming more and more electricity. But when analysing statistics of distributed electricity one discovers that the distribution of high-tension electricity stagnated while the consumption of low-tension electricity increased constantly. This was due to increased electricity consumption by private consumers and by the services sector. Meanwhile the big producers of electrical power decided to invest in additional capacity to be provided by seven nuclear power stations near Antwerp (Doel) and Liège (Tihange) (Dewachter 1992: 210). This heavy investment in new power stations required a further integration of electricity producers. The controlling holding companies (ELECTROBEL, Electrafina, TRACTIONEL and SOFINA) now started to re-organize the sector and after several mergers INTERCOM, a firm operating in the centre of the country, had gained a market share of more than 40 per cent. Electricity supply in the north was controlled by EBES, while in the south Unerg was formed in 1976 out of several smaller firms. Finally, in 1980 the controlling holding companies redistributed their stakes held in the electricity production firms. The SGB became a predominant shareholder in SOFINA, TRACTIONEL and ELECTROBEL, while the Compagnie Bruxelles Lambert (CBL) now controlled Electrafina (Van Broekhoven and Bosman 1981: 62; Lentzen and Vincent 1981: 4–9).

The authorities laid down the concept of a 'rational energy use programme' (Bekx et al. 1983: 1–5; Rigaux 1983: 7–17; Cartrysse et al. 1984: 17–38). Their aim was to reduce energy consumption from the upward trend rate of 3.5 per cent a year for the period from 1948 to 1977 to an average annual growth of 1.6 to 2.5 per cent. The

Table 8.11 Production of electrical power, 1973–81
(in million KWh)

	Total production	By nuclear power plants*	Percentage of total production
1973	39,121.0	68.1	0.17
1974	40,764.3	136.8	0.34
1975	39,019.9	6,408.4	16.42
1976	45,000.6	9,485.1	21.08
1977	44,773.8	11,313.5	25.27
1978	48,356.5	11,871.5	24.55
1979	49,648.0	10,814.8	21.78
1980	51,015.4	11,909.3	23.34
1981	48,179.3	12,219.1	25.36

* Except the Belgian share in Chooz (France)

Sources: De Belgische economie in 1979: 79; *De Belgische economie in 1982*: 141

policy of an adequate return on capital invested in the electricity sector was continued. The government hoped to bring down the proportion of imported oil by means of new power stations, mostly nuclear, and by continuing the policy of converting oil-burning power stations to coal. Following the first oil crisis, the average unit value of BLEU oil imports rose by nearly 200 per cent between 1973–5, whereas between 1978–80 the increase was of the order of 100 per cent. The appreciation of the Belgian franc against the US dollar had exerted a favourable influence on both occasions. On the other hand, the volume of imported oil had increased between 1978–80, whereas it had fallen by more than 20 per cent between 1973–5. The terms-of-trade deterioration due to higher oil prices led to a loss of GNP of the order of 1 per cent in 1979 and 2 per cent in 1980.

THE BELGIAN STEEL CRISIS

During the previous decades the Belgian steel firms had heavily invested in additional production capacity and had realized significant productivity gains. In the years 1953–72 about 10 per cent of total industrial investment made by Belgian firms occurred in the steel industry and was financed by loans provided by Belgian banks and the SNCI–NMKN. In the period 1967–70 the latter provided some 10.6 billion francs or 30 per cent of all invested capital. The SNI–NIM, the savings bank CGRE–ASLK and the ECSC also provided important financial support. Thus total production capacity doubled (see Table 8.12). But in 1975 total output of crude steel had decreased by 4.4 million tonnes to 11.5 million tonnes. In that year only 55 per cent of total production capacity was utilized (Capron 1987: 698–9; De Waele 1983: 25–30).

Table 8.12 Total output of crude steel, 1954–81 (in million tonnes)

1954	4.974	1975	11.519
1966	8.820	1976	12.099
1968	11.486	1977	11.223
1970	12.505	1978	12.578
1971	12.350	1979	13.421
1972	14.452	1980	12.301
1973	15.451	1981	12.267
1974	16.150		

Source: De Waele 1983: 7

Because the Belgian steel firms were exporting 70 to 80 per cent of their produce, they were extremely vulnerable to market fluctuations, monetary instability and dumping. The other EEC countries and North America had become the traditional customers of the Belgian steel merchants. But the fall of the US dollar in 1971–2 and the consequences of the oil crisis forced the Belgian steel firms to find an outlet in Eastern Europe.

The Belgian steel-makers had to face many problems. First, there was the iron ore supply. Iron ore coming from Sweden had always been preferred by the Belgian steel industry, but sharp price increases now forced them to look for cheaper iron ore in Brazil, Venezuela, Liberia, Mauritania and Algeria. Because ARBED and SIDMAR were involved in the iron ore mines of Belo Horizonte Brazilian ore came in. Second, there was the limited capacity of the Belgian ports. Dunkirk and Rotterdam could receive ore carriers carrying 250,000 tonnes, while Antwerp and Ghent received carriers carrying only 65,000 to 85,000 tonnes. There was also the high price of Belgian coking coal. A new purchasing agreement signed by the Belgian steel producers forced them to buy Belgian coking coal, although the steel firms preferred cheap imported coal (Capron 1981: 65–104; Capron 1981–2: 91–144; De Waele 1983: 21).

The Belgian steel industry was divided up into four regional 'poles': Liège, Charleroi, the Walloon 'independents' (the Usines

Gustave Boël, the Fabrique de Fer and the Forges de Clabecq) and Flanders (SIDMAR and Allegheny – Longdoz – ALZ).

In Liège, Cockerill, after several mergers, became the biggest and most diversified steel-maker with managerial baronies imposing their will on central management (Gandois 1986: 129–34). With only 14 per cent of its stock capital the SGB controlled Cockerill. But the other major Belgian holding companies and steelworks also held a stake in Cockerill. The losses accumulated by Cockerill during the first years of the slump were impressive: 4 billion Belgian francs in 1975, 7.3 billion francs in 1977, 6.8 billion francs in 1980. Total accumulated debt amounted to 63.4 billion Belgian francs in 1980. Due to financial difficulties in 1975 Cockerill had to sell its stake in SIDMAR to ARBED. Already in 1973 Cockerill had sold its division Athus to the Métallurgie et Minière de Rodange (MMR), but this steel factory was closed two years later (Capron 1979: 525–39).

In alliance with the Belgian–French holding company COBEPA Albert Frère controlled several steel firms that formed the so-called Triangle of Charleroi (the Société Métallurgique Hainaut-Sambre, TMM and the Laminoirs et Usines du Ruau). TMM also had significant stakes in the SA Société Carolorégienne de Tréfilerie (CARFIL) in Fontaine-l'Evêque, the Laminoirs d'Anvers and minority stakes in the Forges de Clabecq (21.65 per cent) and Cockerill (4.65 per cent). The Laminoirs et Usines du Ruau specialized in long products. Hainaut-Sambre produced 2 million tonnes of crude steel and TMM 1 million tonnes (Capron 1987: 694).

Albert Frère's firm Frère-Bourgeois Commerciale handled all steel products produced by the Triangle of Charleroi and Cockerill. At the beginning of the crisis Frère separated his financial interests from his industrial activities. The holding company Financière du Ruau was split off from the Laminoirs et Usines du Ruau when taking over all financial holdings owned by COBEPA and Frère in the steel firms of the Triangle. Then Frère obliged the CBL to join him in the Financière du Ruau which controlled the Triangle. Meanwhile Frère had already built a new hot wide strip rolling mill SA Société Carolorégienne de Laminage (CARLAM) with a modern blast furnace in Monceau and then he planned new cokeries SA Société Carolorégienne de Cokéfaction (CARCOKE) and a cold rolling mill SA Société Carolorégienne de Laminage à Froid (CARFROID) in the region of Charleroi. The steel crisis prevented him from realizing this project.

The Usines Gustave Boël in La Louvière and the Fabrique de Fer in Charleroi owned by the Boël family stayed out of any alliance with Frère. That was not the case with the Forges de Clabecq in which the Dessy and Germeau families held a majority stake. The Forges de Clabecq were less profitable than the Usines Gustave Boël or the Fabrique de Fer and during the crisis of the 1970s Clabecq accumulated a total loss of 2.5 billion Belgian francs and cut 2,500 jobs. The authorities had to secure Clabecq by providing a loan worth 1.6 billion Belgian francs. Meanwhile the Dessy and Germeau families were fighting for control over the firm. Finally the Germeau family outstripped the Dessy family with the help of Frère.

In Flanders two modern steel firms SIDMAR and ALZ were created in the 1960s. SIDMAR was controlled by ARBED and the SGB, but the authorities provided loans amounting to 42.8 percent of SIDMAR's founding capital. In the 1970s ARBED increased its stake to 63 per cent of SIDMAR's stock capital. SIDMAR produced steel for the European automobile factories. With a total production capacity of 3.5 million tonnes a year SIDMAR became highly profitable. Total employment rose from 5,348 in 1971 to 6,438 jobs in 1981. ARBED also controlled Saarstahl in Germany and in Brazil the Companhia Siderurgica Belgo–Mineira, the Sociedade Mineraçao de Trinidade (SAMITRI) and the Belgo–Mineira Bekaert in Belo Horizonte.

The modern vertically integrated steel firm ALZ in Genk was created in the early 1960s by Evence Coppée and Alleghany–Ludlum Steel. But after the merger of the Espérance–Longdoz steel works with those of Cockerill ALZ became a Cockerill subsidiary. Meanwhile Alleghany–Ludlum withdrew from ALZ. After the restructuring of Cockerill in 1979–80 the German steel firm Klöckner acquired ALZ. Finally the Belgian State took a majority stake in ALZ.

Until the mid-1970s the Belgian steel firms avoided any governmental control over their investment policy. Although on 21 November 1966 a Round Table created a permanent tripartite institution for co-operation (Comité de Concertation de la Politique Sidérurgique), the steel firms refused to discuss their investment plans with this commission (Capron 1987: 703–45). This changed with the outbreak of the crisis. A tripartite National Steel Conference met on 5 March 1977 and examined the problems of the steel sector. A new phase of state intervention in the steel sector was born now the steel-makers were struggling with a deepening crisis and liquidity problems which forced them to beg for loans from the government. Meanwhile the authorities permitted the closure of the Athus department of the MMR and the dismissal of 1,150 workers who received special employment guarantees and social benefits. In the meantime the SNCI–NMKN was urged to allow stand-by credits worth 10.5 billion Belgian francs which were divided among Cockerill, the Forges de Clabecq, Hainaut-Sambre and TMM.

A second Round Table Conference met on 20 May 1978 and discussed a proposal for a general restructuring of the steel sector, which required at least 26 billion Belgian francs in productivity-improving investments and a loss of at least 7,000 jobs. Following the national conference the so-called Agreement of Hanzinelle was signed on 7 June 1978 by the Belgian and Luxembourg governments and the steel companies. Thus ARBED was allowed to make CARLAM in Charleroi a strategic re-roller of Luxembourg steel. Sixty billion Belgian francs were reserved by the government and the holding companies in order to modernize the steel factories. Because the Triangle was integrated within the so-called 'Croissant' formed by Charleroi, SIDMAR and ARBED, this project was violently opposed by Cockerill and the local unions of Liège. Nonetheless, on 23 November 1978 the government accepted the first Claes Plan making the Belgian State a minority shareholder of ALZ (24.3 per cent), SIDMAR (21.97 per cent), Hainaut-Sambre (49.18 per cent), Financière du Ruau (47 per cent), Cockerill (28.9 per cent), UTM (49 per cent), Frère–Bourgeois Commerciale (49 per cent). (The Forges de Clabecq and the Usines Gustave Boël were not concerned with this financial plan.)

Apparently the first Claes Plan solved the problem of financing and restructuring of the steel industry, but its implementation created political confusion. Although the holding companies and the government agreed on the principle that both had to finance a modernization programme estimated at some 60 billion Belgian francs, the holding companies soon contested this part of the agreement, arguing they were not able to raise enough funds on the capital market without governmental guarantees. The plan was also soon overtaken by the impact of a new slowdown on the steel market, making all previously signed agreements inadequate and forcing the government to reconsider a new thoroughgoing restructuring of the Walloon steel industry. Because the Belgian government had to finance the debts of the steelworks, controlling their expenditures was necessary. But Minister of Economic Affairs Claes refused to accept government control of management of the steel firms and ruled out full nationalization (Capron 1987: 711). The government restricted itself to providing the infrastructure required for the short-term survival of the steelworks and the medium-term competitiveness of the steel sector. Although the capital share the State had acquired in the steel firms involved large sums, the State was assigned to the role of a powerless minority shareholder. The average annual cost of paying the interest on the steel firms' debts was 4.2 billion Belgian francs.

In April 1980 a newly created holding company for the steel industry, the Société Financière de la Sidérurgie – Staalfinancier-ingsmaatschappij (SFS), in which the government and the holding companies (SGB, Banque Bruxelles Lambert (BBL), Financière du Ruau, etc.) held shares, had to finance an investment programme drafted by the Comité National de Planification et de Contrôle (CNPC) created in December 1978. The SFS collected its working capital (30 billion Belgian francs) on the international capital market, a task the SFS could not fulfil without full guarantees accorded by the Belgian State. Meanwhile the Belgian holding companies with interests in the steel-holding began to contest their own responsibility regarding their part in the financial needs of the steel industry. In reality the private holding companies decided to withdraw from the steel industry (De Waele 1983: 109).

In the meantime the Belgian government was desperately seeking a solution to the problem of overcapacity and the isolated position of Cockerill. Minister Claes suggested a close collaboration between Cockerill and the Dutch Hoogovens or the German Klöckner, but these proposals met fierce resistance from the steel lobby in Liège. On 16 January 1981 the public announcement of a merger between the steelworks of Hainaut-Sambre (the former Triangle) with Cockerill caused a surprise, because Claes had been excluded from the talks prior to this decision. Cockerill Sambre was officially created on 26 June 1981. On 15 May 1981 the second Claes Plan formulated a 20-point programme, stipulating that a rigorous management contract would be imposed on the private directors and financial support would be provided by two subsidiaries of the SNI–NIM: the SFS and the Compagnie Belge de Financement de l'Industrie (BELFIN). BELFIN was set up in February 1981 with the special task of raising 30 billion Belgian francs in order to cover the contribution of the private groups to the restructuring. The loans contracted by BELFIN received full guarantees from the State.

Because the steel crisis was threatening the survival of the Belgian State, the government had always considered the steel crisis as a 'national problem'. The restructuring of other sectors suffering from the economic crisis, – the (Flemish) textile industry, the (Flemish) coal mines, the (Flemish) shipyards and the glass industry – were promised similar treatment to that accorded to the steel industry and they were all declared 'national sectors' escaping from the responsibility of the regional authorities. They remained object of 'national solidarity' for their borrowing requirement.

This solidarity pact created by the politicians was put under constraint by the rapidly worsening financial situation of Cockerill Sambre. Cockerill Sambre had a total debt of 117 billion Belgian francs of which 42 Belgian billion francs were owed to the SNCI–NMKN. During the summer of 1981 the private sector banks wanted a State guarantee for the credit (30 billion Belgian francs) they had already extended to the steel industry and in addition they asked the same guarantee from the State before agreeing to support the 22 billion Belgian francs package arrangement by the government to cover Cockerill Sambre's future cash drain and before releasing a long-term credit line for 9 billion Belgian francs (Capron 1987: 721). This problem provoked the fall of the Centre–Left coalition government in September 1981 led by Mark Eyskens.

CONCLUSIONS

The economic crisis and necessary adjustments forced the Belgian government to finance expensive unemployment programmes, freeze wages and benefits and impose austerity programmes the population did not want to accept. Meanwhile public debt was soaring. Automatically the authorities discovered the limits of the Keynesian welfare state and its inability to cope with the economic crisis. This reality became apparent in the early 1980s when the Belgian economy moved into a new slowdown and the fiscal crisis of the State necessitated a thoroughgoing economic and financial adjustment programme.

9

BACK TO MARKET CAPITALISM (1981-8)

In the summer of 1981 the coalition government of Socialists and Christian Democrats was rapidly disintegrating. This was due to the growing domestic and external imbalances shown by the Belgian economy. Substantial current account and public sector deficits and high unemployment were forcing down a coalition government that seemed unable to manage the economic crisis (Vandeputte 1982: 23–46; Delpérée 1983: 129–78; Fitzmaurice 1983: 68–72; Verreet and Van Overtveldt 1991: 22–7). But as long as the trade unions refused any change in the automatic wage indexation system, no other policy had much chance of being adopted. Meanwhile entrepreneurs and banks urged reforms. But as long as they feared a proletarian upheaval, a coalition government of Christian Democrats and Socialists constituted the best guarantee for social peace. Notwithstanding the fact that the trade union rank-and-file of the Christian Democrats opposed a break-up of the coalition with the Socialists, leading Catholic politicians prepared for parliamentary elections and a coalition government with the Liberals.

THE FIFTH MARTENS GOVERNMENT (1981-5)

The Eyskens coalition government of Christian Democrats and Socialists was forced down in September 1981 because the Walloon Socialist ministers refused to support the government as long as the funding of the Walloon steel industry was not decided. Parliamentary elections on 8 November 1981 showed that the popularity of the Flemish Christian Democrats had sharply declined. The Flemish Christian Democrats lost fourteen seats in the House of Deputies, while the Flemish and Walloon Liberals and a Poujadist anti-tax party gained eighteen seats. Then the Flemish Christian

Democrat Martens, who had previously led four Centre–Left coalition governments, agreed to lead a Centre–Right government. Martens promised to save the fundamentals of the welfare state. With the support of the Catholic union leader Jef Houthuys, he secretly worked out a plan for economic recovery which the Liberals then endorsed (De Ridder 1991: 145–51; Verreet and Van Overtveldt 1991: 28–9). Martens obtained 'full powers' from Parliament in order to restore competitiveness of industry and implement fiscal reforms. A devaluation of the Belgian franc by 8.5 per cent on 21 February 1981 aimed to restore industrial competitiveness.

This Martens government lasted for four years. Although it paid much attention to competitive problems (Degroote et al. 1983: 15–23), the government did not break with the fundamentals of the employment policy initiated by the previous governments. Labour legislation was made more flexible. The shorter working week had to be paid out of wage reductions and compensated for by job creation (Hansenne Plan) (Hansenne 1985: 50–66). The government refused to adopt a monetarist stance. Supply-side reforms were decided in order to boost profits, but the government did not succeed in reducing its spending deficit.

During the parliamentary election campaign of 1985 Prime Minister Martens stressed his successful economic policy and promised his voters that there was some light at the end of the tunnel. He asked for a new term in order to achieve his economic reforms. Meanwhile the Liberals were forced to accept the government's achievements as theirs. They pleaded for a maintenance of the coalition of Liberals and Christian Democrats, so endorsing the Christian Democratic thesis that no new budgetary cuts would be necessary. The result was that the Flemish Liberals lost six seats in the House of Deputies to the Christian Democrats and Martens reconstituted his coalition with a weakened Liberal Party.

THE CONTINUING CRISIS

The slump of 1980–1 was due to a growing disequilibrium provoked by the second oil crisis combined with rising wage costs. Wages had resisted the impact of the economic crisis by a system of rigid indexation, while social security contributions had been raised throughout the period between the two oil crises in order to finance social welfare and unemployment benefits. Thus real labour costs increased by more than 5 per cent during the 1970s, while corporate incomes declined and bore the brunt of adjusting to the deterioration in the terms of trade.

Belgium continued to pursue a policy of stable exchange rates against the European Monetary System (EMS) currencies (Van der Wee 1986: 479–512). Meanwhile enterprises in the exposed sector (i.e. the exporting industrial firms) had been prevented from passing on the increase in their costs through prices. The overall result was that enterprises were forced to improve their productivity and to close down poorly performing units or to fire workers. Many firms postponed their investment decisions or reduced investment more than in competing countries. During the period 1973–9 industrial investment declined by an annual average of 5.7 per cent. Thus a discussion began about the overall decline of the Belgian economy and the way of modernizing the ailing sectors. The position of the exposed sector had to be reconsidered in the light of a new technological revolution provoking an important shake-out of firms. Although industry still occupied a key position in the Belgian economy, its relative share in total GDP had declined from 31.2 per cent in 1970 to 24.3 per cent in 1982. Meanwhile industrial employment had declined by 30 per cent.

The situation worsened in the wake of the second oil crisis as public finance targets were substantially overrun and the overall net Treasury borrowing requirement exceeded 13 per cent of GDP in 1981 and the current account deficit widened to 4.5 per cent of GDP. At that moment lack of confidence in the Belgian franc resulted in net outflows of private capital equivalent to almost 5 per cent of GDP, whereas in previous years capital flows had almost balanced. Due to large deficits on private sector transactions, massive borrowing abroad by the public sector became necessary, climbing in two years to 10 per cent of GDP or more than 400 billion Belgian francs. Private capital outflows forced the National Bank to intervene on the regulated foreign exchange market, while the downward pressure on the exchange rate on the free market created a difference of more than 12 per cent with the regulated exchange rate.

The causes of the economic crisis (*De economische toekomst* 1981: *passim*) following the second oil crisis were analysed in different ways by the labour movement and the financial world. The Left believed that reflation had to receive priority (*Faire face* 1982: *passim*; *Een socialistisch plan* 1981: *passim*; *SP–alternatief* 1983:

passim), while the financial sector and entrepreneurial organizations cited high labour costs as the main cause of the crisis (Carbonelle 1987: 101–47; Janssen 1981: *passim*; Moden and Sloover 1980: 142–9; Siaens 1985: 86–94, 135–57; Stouthuysen 1980: *passim*; *Voor de regering* 1979: *passim*). But the Centre–Left coalition governments sought to maintain household incomes, although they could not avoid a steep increase in income tax and social insurance contributions. The latter measures did not prevent a rapid deterioration of the position of the Treasury and a fast-growing public debt (Quaden 1984: 129–39). At the same time the government maintained a stable nominal exchange rate, which proved to be an effective instrument to curb price rises, but with no change in the income formation process, also proved to be responsible for an increase in the real effective exchange rate, which aggravated competitiveness problems and provoked high interest rates. High interest rates meant higher expenses for firms investing with borrowed capital and the public sector in need of more cash. Thus Belgium was caught in a vicious circle. The loss of corporate competitiveness caused rising unemployment, and widening public deficits and heavy borrowing by the authorities increased interest rates which obliged many enterprises to postpone their investment decisions (Quaden 1987: 13–18).

MACROECONOMIC ADJUSTMENT POLICIES

Having obtained the backing of the Catholic trade unions the Martens government responded to the crisis by transferring a substantial part of national income from wage earners to enterprises and then to the public sector. Because the contractual nature of wage determination prevented the adjustment process, in February 1982 the Christian Democrats abandoned exchange stability *vis-à-vis* the EMS, a decision on which the Liberal ministers were consulted only when the decision was already taken. In order to restore entreprises' competitiveness the government decided to devalue the franc by 8.5 per cent against all the EMS currencies except for the Luxembourg franc and the Danish krone. But, immediately, the government returned to the traditional objective of exchange rate stability. The principle of indexation of all wages and social benefits was not altered. The normal mechanisms of proportional indexation were only suspended until 1983 and replaced by a flat-rate system confining indexation to that part of remuneration not exceeding the guaranteed monthly wage. Thus only half of the wage bill remained indexed. Total wage indexation was restored again in September 1983.

Meanwhile the so-called 'United Trade Union Front' of Socialist and Catholic Unions, which had dominated the political scene during the 1960s and 1970s, had been broken up. Thus sectoral labour disputes and working-class rebellions in those enterprises exposed to governmental intervention became dominant, but without threatening governmental stability (the airline company SABENA had to proceed to a wage-cut of 1 billion Belgian francs; the employees of the railway company SNCB–NMBS handed in 5 billion Belgian francs; the steel firm Cockerill Sambre was threatened with massive lay-offs and wage cuts) (Mommen 1987: 40).

A temporary suspension of indexation, a freeze of real wages and a reduction in allowances and other variable wage components provoked a sharp decline of the purchasing power of average wages (down 10 per cent in 1981–5). This was more than in the other European countries. Although total wage indexation was restored in September 1983, real wages remained frozen until 1986, when a 'competitiveness standard' was worked out, authorizing the government to intervene in wage formation if the rise were to exceed the average, in common currency terms, of the increases in Belgium's seven main trading partners. Also, various measures were taken to channel savings towards firms and to promote the growth of venture capital. Meanwhile a rapid rise in investment income substantially altered the composition of private income. Whereas wages net of social insurance contributions amounted to almost twice as much as income from property and entrepreneurship in the early 1980s, they were only one-third greater in 1986 (OECD 1987–8: 18).

The benefits of wage restraint and those deriving from the improvement in the terms of trade led to a rapid revival in company profits. The improvement in net profit margins was apparent in industry before it spread to the services sector. The return on equity capital rose sharply, reaching 10 per cent in 1985 after having been close to zero in 1980–1. The investment ratio began to pick up and corporate lending capacity became very substantial at 5 per cent of GDP. In 1981 the current account deficit of the BLEU amounted to 4.5 per cent of GDP, but came close to equilibrium in 1983 and in 1986 was showing a surplus of 2.75 per cent of GDP. This was largely due to cyclical factors. A structural improvement in trade

179

did not occur, because equilibrium was restored as a result of decreased domestic demand achieved through the use of incomes policy and because there was a large domestic demand growth differential with the main trading partners.

Table 9.1 Foreign trade balance of the BLEU, 1982–6
(in billion Belgian francs)

	1982	1983	1984	1985	1986
Exports	2,393	2,651	2,992	3,168	3,070
Imports	2,653	2,821	3,196	3,318	3,065
Balance	−260	−170	−204	−150	+5
Energy balance	−341	−313	−358	−342	−173

Source: Nationale Bank van België 1987: 12

The 1986 surplus was attributable solely to the terms of trade improvement (see Table 9.1) which, for Belgium, was equivalent to 4.5 per cent of GDP, but import and export performances of Belgian products remained poor. The devaluation of the Belgian franc coupled with wage restraints resulted in a sharp reduction in relative unit labour costs, allowing exporters to take advantage of their reduced costs to increase their margins. This improvement in the relative export prices of manufactures was only transitory and within five years relative export prices were almost back to the previous level. The depreciation of the US dollar exchange rate in 1986 forced Belgian exporters to sell their products in European countries instead of on the world market.

The structural weakness of Belgian exports was highlighted in this period by the fact that a very large portion, well above the European Community (EC) average, was composed of products for which demand was growing slowly, while there was little specialization in sectors which were experiencing rapid growth (i.e. electrical and electronic equipment, and data processing and office automation). Belgian manufacturers continued to lose substantial export market shares and they were not able to make serious progress in high-growth products. Thus the impact corrective programmes had on the competitiveness of Belgian products was negligible and only apparent on the domestic market, because the devaluation of 1982 had increased import prices and reduced import penetration. This effect disappeared in 1984 and within a few years the rate of import penetration had risen to the early 1980s' level.

The improvement in the current balance brought investors' confidence back and outflows of private capital dwindled (see Table 9.2). Meanwhile the public sector was forced to continue borrowing abroad in order to preserve foreign exchange reserves, with the result that public external debt amounted to 20 per cent of GDP in 1986 compared with 10.75 per cent in 1981. Because overall borrowing slowed considerably after 1985, foreign borrowing decreased very substantially. Finally, the corrective programme implemented by the government had flattened overall domestic demand, while Belgian foreign trade had been boosted between 1981 and 1986.

BUDGETARY PROBLEMS

Belgium's proportion of public spending, debt and tax and other compulsory transfers relative to GDP was higher than in many other OECD countries. Although Belgium's public debt had always been high, 'it gained almost "explosive" momentum since the end of the 1970s' (OECD 1987–8: 29). As in other OECD countries the public sector had grown in relative importance and in terms of total spending its share in GDP had risen from 38 per cent in 1970 to over 57 per cent in 1981. After 1982 the Belgian government decided to curb the growth of expenditure. This took the form of cutbacks in public investment and a stabilization of civil servants' salaries in real terms and transfer payments were no longer to exceed wage growth. This downturn in public spending was necessary because of increasing interest payments on public debt. High interest payments altered the composition of public expenditure because the share of interest payments in total expenditures increased sharply between 1970 and 1986. This was at the expense of government investment and public consumption, while real wages were falling and government employment kept on rising by an average of 0.5 per cent per annum between 1981 and 1985. The share of government employment in total employment remained above the European average with 14.7 per cent in 1974 and 19.9 per cent in 1985.

Transfers responded less flexibly. Business subsidies did not decline (see Table 9.3). On a national account basis, subsidies represented only a small amount. However, when including capital transfers, loans and equity participation, but excluding 'off-budget

Table 9.2 Current account of the balance of payments, 1981–7
(cash transactions in billion Belgian francs)

1981	1982	1983	1984	1985	1986	1987
−203	−116	−40	−4	+13	+127	+107

Source: Nationale Bank van België 1987: 12

Table 9.3 Subsidies paid to the corporate sector, 1975–84
(in billion Belgian francs)

	1975	1980	1982	1984
1 Nationalized sector				
Railway company	34.9	53.0	59.9	76.7
Public transport	11.6	24.2	30.6	31.2
Post office	12.8	15.6	12.2	16.5
Housing	9.5	33.5	31.0	25.0
Others*	5.3	13.9	12.4	11.1
Total	74.1	140.2	146.1	160.5
2 Industrial sector				
Steel	6.0	18.9	40.4	25.6
Coal	5.2	12.3	8.7	9.7
Shipbuilding	2.8	8.8	4.6	6.0
Textiles/glass	0.3	1.5	3.7	4.3
Total	14.3	41.5	57.4	45.5
3 Private sector	14.6	32.3	54.5	62.0
General total	103.0	214.0	258.0	268.0

* SABENA, air traffic control, ferries, SNI–NIM

Source: 'De overheidshulp' (1987): 10

assistance', total government aid to the corporate sector amounted in 1985 to 5.2 per cent of GDP. When including also fiscal advantages, aid to the corporate sector was 6.2 per cent of GDP (Mommen 1987: 145). Transfers to individuals stabilized after 1981. They remained higher than in Germany and Denmark, but lower than in the Netherlands and France (see Table 9.4).

The abrupt policy switch from a counter-cyclical Keynesian policy in 1970s to a restrictive neo-liberal one is reflected in the

Table 9.4 Transfer payments as a percentage of total household incomes, 1970–86

	1970	1975	1980	1985	1986
Belgium	16.2	19.2	20.6	21.4	21.2
Germany	15.8	19.8	19.2	19.2	18.9
Denmark	14.5	17.6	21.1	20.0	19.7
France	17.8	19.6	24.0	27.1	27.4
Netherlands	17.6	24.0	26.7	28.8	28.9

Source: OECD, 1987–8: 32

structural budget deficit excluding interest payments. Budget savings resulted in declining family allowances in real terms and the expenditure on education increased only slightly. The purchasing power of retirement and old-age pensions declined by 0.8 per cent on average a year and real wages were falling by 0.1 per cent in the private sector and by 1.4 per cent in the public sector. Spontaneous demographic trends had a beneficial impact on family allowances and pensions. But problems remained in several sectors, such as the health service and education. The teacher/pupil ratio and the high level of capital equipment in the health sector made these services expensive. Aid to the ailing industrial sectors was taken 'off-budget', with only the total interest payments given in the budget. Regionalization introduced in the early 1980s vested more power in regional authorities still seeking subsidies. All these negative factors made efforts to achieve fiscal consolidation difficult and fuelled steep increases in expenditure, making the share of general government receipts in GDP steadily expand. The rise of the level of income tax and social insurance contributions was exceptional in the early 1980s. Until 1986 tax scales and allowances were not inflation-linked and the levying of special surcharges meant a heavy burden for all wage-earners. Meanwhile the authorities were reluctant to increase the corporation tax and in 1987 it was brought down to 43 per cent. These developments resulted in comparatively high marginal tax rates on the use of labour and low rates on the use of capital.

High tax pressure on household income was compensated by high expenditure in favour of individuals and amounted to 40 per cent of revenues from personal income tax in 1985. This was the reason why resistance to the increasing burden of taxation had grown and especially fringe benefits in kind became popular. Tax evasion on investment income remained very high, because the withholding tax on income from securities provoked leakages. Because of the progressive nature of direct taxation combined with inflation taxation of wage-earners, revenues could grow as they came into higher tax brackets (Cantillon et al. 1987: 191–226; Deleeck 1992: 163–88).

PUBLIC DEBT

Meanwhile deficit spending had accumulated a high level of debt provoking ballooning interest payments in a period when real interest rates were high. Therefore the central authorities tried to set up a system of tough budget control. In December 1982 a decree forced local authorities to balance their budget at last in 1987 while transfers from central to local authorities were stabilized. Thus local authorities were forced to cut their infrastructural expenditures and to raise local taxes. The social security system had to balance its accounts by raising contribution rates and receipts from 'index skips'. Now the central government was better able to control the trend in the public sector deficit. But financing the public sector deficit remained a critical affair. Up to 1977 private sector saving financed the public sector deficit, but from 1979 on the deficit was financed to a very large extent from massive foreign borrowing and from monetary sources (see Table 9.5) (OECD 1987–8: 44–6).

The accumulation of large public deficits resulted in a rapid build-up in gross central government debt. If the off-budget debt, the social security and local government debt are included, gross public debt was the equivalent of 122.2 per cent of GDP in 1986 and 127.2 per cent in 1987. In the 1970s the acceleration of inflation eroded the real value of Belgian public debt, but in the 1980s the apparent interest rate on debt adjusted only slowly to current nominal rates. Loans in excess of five years accounted for a substantial proportion of the public debt (more than 50 per cent in 1979 and 37 per cent in 1986) in a period when inflation and interest rates were slowing down. Moreover, there was a tendency for the public debt to grow faster than nominal GDP, which was largely due to increased interest payments. In 1987 interest payments by the government reached 523 billion Belgian francs or the equivalent of 9.9 percent of GDP.

Stopping the self-perpetuating impact of interest payments (the so-called 'snowball effect') became an urgent problem, but despite

Table 9.5 Financial accounts of the institutional sectors and structure of financing of the central government financial deficit, 1972–86

Years	Gross saving as % of GDP	Deficit of general government as % of GDP	Structure (%) of financing central government deficit		
			(1)	(2)	(3)
1972–7	23.1	−6.2	58.4	54.3	−5.8
1978	22.0	−7.9	39.3	54.4	6.3
1979	20.9	−8.8	27.4	52.6	20.0
1980	21.6	−11.5	11.4	57.5	31.1
1981	22.1	−16.3	21.4	31.5	47.1
1982	20.7	−14.3	32.4	31.2	36.4
1983	22.5	−14.8	27.9	47.8	24.3
1984	21.6	−12.0	34.2	34.8	30.9
1985	21.1	−11.3	55.7	39.3	4.9
1986	24.3	−11.1	42.5	44.3	13.2

(1) Non-monetary financing
(2) Monetary Belgian franc financing
(3) Monetary foreign currency financing

Source: OECD 1987–8: 45

all restrictive measures the level of net general government debt (including local government and social security) increased to 6,743.8 billion Belgian francs. Although overall borrowing was stabilized and massive foreign borrowing finally declined in 1987, the foreign-denominated share of the public debt remained considerable (see Table 9.6).

Table 9.6 Belgian public debt in foreign currencies, 1980–7
(in billion Belgian francs)

1980	1981	1982	1983	1984	1985	1986	1987
153.5	388.3	642.4	823.9	976.2	990.0	1,021.0	1,013.0

Source: Conjunctuurbrief

THE SIXTH MARTENS GOVERNMENT (1985–7)

The parliamentary elections of 13 October 1985 resulted in a victory for the Christian Democrats, which enabled Martens to reconstitute his coalition with the Liberals and to prevent a thoroughgoing restructuring of the welfare state the young neo-liberals of Guy Verhofstadt expected (*Er is opnieuw* 1985: *passim*; *Manifest van Kortrijk* 1982: *passim*; Raes 1983: 30–61). Verhofstadt became Minister of the Budget and started striving for a radical reduction of the spending deficit. But under pressure of the Christian Democrats the government decided that a lowering of the annual spending deficit to the level of 7 per cent of GDP only should have to be reached in 1989. This defeat of the neo-liberals provoked serious rifts in the coalition which were mainly due to ideological disputes which erupted as soon as Verhofstadt wanted to discuss tax reforms, a privatization of all state enterprises and incisive spending cuts. Meanwhile the spending deficit of the Belgian central government remained higher than in the other industrialized countries (see Table 9.7) and caused the fall of the government in 1987 (De Ridder 1991: 159–61).

Table 9.7 Central government spending deficit, 1980–7 (in percentages of GDP)

	1980	1981	1982	1983	1984	1985	1986	1987
USA	−1.2	−1.0	−3.5	−3.8	−2.8	−3.3	−3.5	−2.4
Germany	−3.1	−3.7	−3.3	−3.6	−3.9	−2.9	−2.6	−2.1
UK	−3.8	−2.8	−2.8	−3.2	−2.7	−2.9	−2.6	−2.8
France	+0.2	−1.8	−2.8	−3.2	−2.7	−2.9	−2.9	−2.1
Italy	−8.0	−11.9	−11.3	−10.7	−11.5	−12.3	−11.2	−10.3
Netherlands	−3.9	−5.4	−7.1	−6.4	−6.2	−4.8	−5.6	−6.3
Belgium	−9.3	−13.6	−11.6	−11.8	−9.8	−8.7	−9.1	−8.1

Source: Nationale Bank van België

COSTS, PROFITS AND INVESTMENT

After 1981 the objective of the authorities consisted of mastering the spending deficit and lowering production costs of enterprises. More tax facilities were created, such as a reduction of corporate taxes, tax-free zones, co-ordination centres for multinational enterprises, fiscal incentives favouring venture capital, etc. After 1985 the exchange rate of the US dollar made imports of crude oil cheaper permitting the energy-intensive Belgian industry to recuperate from the second oil crisis. Finally, different forms of labour flexibility stimulated enterprises to hire more (part-time) workers and to lower labour costs. Thus profits could pick up while many enterprises could start paying back many of their long-term loans contracted in the early 1980s (see Table 9.8).

This operation of repaying long-term debts was eased by the so-called 'Monory Act' (or the 'Cooreman and De Clercq Acts', i.e. the Royal Decrees nos 15 and 150) the government had approved in 1982. Investment funds subscribing to new issues obtained special tax reductions for their clients. In order to improve entreprises' capital structure these enterprises created a new category of capital shares paying very high dividends (Avantages Fiscaux – Fiscale Voordelen – AFV shares). In combination with decreasing interest rates these measures created a euphoric mood on the Brussels stock market. In 1983 the stock market index increased by 35 per cent. During the twenty-one months the 'Monory Act' was in force, enterprises considerably increased their share capital. The government estimated total capital increases at some 300 billion Belgian francs, of which 83 billion Belgian francs consisted of issues on the stock market (Mommen 1987: 119–20). This provoked a real 'democratization' of capitalism so that about 10 per cent of the population now owned shares. Although the government pretended that 'popular capitalism' would stimulate investment, enterprises and holding companies started paying off their long-term loans, which also reinforced the tendency of overinvestment in low-risk shares, especially those issued by holding companies, banks and the electricity industry (see Table 9.9).

The special investment funds were successful because they were founded and managed by big banks able to pre-finance this operation. At the end of 1984 special investment funds owned 5 per cent of the total market value of Belgian stock capital, which increased the influence of the big banks on enterprises in which they held shares in their investment funds. In order to attract multinational enterprises to Belgium and to stop tax evasion the Royal Decree no. 187 of 30 December 1982 stimulated big enterprises to establish 'co-ordination centres' which received important reductions on their company taxes.

COPPEE–RUST AND EMPAIN

During the crisis of the 1970s the Belgian holding companies saw their source of income dry up as dividends paid by companies they controlled decreased and their borrowing requirements increased. Because of the low return on their capital investment and high

Table 9.8 Profitability of Belgian industry, 1970–86
(in percentages)

	Profitability		Long-term debt	
Year	Total	Except steel	Total	Except steel
1970	7.7	–	30.7	–
1973	8.6	–	45.4	–
1976	5.7	–	62.5	–
1979	5.9	8.2	74.2	68.0
1980	3.8	7.0	76.2	66.5
1981	3.3	8.0	77.6	71.5
1982	6.1	9.7	78.9	70.1
1983	6.7	9.4	66.3	60.1
1984	9.7	11.0	56.5	52.9
1985	10.4	11.5	54.3	49.7
1986	10.2	11.2	46.1	41.6

Source: Paribas Bank België

Table 9.9 Sectoral spread of AFV capital increases
(in billion Belgian francs)

Sectors	(1)	(2)	(3)
Holding companies	25.2	30.5	16
Gas and electricity	20.6	24.8	3
Banks	12.1	14.6	6
Electricity holdings/ engineering firms	7.0	8.5	3
Non-ferrous metals	3.2	3.8	3
Chemicals	3.1	3.7	4
Insurance companies	2.5	3.1	3
Building	2.0	2.4	2
Transport	1.4	1.7	4
Department stores	1.1	1.4	2
Glass	1.0	1.3	1
Others	3.6	4.3	13
Total	82.8	100.1	60

(1) In billion Belgian francs
(2) In percentages of total
(3) Number of companies

Source: Een energie-onderneming in de samenleving 1984: 81

interest rates they had to pay on their loans they were cut off from the capital market. Thus at the end of the 1970s all holding companies were heavily in debt and making losses on their portfolio investment.

In 1980 the Coppée–Rust group (CDI) was acquired by the French cement group Lafarge. The decline of the Coppée group started in the late 1960s when Coppée had to withdraw from heavy industry (steel, coal, coking coal and fertilizers). Then Coppée allied with the American firm Wheelabrator when expanding its engineering activities and laboratories (Dubois 1988: 258–63). Because Coppée–Rust's activities were all concentrated in France, a marriage with the French cement firm Lafarge was a logical step.

During the 1960s Baron Empain acquired the French Schneider Group, but in the late 1970s liquidity problems obliged Empain to reorganize his industrial empire. In 1980 he ceded his control over the Banque Belge pour l'Industrie to the Royal Bank of Canada. The glass-holding company Verlica–Momignies invited the Belgian authorities to float Verlipack (glass products). Meanwhile Empain's holding company Compagnies Réunies d'Electricité et de Transports (ELECTRORAIL) was shut out of the electricity sector. In the sector of rolling-stock production Empain's ABR came under control of the SNI–NIM and then merged with the contracting firm SA Imsay–Ets (Lentzen and Vincent 1981: 19–20). In February 1981 Baron Empain sold his 35 per cent holding in the Auxilière d'Entreprises Industrielles et Financières to Paribas and retired from business (Empain 1985: 193). ELECTRORAIL liquidated Verlica–Momignies. Empain's group (which owned the holding companies Société pour la Fabrication du Gaz (FAGAZ), Compagnie Belgo-Africaine du Kivu (SOBAKI), Cofibel and Compagnie Financière, Minière et Industrielle (COFIMINES)) allied with the Groupe Bruxelles Lambert (GBL) when merging in 1987 the Compagnie des Grands Lacs with Cometra Oil. After having ceded its stake in the French firm Patience et Beaujonc to FAGAZ, ELECTRORAIL became an empty shell which later was sold to Kamolux.

THE GROUPE BRUXELLES LAMBERT (GBL)

During the 1960s Léon and Philippe Lambert tried to supplant the SGB when they launched into battle for the control of SOFINA in 1964. In 1967 the Lamberts allied with Mobutu who was then looking for foreign investment in the copper mines he had nationalized. Although the Banque Lambert had absorbed the Banque de Reports et de Dépôts in 1953 its retail banking activities had remained underdeveloped. As investment bankers the Lamberts still sought opportunities. In 1972 the Lamberts acquired the remnants of the empire (BRUFINA, COFININDUS, Compagnie Financière Internationale (COFINTER) and Banque de Bruxelles) controlled by Comte Paul de Launoit. The Lamberts merged their Compagnie d'Outremer with de Launoit's companies, forming the Groupe Bruxelles Lambert (GBL). In 1975 the Banque de Bruxelles merged with the Banque Lambert, establishing the BBL. Because the Banque de Bruxelles had made heavy losses (about 1 billion Belgian francs) on the hard currency exchange market and both banks had to integrate their staff the BBL had to undergo a painful reorganization.

The Mutuelle Lambert and the Mutuelle de Launoit representing both families controlled the GBL which was a 'passive holding company' heading the commercial bank BBL and the CBL (an 'active' holding company). Like other holding companies the CBL ran into an acute liquidity crisis. In 1981 CBL's balance sheet reported a total debt of some 17 billion Belgian francs while share capital and reserves did not exceed 4 billion Belgian francs and interest payments on the contracted loans by far exceeded earned dividends on portfolio investment.

In the autumn of 1981 two CBL directors (Jean-Pierre de Launoit and Jacques Moelaert) found a 'white knight' in the person of the Walloon steel merchant Albert Frère who at that time was on the point of abandoning the steel industry (Mommen 1985: 36–9). An alliance with Frère was logical, because Frère had accumulated significant working capital while the CBL held a stake of 10.04 per cent in Frère's Financière du Ruau. In 1982 the GBL absorbed the subsidiary CBL and the Financière du Ruau when a new group of shareholders led by Frère moved in. Share capital increased from 4,000 million Belgian francs to 8,232 million Belgian francs and a significant part of GBL's portfolio investment was sold. Thus debts could be paid off and investment in new activities financed. Although Baron Léon Lambert remained chairman of the board of directors, Frère and Gérard Eskenazi, representing as vice-presidents the group of majority shareholders, put their stamp upon the GBL. This group of majority shareholders was constituted by Pargesa Holding SA (in which Frère–Bourgeois, Volvo International and

Power Corp. of Canada were present), Etablissements Frère–Bourgeois, Banque de Paribas Suisse, COBEPA, Gevaert Photo-Producten (GPP) and the SOCFIN Group held 39.5 per cent of GBL's stock capital.

Frère's strategy consisted of reorganizing the whole GBL group to work within a transnational financial strategy carried out by Pargesa Holding SA. Meanwhile the GBL, together with Pargesa Holding SA, developed its principal activities through the Drexel Burnham Lambert Group (DBLG), an important New York broker and investment banker with branches in several states.

In 1983 the DBLG stake accounted for 36.4 per cent of GBL's total assets, while stakes in Belgian firms only represented 25.8 per cent of total portfolio investment (Mommen 1985: 36–45). In 1987 the DBLG employed 10,500 employees. Among them was 'junk bonds' inventor Michael Milken (Bruck 1988: 78–102) who was convicted of 'insider trading' after an investigation carried out by the Securities and Exchange Commission and the New York Court. Subsequently the DBLG was sentenced to pay large fines and finally liquidated. Thus Frère had to return to his Belgian and French affairs now his ambition of building a transnational financial group had been curtailed. Meanwhile Frère had liquidated an important part of GBL's portfolio investment in the Compagnie Auxilière des Chemins de Fer and the Compagnie Industrielle et Financière des Produits Amylacés (CIP) and acquired significant stakes in the Belgian oil (Pétrofina) and electricity sectors. In reality the GBL had become a subsidiary of Pargesa Holding SA, which was now jointly led by Frère and Paul Desmarais's Power Corp. of Canada.

COBEPA AND GEVAERT

COBEPA is a subsidiary of the French Compagnie Financière de Paribas (*Een eeuw vestiging* 1972: 31; Baumier 1988: 185–202) which stresses its Belgian character by allying with entrepreneurs and managers active in the Walloon steel industry (Hainaut–Sambre, Forges de Clabecq, Frère) and the port of Antwerp. In Antwerp André Leysen (Ahlers Lines & Stinnes Group) acquired a stake in Investerings- en Beleggingsmaatschappij Lacourt – Financière Lacourt (IBEL) in which COBEPA also held a stake. IBEL in turn had an important investment in GPP, a Flemish group which had formed a joint venture with the German Agfa group, the latter a subsidiary of Bayer. In 1978 Leysen became president of the joint venture Agfa–Gevaert, an important producer of photographic paper. Two successive problems, namely the silver crisis caused by the speculative move of the Hunt brothers (1979–80) on the one hand, and the rapidly deteriorating competitive situation of the camera manufacturing unit of Agfa in Munich on the other hand, forced Agfa–Gevaert to strengthen its capital base (Leysen 1984: 21–33; Govaert 1985: 18–19).

The Flemish shareholders whose 50 per cent interest in the joint venture Agfa–Gevaert was regrouped in the holding company GPP (now called Gevaert NV) thus became a portfolio company which over the years greatly diversified its holdings. André Leysen became President of Gevaert NV in 1985 and under his presidency Gevaert further diversified its investments, among others in the shipping industry (Hapag–Lloyd and CMB) and in Dutch companies like Aegon, Stork, and Verenigde Nederlandse Uitgeversbedrijven NV (VNU). Gevaert also has a rather important interest in the ALMANIJ-Kredietbank group which dates back to long before the 1980s.

In 1981 the French socialist government decided to nationalize all big banks and industrial companies. In Belgium this provoked a reaction because an eventual nationalization of the Compagnie Financière de Paribas implied that the French would acquire control over COBEPA. With the help of Paribas president Pierre Moussa Albert Frère and his Swiss friends acquired control over COBEPA and Paribas Suisse. An exchange of stock capital by both holding companies was combined with the awakening of the sleeping Swiss holding company Pargesa Holding SA which became the controlling shareholder of COBEPA and Paribas Suisse. Although the French socialist government did not appreciate this manoeuvre, the cold war between Frère and the French ended in 1984 when a compromise was reached on Paribas Suisse (Baumier 1988: 211–12). After his compromise with the French government Frère allied with the French group Union des Assurances de Paris (UAP) in order to acquire control over the Belgian insurance company Royale Belge and to obtain stakes in French firms which were denationalized by the conservative Chirac government (1986–8). Frère's Parfinance (formerly GBL France) formed a syndicate with Paribas, Axa and Assurances Générales de France (AGF) that acquired a controlling interest in the Société Parisienne d'Entreprises et de Participations (SPEP, the holding company heading the Schneider Group).

Parfinance also obtained minority stakes in French trading firms like Compagnie Française de l'Afrique Occidentale (CFAO) and Imétal. Meanwhile Gevaert and COBEPA remained shareholders of Pargesa Holding, but both holding companies did not influence Frère's strategic initiatives because the former steel merchant trusted his Canadian acquaintance Paul Desmarais when developing strategic initiatives in Canada.

Apart from COBEPA, Leysen's Gevaert also developed a special relationship with the Flemish ALMANIJ–Kredietbank group. Perhaps it is useful to remember that the Kredietbank was the successor bank of the Algemeene Bankvereeniging that had collapsed in 1934. After the Second World War the Kredietbank expanded in Flanders as a bank specializing in small and medium-sized enterprises. Because of its Flemish character the Kredietbank prospered now that linguistic reforms favoured Flemish as a business language in Flanders. Although the Kredietbank preserved its ties with the mighty Boerenbond, this relationship was not explicitly stressed. As all other major Belgian banks, the Kredietbank was headed by the holding company ALMANIJ controlling the Kredietbank and its affiliated banks (Crédit Général, Kredietbank SA Luxembourgeoise) and financial subsidiaries.

THE SOCIETE GENERALE DE BELGIQUE (SGB)

With its very diversified portfolio investment in heavy industry, non-ferrous metals, electric power stations, cement, diamonds, shipping companies, and banking activities the Société Générale de Belgique (SGB) was by far the largest and powerful holding company in Belgium. Apart from a few rich families the SGB's shareholders represented at the annual general meeting comprised a group of some forty Belgian insurance and investment companies representing about 10 per cent of total stock (Lamy 1990: 10). The SGB held interests in some 1,600 firms, but its control exercised over these firms was rather loose, permitting important financial groups like SOFINA or ELECTROBEL to preserve their autonomy. However, this autonomy was soon curtailed. In July 1980 the GBL and SGB decided to exercise joint control over the two strategic holding and engineering companies, TRACTIONEL and ELECTROBEL, while the holding company Electrafina became a GBL subsidiary. In 1980 René Lamy was appointed governor of the SGB. He drafted a strategy for the group and started reforming its structure and management. Because of a depressed stock market and its low profitability the SGB was unable to raise funds on the capital market. Therefore in 1981 the SGB decided to absorb the Union Minière and its two controlling holding companies TANKS Consolidated and FORMINIERE. Then a new Union Minière was founded receiving the SGB's interests in the non-ferrous metals industry (Lamy 1990: 13–15). After this exchange of shares the SGB increased its share capital from 7 billion to 13.5 billion Belgian francs (see Table 9.10).

Table 9.10 The SGB's comparative balance sheets, 1977–87
(in million Belgian francs)

Year	(1)	(2)	(3)	(4)	(5)	(6)	(7)
1977	7,000	9,505	13,696	144.09	856.3	1,392.6	1,292.5
1978	7,000	9,505	15,157	159.46	1,025.4	1,469.5	1,178.0
1979	7,000	9,435	14,033	148.74	1,187.7	1,520.1	889.0
1980	7,000	9,435	14,566	154.13	1,426.7	1,746.7	955.8
1981	13,500	25,855	16,892	65.33	1,668.0	1,731.1	1,082.9
1982	13,500	26,716	17,957	67.21	2,053.3	1,997.0	2,763.5
1983	20,000	34,787	13,925	40.03	1,791.8	2,254.6	4,182.8
1984	24,100	39,842	12,252	30.75	1,314.5	2,877.3	5,223,9
1985	27,220	45,519	14,873	32.66	890.1	3,270.9	5,974.8
1986	30,100	52,810	19,790	37.47	892.2	3,680,6	9,905.9
1987	35,254	67,556	23,135	34.25	922.9	4,085.1	10,888.2

(1) Share capital
(2) Share capital and reserves
(3) Debts
(4) Capital and reserves/debt (in percentages)
(5) Charges on debts
(6) Dividends earned
(7) Total earnings

Source: Société Générale de Belgique 1979–87

Although Lamy had promised that in the near future priority would be given to the development of financial services, international trade, electronics, telecommunications and the media industry, he had to pay much attention to the SGB's traditional activities which were not generating enough profits and therefore had to be reorganized. Interests without strategic importance were disposed of (MECANIVER in 1984, Genstar and UCO in 1986, BN in 1986–7). The recovery of the stock market allowed the SGB to raise significant funds. Thus between 1982 and 1987 SGB's share capital plus reserves increased from 17.9 billion to 67.5 billion Belgian francs.

The SGB was rather slow to adapt its management to the rapidly changing economic environment and met difficulties when seeking partners in its non-ferrous metals activities. Nonetheless important reforms were carried out in this sector. First, the Union Minière withdrew from its mining activities in Brazil, Australia, and Canada. Second, the Métallurgie Hoboken–Overpelt concentrated all its efforts on copper, cobalt, germanium and rare metals, while the refineries of Vieille Montagne (Belgium) and Union Zinc (USA) concentrated on the zinc industry. Third, the Compagnie Asturienne des Mines remained an independent mining firm. Fourth, the engineering firm Génie Métallurgique et Chimique (MECHIM) continued selling the group's technology.

The SGB did not retreat from heavy industry. Apart from the non-ferrous metals industry the SGB remained present in the Belgo–Luxembourg steel industry. After having sold its stake in SIDMAR to ARBED the SGB increased its investment in ARBED. Then the SGB reorganized its chemical firms (Carbochimique and Société d'Applications de la Chimie d'Electricité et des Métaux – SADACEM) and merged them in 1985 with PRB. The new firm, now called Gechem, had to develop new 'synergies'. But Gechem proved to be a failure because only its polyurethane division was profitable. The fertilizer factories were sold to the Finnish group Kemira Oy, while Montedison and Hercules Chemicals bought the plastic film division. Finally, in 1987 all factories producing explosives were grouped into a new PRB which soon went bankrupt, while Gechem continued the production of polyurethane foam in its Recticel plant.

The SGB was more successful when reinforcing its control over the electricity sector. With the consent of the GBL the two electricity holding companies TRACTIONEL and ELECTROBEL were merged in 1986 into TRACTEBEL (Verenigde Maatschappijen Electrobel en Tractionel). In 1988 the SGB sold its stake in SOFINA to Boël's Union Financière. Then the GBL and the SGB acquired CONTIBEL Holdings, a British company with a rich portfolio investment in Pétrofina and the Belgian electricity firms. Finally, in 1990 this reshuffling led to the merger of the three big electricity producers EBES, INTERCOM, and Unerg with Interescaut, the Société Auxiliaire pour la Fourniture d'Energie de Traction (SAUTRAC), the Société d'Electricité d'Eupen et

Extensions (SEEE), and Electronucléaire into Electrabel. Unerg ceded its electricity network to Electrabel and was transformed into a holding company called Powerfin which was controlled by TRACTEBEL. TRACTEBEL also owned the Compagnie Générale pour la Diffusion de la Télévision (CODITEL) (TV and radio distribution) and the engineering and contracting firm SA pour le Commerce et les Fabrications Industrielles (FABRICOM) and was an important shareholder (33 per cent) in the gas firm Distrigaz. Because of its high investment need (see Table 9.11) and the maintenance of seven nuclear power plants, financial control exercised by one firm had become a necessity in a period when the EC was establishing a competitive electricity market.

Table 9.11 Main indicators of the electricity sector, 1980–8

	1980	1984	1988
Output GWh	51,015	51,851	61,913
Index 1980=100	100	102	121
Primary energy source (%)			
– coal	24.4	28.5	21.2
– oil	33.9	7.9	2.5
– gas	16.8	10.3	8.4
– nuclear	23.3	50.8	66.0
– hydro-electric	1.6	2.5	1.9
Investment*	34,612	36,802	30,088
Employment of the sector	18,169	17,800	17,336
Turnover*	99,573	157,354	159,289

* In million Belgian francs

Source: Herremans 1990: 78

The SGB also reorganized its shipping activities by merging the CMB with several smaller shipping firms, like Bocimar (1982), Armement Deppe (1984), Methania (1986) and Hessenatie, and by allying with several Flemish ship-owners' families (Leysen, Saverys).

The SGB's laborious attempt to penetrate into high-tech activities, such as electronics, telecommunications and automation received a new impetus in 1984 when an agreement was signed with the French firm CGE. At that moment ITT wanted to withdraw from its electronics and telephone manufacturing division in France and Belgium. Thus the CGE acquired an important stake in ITT's Bell Telephone Company in Antwerp, which was jointly controlled by Alcatel NV, a CGE and ITT joint venture in which the SGB obtained a 5 per cent stake. In 1985 the SGB acquired the stake Westinghouse still held in ACEC and integrated ACEC into the Compagnie Européenne pour le Développement Electrique et Electronique (CEDEE), a joint venture by SGB, Telfin and CGE. But soon the CGE acquired majority stakes in all ITT's telecommunication firms in Europe and in 1989 the SGB–CGE alliance was dissolved.

Because of SGB's annual capital increases, the company's stock was dispersed over a multitude of small shareholders. Only 6 per cent of its share capital was concentrated in the hands of 'stable shareholders', (i.e. Belgian insurance companies and investment funds), whose delegates attended the shareholders' meetings but who did not control the SGB's board of directors. Therefore Governor Lamy tried to bring together a block of stable shareholders (Lamy 1990: 16–19), but when in the summer of 1987 SGB's stock became the target of a speculative move the SGB directors had to discuss the creation of a 'poison pill'. Meanwhile a group of stable shareholders announced themselves. Among them were the Italian industrialist Carlo De Benedetti and the French investment bank Duménil–Leblé. The Wall Street crash of October 1987 provoked a sharp price fall of all shares which enhanced the chance of a 'predator' wishing to acquire the low-priced SGB shares. Indeed, at the beginning of January 1988 De Benedetti revealed himself as the 'raider' aiming to control the SGB (Turani 1988: 290–314). So the 'battle of the Société Générale de Belgique' was launched and within a few weeks the French Compagnie Financière de Suez also entered the fray. Finally, De Benedetti and his occasional allies (Gevaert, COBEPA) lost the battle, and Suez, with a small group of Belgian shareholders (Assurances Générales–AG) moved in (Cottenier et al. 1989: 219–76; Cuypers 1988: *passim*; Dethomas and Fralon 1989: 58–169; Lamy 1990: 38–195; *Raid sur la Générale* 1988: *passim*; Vanden Driessche 1988: 49–274).

Suez, now holding a majority stake in the SGB, appointed a new management team headed by Etienne Davignon. Then Suez started to carry out the rest of the 'Lamy Plan' which wanted to concentrate all SGB's efforts on a limited number of core activities. Within a couple of years significant interests were disposed of or liquidated and lame ducks closed down. In 1988 the SGB sold its 23.6 per cent stake in SOFINA to Boël's Union Financière; in 1989 the contracting firm Compagnie François d'Entreprises (CFE) was ceded to the French firm Dumez, Franki (contracting) was sold to the Van Roey Group, Pabeltec (formerly Papeteries de Belgique) was acquired by Feldmühle, and CIG–Intersys was ceded to Computer Sciences Corp. Although the SGB had floated the small arms manufacturer FN this interest was sold. FN Moteurs was acquired by the French aviation firm Société Nationale d'Etudes et de Construction de Moteurs d'Aviation (SNECMA) and FN's civil and military weapon division (Browning and FN's stake in Beretta) was bought by the French weaponry firm Groupement des Industries d'Armements Terrestres (GIAT). In 1991 the SGB even sold its 49.5 per cent stake in the shipping firms CMB to Algemene Maatschappij Boel (ALMABO) and Compagnie Belge d'Expansion Maritime (EXMAR), and in 1993 CBR was sold to the German firm Heidelberger Zement AG.

The take-over of the SGB by Suez provoked a debate in Flanders on the presumed danger of a creeping Frenchification of the Belgian economy which was now influenced by French companies (Suez, Paribas, BSN, UAP, AGF, Hersant).

THE CHEMICAL AND OIL INDUSTRIES

Of all industrial sectors the chemical industry was the most prosperous. Although in the 1970s and the early 1980s problems appeared making some structural adjustment necessary, investment never declined seriously and total employment had increased in 1989 to 95,281 people. Wallonia was still lagging far behind Flanders, apparently because of the decline of the Walloon coal industry (see Table 9.11). Antwerp (with BASF, Bayer, DEGUSSA, Solvay, BP Chemicals, Amoco Fina, Pétrochim, Finaneste, Polysar, Exxon Chemical, Monsanto, QO Chemicals, Union Carbide, 3M, and L'Air Liquide) and Ghent (with Rhône–Poulenc, UCB, Oléofina) remained centres of the petrochemical and basic chemical industries, while Feluy (Hainaut) in Wallonia developed as a new chemical centre. In Wallonia many big chemical processing units were still concentrated in the triangle of Couillet–Charleroi (Solvay, L'Air Liquide), Tertre (Carbochimique, SADACEM, Crompton & Knowles) and Feluy–Manage–Seneffe (Montefina, Calgon Carbon

Corp., Sigma Coatings, Dow Corning, Staffer Chemical), while in Liège Pneu Uniroyal Englebert (tyres) and the Société Chimique Prayon–Rupel (phosphorous acid and fertilizers) remained the biggest employers. After having sold the fertilizers division of Carbochimique to Kemira Oy the SGB practically retired from heavy chemicals. The combination Solvay–UCB remained the largest Belgian chemical enterprise. During the 1970s Solvay sold its last stake in Allied Chemicals and ICI. Solvay's decline was caused by the Second World War and its aftermath when Solvay lost about a half of its assets. Today Solvay has diversified into pharmaceuticals (in 1980 Duphar was bought from Philips and in 1986 Reid Rowell was acquired) and into plastics (polyethylene and polypropylene) and peroxides. Solvay employs about 45,000 people worldwide. The company is still controlled by the Solvay family (about 4,000 people) through their holding company Solvac.

The Belgian chemical industry is strongly internationalized and imports most of its raw materials. About 80 per cent of its produce is exported. Heavy chemicals account for 40 per cent of total output and rubber and plastics for 11 per cent, while pharmaceuticals represent 10 per cent and detergents and cosmetics 6 per cent of total turnover (Herremans 1990: 27). Because of its cyclical character investment and profits fluctuate sharply (see Table 9.12).

The Belgian oil industry underwent important changes during 1982, because several refineries had to close down as a result of the second oil crisis (1979). BP and Shell stopped their primary refining activities in Belgium, while the big refineries of Texaco in Ghent and Chevron in Feluy were closed in 1982. The RBP in Antwerp was taken over by Nynas Petroleum and Universal Refining, while the old Albatros refinery continued under the name of the Belgian Refining Corporation. As a result of this shake-out, refining capacity diminished by 20,000 tonnes making Fina (Pétrofina) by far the most important refiner of crude (see Table 9.13). The import of crude from the Middle East declined steadily as production in the North Sea fields increased. In 1979 49.5 per cent of all crude was imported from Saudi Arabia. Subsequently the Arabian sheikhs lost this position in favour of the North Sea and Iran. In 1990 26.1 per cent of all imported crude came from the North Sea, while the Saudi market share had shrunk to 7.2 per cent. With a market-share of 31.2 per cent the North Sea had become by far the most important provider of crude oil. As a result of the shake-out in the sector and rationalization in the remaining factories, sectoral employment

Table 9.12 Investment in the chemical industry, 1980–9 (in million Belgian francs)

Year	Wallonia	%	Brussels	%	Flanders	%	Total
1980	4,177	29.2	207	1.5	9,919	69.3	14,303
1981	5,037	37.1	135	1.0	8,390	61.9	13,562
1982	3,507	22.4	105	0.6	12,065	77.0	15,677
1983	3,324	17.2	299	1.6	15,687	81.2	19,310
1984	5,172	24.1	563	2.6	15,768	73.3	21,503
1985	7,419	28.1	994	3.8	17,977	68.1	26,390
1986	9,315	29.2	1,062	3.3	21,567	67.5	31,944
1987	8,413	23.1	1,769	4.9	26,198	72.0	36,380
1988	10,394	18.2	3,635	6.3	43,177	75.5	57,206
1989	11,606	16.7	2,621	3.7	55,408	79.6	69,635

Source: Herremans 1990: 18

declined sharply from 11,264 employees in 1973 to 7,413 in 1983 and 6,773 in 1990. Compared to the chemical industry the oil sector is a stagnating sector.

Although the pipeline networks expanded and the total number of consumers increased during the 1980s total sales of natural gas stagnated because of shrinking domestic consumption. While household consumption did not increase as a result of better insulation of houses, industrial consumption declined after 1980 by about 25 per cent because of price competition from other primary energy sources (after 1986 oil prices fell sharply). In the 1980s Belgium started to import natural gas from Algeria and increased its import from the Norway, while import from the Netherlands decreased. In 1991 41 per cent of all imported gas came from Algeria, 36 per cent from the Netherlands and 23 per cent from Norway.

NON-FERROUS METALS

With an annual output of 1.850 million tonnes Belgium remains an important producer of non-ferrous metals (copper, zinc, silver, lead, indium, tellurium, cobalt, germanium and selenium). About 70 per cent of its produce must find an outlet abroad, mainly in Europe. All raw materials have to be imported from other continents. A cyclical market and fluctuating exchange rates have forced the refineries owned by the SGB firms to group under the aegis of the Union Minière. The aluminium branch (20 per cent of total sectoral turnover) is dominated by subsidiaries of multinational companies which were established in Belgium after the Second World War. Defensive investment meant that employment decreased during the first half of the 1980s by a quarter (see Table 9.14) and stabilized in 1989 at 14,500 workers in the whole sector.

THE METAL, ELECTRONICS AND MECHANICAL INDUSTRIES

During the 1980s Belgium remained an important producer and exporter of metal products, vehicles, heavy construction units and electrical equipment. Casting techniques made significant progress as did sophisticated amalgamation technology. High-precision work was required when producing cylinders for rolling mills. In the packaging industry canneries could easily switch from the use of tin to cardboard and plastics, provoking fierce competition among

Table 9.13 Primary refining capacity of the Belgian refineries, 1973–90 (in '000 tonnes)

	1973	1979	1985	1990
Belgian Refining Corporation (a)	3,500	4,600	4,600	4,800
BP Belgium	40	–	–	–
Chevron (b)	5,000	7,000	–	–
ESSO Belgium	4,730	12,000	12,000	11,900
Raffinerie Belge des Pétroles (c)	5,000	5,000	3,750	–
Nynas Petroleum	–	–	–	720
Universal Refining	–	–	–	2,570
Fina (d)	7,000	17,000	15,000	15,000
Belgian Shell	544	544	460	–
Texaco Belgium (e)	7,270	9,370	–	–
Total	33,084	55,514	35,810	34,190

(a) Albatros from 1973–79
(b) Closed down on 1 September 1982
(c) Taken over by Nynas Petroleum and Universal Refining
(d) SIBP until 1987
(e) Closed down on 1 February 1982

Source: Belgische Petroleum Federatie 1978–91

Table 9.14 Main indicators of the non-ferrous metals industry, 1980–9

	1980	1983	1985	1987	1989
Output*	1,602	1,505	1,584	1,614	1,853
Index 1980=100	100	94	99	101	116
Investment[†]	2,706	2,113	4,538	3,699	4,000
Index 1980=100	100	78	168	137	148
Employment	19,110	15,687	15,480	14,328	14,460
Index 1980=100	100	82	81	75	76
Added value[†]	14,244	19,201	24,754	22,118	–
Index 1980=100	100	135	174	155	–

* In '000 tonnes
[†] In current million Belgian francs

Source: Herremans 1990: 24

these firms. The rolling-stock industry which had been reduced to one single firm (BN), still exported city transport systems. Meanwhile the SNCB–NMBS had designed its 'Star 21 Plan' aimed at modernizing the highly dense but outdated railway system and building trunk lines for the high-speed train crossing the territory.

In the mechanical industry foreign firms or their subsidiaries (Atlas Copco, Caterpillar, Hansen Transmissions, Ford New Holland, Pégard) became dominant. The Flemish producers of weaving looms or machinery (Picanol, Van de Wiele, Lefebvre–Vanneste–Dewulf (LVD)) preserved their independence, while Hayen–Mommen–Zepperen (HMZ) with its factories in Belgium and the USA producing high-tech windmills, was acquired in 1990 by the Dutch Begemann group.

During the period 1980–7 yearly average growth of the sector did not exceed 3 per cent. This growth was largely due to the automobile industry. Recovery only came at the end of the 1980s when the export markets expanded and all industries, except the shipyards, took advantage of booming investment in other sectors. As a result of the shake-out during the early 1980s employment declined by an average of 3 per cent a year and then stabilized at an average sectoral level of 230–240,000 people (see Table 9.15). The automobile industry with its five major assembly plants (Ford, General Motors, Volvo, Volkswagen, Renault) in 1988 produced 1,230,000 vehicles and employed about 50,000 manual workers. The automobile industry was by far the most important purchaser of the metal, glass and plastic components manufactured by Belgian firms. In 1988 the automobile industry's share of total added value realized in the sector had risen to 30 per cent (27.6 per cent for the machinery building industry, 21.4 per cent for the electro-technical industry and 21 per cent for the metal products industry) (Herremans 1990: 3).

THE FOODSTUFFS AND PAPER INDUSTRIES

Notwithstanding the economic crisis, the foodstuffs industry, with its multitude of small and medium-sized enterprises, was continuously developing. In 1988 4,833 enterprises out of a total of 7,330 employed less than five employees and 2,190 between five and forty-nine employees. Producers of primary foodstuffs (sugar, vegetable oils, milk and milk powder) exported an ever-increasing share of their output to Eastern Europe and the developing countries. End-products with high added value like chocolates and

Table 9.15 The metal, machinery building, plastics transforming, electronic, and electro-technical industries, 1981–90 (1980=100)

	1981	1982	1983	1984	1985	1986	1987	1988	1989	1990
The sector										
Volume	98	102	104	104	113	118	119	126	134	140
Investment	91	98	88	103	117	126	114	116	131	139
Employment	94	89	86	85	84	83	80	78	81	84
Metal products										
Volume	92	91	92	91	95	90	88	100	n.a.	n.a.
Investment	73	71	73	72	99	89	88	103	n.a.	n.a.
Employment	95	87	84	79	80	77	72	71	n.a.	n.a.
Machinery building										
Volume	99	94	92	99	110	105	101	109	n.a.	n.a.
Investment	65	68	68	72	89	106	106	120	n.a.	n.a.
Employment	96	92	88	87	87	85	82	80	n.a.	n.a.
Electro-technical industry										
Volume	96	99	97	99	105	116	111	113	n.a.	n.a.
Investment	93	93	97	103	134	156	141	145	n.a.	n.a.
Employment	93	87	84	84	83	83	80	74	n.a.	n.a.
Automobile industry										
Volume	104	121	130	123	136	155	165	172	n.a.	n.a.
Investment	128	150	115	158	137	148	105	88	n.a.	n.a.
Employment	91	89	88	88	89	89	90	92	n.a.	n.a.

Sources: Herremans 1988: 36–44; Herremans 1990: 6; *Statistieken–Statistiques (1970–1991)*, 1992: 4

biscuits remained successful. At the end of the 1980s important Belgian firms controlled by family capital were acquired by foreign firms. The sugar giant Sucre Tirlemont was sold to the German Südzucker and the chocolate producer Côte d'Or to the Swiss Jacobs–Suchard conglomerate. In the sugar industry production was determined by rules set by the EC. Here total output stabilized at the level of 800 to 1,000 million tons a year. The breweries faced decreasing consumption of Pilsner beer because consumers increasingly preferred special beers and wine. Thus total output of all breweries declined by 4 per cent during the 1980s and stabilized at an annual production level of 13.8 million hectolitres of which an increasing part was exported (in 1991 3.1 million hectolitres). Meanwhile the number of breweries had fallen from 232 in 1970 to 121 in 1991. The biggest firm Interbrew (Artois–Piedboeuf) controlled half of total output while the BSN breweries of Alken–Maes remained the second largest producer of Pilsner beer.

The tobacco industry had to face a declining total output of cigarettes (from 28 billion cigarettes in 1983 to 26 billion in 1991) while total employment fell from 6,014 employees in 1983 to 4,840 in 1990. This was mainly caused by anti–smoking campaigns launched by the authorities and/or changing habits.

During the early 1980s the paper industry, which employed 20,000 workers, had to recover from the consequences of the recession, but in the second half of the decade additional production capacity of some 40 per cent was created. About 85 per cent of the sector is controlled by foreign groups. Feldmuehle acquired Pabeltec (formerly Papeteries de Belgique) and the Spanish group Torras (which belonged to the Kuwait Investment Office – KIO), Intermills in Malmédy and the Cellulose des Ardennes. But in 1992 Torras went bankrupt which caused a crisis in the Walloon paper industry. Finally in 1993 the Italian firm Cartiere Bourgo acquired a majority stake in the Cellulose des Ardennes. About 65 per cent of the sector's total output is destined for the packaging industry.

THE GLASS AND CEMENT INDUSTRIES

The glass industry can be divided up into three branches of which the 'flat glass' branch is the most important. Glass products such as bottles and other containers, with 22 per cent of total output, were hit by the crisis and the bankruptcy of the main producer Verlipack. But the branch of special products like glass wool and fibres expanded, although its share of total output was relatively low (8 per cent). Of the total output of 1,380,000 tons in 1988 about three-quarters was exported, making the sector extremely vulnerable to external fluctuations.

The building industry is an important buyer of glass, wood, cement and steel and employed 242,000 people in 1980. But due to the economic crisis and high real interest rates building activities declined sharply and within a few years the total number of workers employed in the sector had declined to 156,000. This crisis was also felt upstream in the cement industry that saw its total output of cement decline from 6,797 tonnes in 1980 to 4,744 tonnes in 1985. Recovery came slowly because the authorities had practically stopped investing in large-scale building activities and infrastructural works, and the cement industry had to sell an increasing part of its output to the housing sector. Concentration of cement production increased and two big firms, Ciments d'Obourg and CBR, now monopolize the market.

DIAMONDS

Antwerp remains an important diamond centre, with specialist diamond banks and companies. The top-quality diamond industry employs some 7,000 workers in 350 workshops in Antwerp and the surrounding area. Most of the diamonds are exported to the Far East. Important suppliers of diamonds are Zaïre and Australia for industrial diamonds and Southern Africa for gem quality diamonds (*Cut in Antwerp* 1982: 63–85). Meanwhile Russia has become a very important supplier providing 25 per cent of all imported diamonds. Belgian trade of the world supply of rough diamonds accounts for approximately 85 per cent and trade and manufacturing polished diamonds for 50 per cent. The diamond industry contributes about 2 per cent to GDP and 6 per cent to the Belgian balance of trade.

THE NATIONAL SECTORS

The fifth and sixth Martens governments still had to solve the problem of financing the so-called 'national sectors in difficulties' (i.e. the steel, coal, shipbuilding, textile and glass products industries). The most urgent problem was that of the Walloon steel industry. In Wallonia the Cockerill Sambre merger forced the Belgian government to increase the capital of the ailing steel firm by 5.2 billion Belgian francs and, according to the EC code, to implement an adequate restructuring programme aimed at reducing Cockerill Sambre's production capacity below the ceiling of 8 million tonnes of crude steel. Meanwhile the Belgian government had to promise the EC that Cockerill Sambre would return to profitability (Capron 1987: 722). After some equivocations the fifth Martens government concluded an agreement with the private banks in order to assure a new credit line and the new Cockerill Sambre director Michel Vandestrick worked out a new industrial plan limiting crude steel production to 6.1 million tonnes and reorganized the firm around four vertically integrated networks. But at the end of 1982 Cockerill Sambre had already swallowed the funds earmarked to cover its operating losses between 1981-5 and the government refused to sink more billions into the bankrupt steel firm.

At the beginning of 1983 the government hired a new manager, the Frenchman Jean Gandois, who was given the task of reorganizing Cockerill Sambre. Gandois began by purchasing Frère–Bourgeois Commerciale, the firm promoting all steel products sold by Cockerill Sambre (Gandois 1986: 73–86). Gandois made public a new plan which proposed a maximum level of rolled products of 4.45 million tonnes or 5.1 million tonnes crude steel. The Gandois plan was based on two steel forges (Chertal and Marcinelle) instead of four, four cold-rolling mills instead of five and the release of 7,900 workers (out of a total of 22,000), the abandonment of a high-quality plant (Seraing) and the non-integration of subsidiaries such as Phénix Works and the Usines et Laminoirs du Ruau and the dependence of Valfil (if maintained in operation) and CARLAM on external supplies (De Waele 1983: 152–8). Influential pressure groups (e.g. the Flemish Catholic trade unions) pleaded for a regionalization of all national sectors including a devolution of financial responsibility and the replacement of the existing system of regional 'endowments' with a specifically regional tax base. An acrimonious discussion started on the overall distribution of public aid to the five national sectors. This debate revealed that the coal mines situated in the North were consuming subsidies equal to the Walloon steel industry and that the Flemish textile industry and shipyards required more funds than the Walloon steel industry (Capron 1987: 745).

It became obvious that Belgium would be divided into two distinct economic regions with different regional economic policies and tax systems. With the publication of the Gandois Report in 1983 all contending parties had to recognize that the sums involved were now surpassing by far those envisaged in 1982. On 21 June 1983 the government agreed on the principle that national financing would cover all past financial costs of Cockerill Sambre (55 billion Belgian francs) and that for future financial needs new arrangements would be necessary with resources attributable to the regions. In practice the decision was taken that the national sectors were 'regionalized'.

The main stumbling-block remained the code for the distribution of funds among the regions. On 26 July 1983 an agreement was reached on the question of national budgetary cover for the regions' past financial costs which the regions were not able to repay. Past costs amounted to 76.5 billion francs for Flanders and 51.3 billion francs for Wallonia. The agreement of 26 July covered these inherited debts. The balance of regional funds was intended for settling the regional debts with the State Treasury and for financing any expenditure beyond the original financial packages of the national sectors (Capron 1987: 753). Supplementary financial needs would be met by a portion of the regional balance which remained after past costs had been covered and debts with the State Treasury settled. To this end the Société Nationale de Restructuration des Secteurs Nationaux – Nationale Maatschappij voor de Herstructurering van de Nationale Sectoren (SNSN–NMNS) created two regional subsidiaries. Meanwhile several problems remained unsolved. For instance, Gandois estimated Cockerill Sambre's total past and future borrowing requirements at 95 billion Belgian francs (107 billion Belgian francs if all social costs were included) which was much more than envisaged.

The Cockerill Sambre case gave a strong impetus to a further regionalization of the Belgian State, because a progressive liquidation of the charges incurred by the regions in the past and responsibility of the regions for financing expenditures supplementary to the total sums originally set had been recognized by the compromise of 21 June–26 July 1983. The problem remained that the Walloon Regional Executive would be responsible for Cockerill Sambre's financial needs. The Walloon ministers in the national government still had to protect the firm, because the rescue of Cockerill Sambre was exhausting all financial sources of the Walloon region.

A PROLIFERATION OF INVESTMENT COMPANIES

The economic crisis of the 1970s and 1980s provoked the creation of a wide variety of industrial development institutes and state-owned holding companies. The Fonds d'Expansion Economique et de Reconversion - Fonds voor Economische Expansie en Reconversie (FEER) created in 1970 took on the task of funding industrial initiatives and economic expansion. FEER received subsidies from the Ministry of Economic Affairs and the three regional authorities (Mommen 1987: 144). The Fonds de Solidarité National (1972) had to provide distressed regions and sectors with funds. The Act of 15 July 1970 created a number of new institutions, such as the Office de Promotion Industrielle and the Bureau du Plan created three departments responsible for regional planning. Three regional economic councils were put in charge of economic and social planning and regional development agencies were created (only one in Wallonia and five provincial agencies in Flanders). The Act of 4 August 1978 created regional investment agencies and supplanted the regional development agencies which now were considered as failures. The SNI–NIM incited the government to create the national Fonds de Rénovation Industrielle–Fonds voor Industriële Vernieuwing (FRI–FIV) which contributed to industrial redevelopment in areas affected by the industrial crisis in the steel, textile and shipbuilding industries. Then redevelopment agencies were created at local levels with the task of selecting new industrial projects in each modernization area.

Gradually a wide variety of redevelopment and industrial diversification agencies and holding companies emerged during the restructuring of the national sectors. Apart from the short-lived SFS created jointly in 1980 by the State and the private holding companies to finance the steel industry, the government invited the SNI–NIM to found specialist holding companies for the different national sectors. Three specialist investment companies were created in 1981 for the textile, steel and coal industries, but in 1982 they merged to form the SNSN–NMNS which was allowed to borrow on the Belgian capital market or abroad up to a maximum of 70 billion Belgian francs to finance its activities (Capron 1987: 760). Several specialist subholdings financed jointly by the SNI–NIM and private groups which formulated requests for aid from the SNSN–NMNS were created: Sidinvest (SIDMAR); Alinvest I and Alinvest

II (ALZ) in Limburg; Boëlinvest (Boël and Fabrique de Fer). Many other investment concerns followed: Clabecqlease, Investsud, Meusinvest, Nivelinvest, and Sambrinvest. Shipinvest was created for the restructuring of the shipbuilding industry and Midship for the restructuring of the wharves building barges (Capron 1987: 760–1; Mommen 1987: 147; *NMNS 1988*: 22–7). These investment companies had to find working capital on the capital market or to contract loans in cases where the financial aid and subsidies coming from the central government or the regional authorities were not sufficient to cover their expenditures.

CONCLUSIONS

During the 1980s the Belgian economy had to face a structural crisis the Centre–Right governments had underestimated. Meanwhile the spending deficit had remained high and public debt was well above the EC average. At high cost the government had saved a good part of the Walloon steel and glass products industries and the Flemish textile industry, but meanwhile the closure of the last Flemish coal mines and wharves still had to be decided and financed.

10

THE LAST TRUMP

During his parliamentary election campaign of 1985 Prime Minister Martens had stated that 'there was light at the end of the tunnel'. But hard times were not over because there was still an important spending deficit. In 1987 the Centre–Left coalition government disintegrated, apparently because of linguistic problems between the Flemings and Walloons, but in reality because of serious rifts caused by the Liberal ministers when contesting the continuing deficit spending. But this also proved that the Christian Democrats were still setting the rules of the political game. As in the past, the Christian Democratic Party determined the guidelines of economic and social policy-making (De Ridder 1983: 94–5; De Ridder 1986: 75–109).

Parliamentary elections held on 13 December 1987 were not a success for the coalition parties as a whole. Walloon and Flemish Christian Democrats together lost eight (two plus six seats) in the House of Deputies. The Flemish Liberals gained three seats but the Walloon Liberals lost one seat in the House of Deputies. Thus the Liberals and Christian Democrats only held a narrow majority in the House of Deputies and the Senate. Although the Flemish Christian Democrats had to face a set-back, they could use all their 'experience, inventiveness and skill in order to transform their defeat into power' (De Ridder 1989: 35; tr. A.M.). The Flemish Christian Democrat Jean-Luc Dehaene formed a coalition government with the Socialists and Flemish Nationalists which could count on a broad majority. This government aimed to reform the Constitution in a federal sense. Because a large minority in the Flemish Christian Democratic Party opposed a coalition with the Socialists, Dehaene pressed Martens to lead a Centre–Left coalition.

ECONOMIC AND FISCAL PROBLEMS

Because of the openness of the economy in 1989 the Centre–Left government was forced to safeguard the country's competitiveness by translating this principle into a law which would require an annual assessment of competitiveness by the social partners and also enable the government to intervene if necessary. The system of automatic indexation of wages and social benefits was not contested. In June 1990 the government adopted a firm exchange rate link with the Deutschmark and the EMS. With the Maastricht agreement of December 1991 the government had additional reasons to carry out fiscal and budgetary reforms in order to keep the Belgian franc within the narrow margins of the EMS.

The government tried to reduce the spending deficit by using its hard currency policy for a reduction in the effective interest rates and obtaining a good performance by the economy. Thus it was possible to reduce interest payments and maintain price stability. Meanwhile the traditional two-tier foreign exchange market was abolished. Fiscal reforms (the reduction in the withholding tax on dividend and interest payments on financial assets from 25 to 10 per cent) completed these reforms (OECD 1991–2: 25–6). All these reforms enabled the Belgian government to decrease the effective interest rate on the entire public debt (see Table 10.2) and to consolidate a part of the floating debt. As a result of this hard currency policy structural outflows of capital stopped because of reduced purchases of foreign securities by residents and an increased demand by foreign investors for Belgian stock. Notwithstanding these promising results the level of public indebtedness (see Table 10.2) and the spending deficit remained higher than in other OECD countries (see Table 10.1).

In 1988 the government decided to control public expenditure by setting a double norm: primary expenditure (i.e. excluding interest payments on the public debt) by the national government should not increase in real terms and the deficit should not increase in nominal terms. But the lower levels of government and the social security system were excluded from this norm. Because of a favourable economic development in the late 1980s the overall general government deficit continued to decline as a proportion of GNP, especially as a result of a decrease in transfers to the social security system. But in the early 1990s economic growth slowed down and the budget position deteriorated once again thereby provoking a

Table 10.1 Net public spending deficit, 1987–92 (in percentages)

	1987	1988	1989	1990	1991	1992
Belgium	− 7.5	− 6.8	− 6.7	− 5.8	− 6.7	− 6.9
USA	− 2.5	− 2.0	− 1.5	− 2.5	− 3.4	− 4.7
Japan	0.5	1.5	2.5	3.0	2.4	1.3
Germany	− 1.9	− 2.2	0.2	− 2.0	− 3.2	− 3.2
Italy	− 11.0	− 10.7	− 9.8	− 10.9	− 10.2	− 11.1
UK	− 1.3	1.0	0.9	− 1.3	− 2.8	− 6.6
Netherlands	− 6.5	− 5.1	− 5.1	− 5.3	− 2.6	− 3.8
EC	− 4.0	− 3.5	− 2.6	− 3.9	− 4.5	− 5.3
OECD	− 2.3	− 1.7	− 1.0	− 1.8	− 2.7	− 3.8

Source: Nationale Bank van België 1992: 5

new 'snowball effect' (i.e. the self-sustaining increase in the debt/ GNP ratio as a result of interest payments; see Table 10.2).

The growth of primary expenditure accelerated, which was entirely due to growing transfers to households (unemployment benefits), health care and pensions. To prevent the deficit from exceeding the ceiling set by the 'double norm', the 1992 budget had to include several corrective measures.

After the 24 November 1991 elections Socialists and Christian Democrats formed a new coalition in March 1992 which had to complete federalism. Meanwhile a new slump incited the Dehaene government to budgetary measures estimated at 135 billion Belgian francs in 1992 and 113 billion Belgian francs in 1993. All these measures were aimed at keeping the deficit within the ceiling and at restoring equilibrium in the social security system (OECD 1991–2: 31–2). Furthermore the Maastricht Treaty of December 1991 required the Belgian government to reduce the expenditure deficit of 6.3 per cent of GNP in 1991 to a maximum deficit of 3 per cent in 1996 and to lower total debt from 123 per cent of GDP to a maximum of 60 per cent of GDP which would entail a sharp increase of the primary surplus from 4.1 per cent of GNP in 1991 to 7 per cent in 1996. The adjustment required by the Maastricht agreement will have to take place in a context which may not be as favourable as in the early 1980s, because after a decade of fiscal consolidation the least painful ways of achieving savings had been largely exhausted which could provoke a 'certain battle fatigue' (OECD 1991–2: 34). The bulk of savings should come from current expenditure (social benefits and other subsidies, health care and pensions).

Table 10.2 The mechanism of the 'snow-ball' effect

	1986	1987	1988	1989	1990	1991	1992
Spending deficit*	− 504	− 424	− 428	− 431	− 421	− 405	− 472
Local authorities*	− 15	− 1	− 5	− 31	− 14	− 42	− 24
Social security*	31	21	16	47	47	− 14	− 9
Interest payments/ GDP ratio	−	10.8	10.3	10.6	11.0	10.6	11.2
Debt/GDP ratio	115	119	119	117	117	119	121
Interest rate minus GDP growth rate	4.5	4.4	1.5	− 0.1	2.6	3.6	4.0
Implicit interest rate[†]	9.8	8.9	8.4	8.6	8.8	8.2	8.6
Nominal GDP growth rate	5.3	4.5	6.9	8.6	6.2	4.6	4.6
Real GDP growth rate	1.5	2.0	5.0	3.8	3.4	1.9	0.8
Real implicit interest rate	6.0	6.5	6.6	3.9	6.1	5.5	4.8

* In billion Belgian francs
† Ratio of paid interests and debt

Source: Nationale Bank van België 1992

MASS UNEMPLOYMENT

One of the striking features of the Belgian economic situation was the very low rate of active labour-market participation which was caused more by insufficient growth in employment, than by a rapid increase of the labour force. The female participation rate was largely offset by a declining male participation rate (see Table 10.3). The composition of unemployment showed a large incidence of female and youth unemployment and unbalanced regional dispersal of unemployment (9 per cent in Flanders and 19 per cent in Wallonia).

By international standards unemployment duration remained high and unemployment duration was worse for older people and those with lower qualifications. Since 1983 a growing number of people have joined a variety of government programmes. Moreover, the government has made considerable efforts to improve the flexibility of the labour market. Nonetheless, the number of unemployed people exceeded 600,000 in 1991.

The root causes of the unemployment problem are complex and difficult to disentangle (Deleeck 1992: 68–83), but the emergence of

Table 10.3 Unemployment statistics, 1983–91

Year	Employed			Unemployed		
	Men	Women	Total	(1)	(2)	(3)
1983	1,813,337	1,015,132	2,828,469	81,181	482,848	564,029
1984	1,795,621	1,031,798	2,827,419	71,264	501,370	572,634
1985	1,792,460	1,052,164	2,844,624	67,302	515,538	582,840
1986	1,786,804	1,075,726	2,862,530	62,381	527,390	589,771
1987	1,788,067	1,100,644	2,888,711	63,508	546,180	609,688
1988	1,826,974	1,175,654	3,002,628	49,575	534,376	583,951
1989	1,857,692	1,224,285	3,081,977	38,715	523,648	562,363
1990	1,879,185	1,266,105	3,145,290	37,917	518,639	556,556
1991	1,872,583	1,280,913	3,153,496	51,498	540,383	591,881

(1) Occasionally unemployed
(2) All categories of secured unemployed
(3) (1) + (2)

Source: Rijksdienst voor Arbeidsvoorziening 1992: 14–16

the problem can be traced back to the 1970s, when international competitiveness deteriorated and contributed to unemployment. But steps to solve this problem have been taken.

Real total labour costs – reflecting among other factors a sizeable tax wedge – and associated substitution of capital for labour are considered to be major causes of high unemployment. In Belgium unemployment became essentially a structural problem. Furthermore, Belgium still had a generous unemployment insurance with long statutory benefit duration and limited decrease in benefit levels, which created a large pool of unemployed who became progressively more difficult to place. In similar cases in other countries claimants would drop out of the unemployment insurance system and eventually qualify for social assistance. The extremely high long-term female unemployment rates were certainly favoured by this system of generous benefits, because replacement rates are lowest for those women with a working spouse. Confronted with these problems the Dehaene government discussed the necessity of a thoroughgoing overhaul of the social security system in order to reform the method of financing unemployment benefits and old-age pensions. Therefore in 1993 Prime Minister Dehaene launched the idea of negotiating with the entrepreneurial organizations and the trade unions a new 'Social Pact' replacing the 1944 Agreement which established the basic principle of the welfare state.

These proposals were contested by the Flemish Liberal Party which had broadened its political base in 1992 when it formed the Party of Flemish Liberal Democrats. Its leader Verhofstadt now pleaded for a radical change in the social security system, a negative income tax, tax reductions for the higher-income groups and a dismantling of the neo-corporatist system of interest intermediation which he felt was responsible for the high spending deficit.

Although international competitiveness was restored, real labour costs were still very high and had risen by 47 per cent since 1974 compared to 37 per cent on average in all OECD countries. Labour-saving was facilitated by strong growth of gross fixed-capital stock, generally surpassing that in neighbouring countries. Firms were striving for reduction of labour inputs per unit of output. In spite of high unemployment, downward pressure on real wages was prevented by the role played by the trade unions in the wage formation system and the automatic mechanism of wage indexation. Although total union membership was stagnating and the unions were unable to maximize their votes during the workers' councils elections

(Hancké 1991: 463–87; Pasture and Mampuys 1990: 102–3) the unions were still influential (Dewachter 1992: 127–62). After the Act on Competitiveness (1989) and full freedom of wage negotiations (1987) was restored, the social partners meeting in the Conseil Central de l'Economie were required to examine the international competitive position of the Belgian economy on the basis of specific criteria. The evolution of the export performance and comparative labour costs were examined by the social partners and then they presented a report with recommendations to the government. Where competitiveness was threatened government and Parliament could take measures.

The government did not succeed in reducing the extremely high costs of all sorts of labour-market related programmes. Special programmes accounted for half the budgetary costs of unemployment. Meanwhile the government tried to reduce the costs of unemployment in order to save the system of unemployment benefits. In 1992 and 1993 measures were taken to suppress the system of partial unemployment benefits and the improper use of temporary lay-offs. Long-term unemployed and school-leavers were forced out of the unemployment system and a system of monitoring was introduced in order to prevent the growth of the number of unemployed without a chance on the labour market.

COAL, STEEL, TEXTILES, GLASS PRODUCTS AND SHIPYARDS

The Act of 8 August 1988 on regionalization of the economy forced the national authorities to a regionalization of the stakes the Belgian State held in enterprises of the so-called 'national sectors' (steel, coal, textiles, shipyards, glass products). These interests had been administered since 1982 by the SNI–NIM subsidiary SNSN–NMNS and via the Act of 16 January 1989 concerning the funding of the regions and the cultural communities they were handed over to the regional investment companies.

Already well before the regionalization of the former 'national sectors' the national government had to decide on the future of the coal mines in the Campine Basin when accepting in 1986 the Thyl Gheyselinck Plan proposing the closure of all pits before 1996. Total costs to be paid by the government were estimated at some 100 billion francs. The decision to close the mines had met a fierce resistance from the miners who feared job losses. Because 19,000

217

jobs would disappear in an area with high unemployment the government and the EC worked out a programme for social and economic recovery. Meanwhile the SNSN–NMNS received the stake the State held in the KS and the private shareholders had ceded theirs, making KS a 100 per cent state-owned firm, and in 1987 the government appointed Thyl Gheyselinck as general manager of KS. As losses made by KS increased, a consensus was reached to close the remaining northern pits as soon as possible. In September 1992 the last mine was closed down. The funds KS saved were destined for new industrial initiatives. But when starting its diversification policy outside of the coal sector KS met many problems. In 1993 a Parliamentary Investigation Commission had to concede that corruption, mismanagement and a multitude of public investment companies had contributed to the KS failure.

The steel industry took advantage of high prices paid for steel products. Especially in the years 1988–90 the steel industry made high profits which fuelled investment in downstream activities and modernization programmes. In 1991 investment reached 890,000 Belgian francs per worker, which was about twice as high as in 1985. This shows that the Belgian steel firms wanted to enhance their competitiveness in a highly competitive market. In 1991 about 93 per cent of all crude steel (11.277 million tonnes) was produced by continuous casting blast furnaces against only 61 per cent in 1985 (see Table 10.4). Meanwhile total employment in the sector decreased from 37,491 people in 1985 to 28,229 people in 1991. The steel industry concentrated its activity on flat products – whose evolution in the long run is more assured – and, in this vast product group, by giving precedence to those products that meet the most severe requirements of the consumers, very large coils and plates, ultra-thin plates, coated plates, stainless steel, etc.

Although the steel industry did not account directly for more than some 1.2 per cent in the Belgian GNP, its indirect contribution to the Belgian economy remained substantial. Among the heavy industries the steel industry was still the main consumer of transport by rail and waterways, and was the second Belgian electricity consumer after the chemical industry.

The Textile Plan which aimed to stabilize employment in the textile and clothing industries at 100,000 people must be considered as an example of successful sectoral recovery. Although total employment in 1991 had fallen well below the level of 90,000, the Belgian textile and clothing industries had recovered from the slump

Table 10.4 The Belgian steel industry, 1987–90 (in billion Belgian francs)

Year	Turnover	Gross profits	Net profits	Steel output*
1987	165	+ 13	− 1	9,722
1988	197	+ 33	+ 19	11,163
1989	230	+ 44	+ 30	10,894
1990	209	+ 29	+ 18	11,360

* In '000 tonnes

Source: Staalindustrie Verbond, Brussels

of the 1970s and the 1980s. Between 1985 and 1990 productivity increased by 35 to 45 per cent and exports picked up (see Table 10.5). A sharp decrease of total output in cotton spinning was compensated for by an increased output in other branches (weaving, clothing). In 1990 textile products still counted for 7.3 per cent of total Belgian exports.

Table 10.5 Export of textiles, 1980–91

Year	(1)	1985=100	(2)	1985=100
1980	119,860	60	941,615	84
1981	127,211	64	954,018	86
1982	140,932	71	929,456	83
1983	161,292	81	1,006,526	90
1984	189,072	95	1,129,406	101
1985	199,875	100	1,115,436	100
1986	192,939	97	1,112,517	100
1987	193,586	97	1,142,139	102
1988	205,916	103	1,192,399	107
1989	232,776	116	1,357,768	122
1990	236,860	119	1,402,387	126
1991	239,094	120	1,454,310	130

(1) In million Belgian francs
(2) In tonnes

Source: Conseil Central de l'Economie, Brussels

The Belgian State acquired minority stakes in some 200 (Flemish) textile firms. Among them were big companies like De Witte-Lietaer, Imperial Tufting, Lano, Neyrinck, and UTEXBEL. A famous case was the take-over of FABELTA (a major producer of nylon fibres owned by the Belgian State) by the carpet weaver Beaulieu. Beaulieu invested about 1 billion Belgian francs in a new FABELTA factory. Beaulieu's investment was largely financed by a governmental loan the Belgian authorities had provided by infringing EC directives. Finally the Beaulieu refused to pay back these subsidies the government wanted to recover (Verduyn 1992: 97–123).

The Verlipack group (glass products) went bankrupt in 1985 and was taken over by Walter de Backer. De Backer received a subsidy of 200 million Belgian francs to be invested in the Verlipack glass factories. But in 1989 it was revealed that the real Verlipack owner was the Beaulieu group (Verduyn 1992: 201–2). The Verreries de Momignies were reorganized and in 1988 sold to the Heinz group.

The Belgian shipyards could not overcome their difficulties because subsidies paid by all governments to their own shipbuilding industry disadvantaged the Belgian wharves, especially the Boelwerf which specialized in building carriers and tankers. The authorities subsidized the Belgian shipping firms when modernizing their fleet, but subsidies could also be obtained for new ships built on foreign wharves. All wharves (Boelwerf, Mercantile–Béliard, Meuse et Sambre, Fulton Marine, Scheepswerven van Rupelmonde, Scheepswerven van Langerbrugge, Nieuwe Scheldewerven, Nieuwe Scheepswerven St Barbara) had to be floated via the regional investment companies. Nevertheless in 1992 the Boelwerf (1,800 employees) went bankrupt because its private partners, after having heavily invested in shipping activities (in 1991 they had taken over CMB from the SGB), refused to conclude a settlement proposed by the Flemish authorities. In 1993 the heavily indebted Dutch Begemann group acquired a majority stake in the new Boelwerf, a transaction the European Commission criticized because of the fact that the Begemann group was unable to finance its shipbuilding activities in Flanders.

PRIVATIZATIONS

In May 1988 Prime Minister Martens announced in his governmental declaration that a Commission on Privatization would study a reform of the public banks and insurance companies. The commission advised a complete reorganization of the public financial sector. The government adopted these conclusions (Act of 17 June 1991). In 1992 a public holding company ASLK Holding, grouping the public savings bank CGER–ASLK, the CGER–ASLK insurance company and two minor sectoral credit banks for craftsmen and peasants, was formed and then started negotiating with the Belgian–Dutch insurance company Fortis (Algemene Maatschappij tot Exploitatie van Verzekeringen – AMEV) on ceding a 50 per cent stake in its capital. Furthermore, the Commission on Privatization advised that the municipal credit bank (Crédit Communal – Gemeentekrediet) would absorb the SNCI–NMKN and the central mortgage company CBHK–OCCH. But the municipal credit bank opposed this merger because the 50 per cent stake the State held in the SNCI–NMKN would cost 4 to 5 billion Belgian francs.

Meanwhile in 1993 budgetary problems incited the Dehaene government to start a debate on a complete privatization of the public sector. The Dehaene government estimated that ASLK Holding, the SNI–NIM, the regional investment companies with their subsidiaries, Distrigaz, Belgacom (telecommunications), and the National Lottery, all could be completely privatized for 140 to 170 billion Belgian francs.

For many years the Belgian government had subsidized SABENA. The last reorganization of SABENA dated back to the early 1980s. Meanwhile the airline company was looking for a foreign partner. But all potential foreign partners hesitated to get involved in SABENA as long as this firm was accumulating losses (in 1989 1.3 billion Belgian francs and in 1990 7.2 billion Belgian francs). In 1991 the Belgian government decided to float its airline company after having obtained the approval of the European Commission. SABENA's capital was increased by 43.4 billion Belgian francs in order to compensate all previously accumulated losses and depreciations. Then Air France was invited to move in. But in the summer of 1993, when SABENA World Airlines was facing another liquidity crisis, the government refrained from floating the company. Apparently, the government had become more interested in enlarging Brussels Airport than in keeping afloat a relatively small and undercapitalized airline company operating in a highly competitive market.

LAST TANGO IN BRUSSELS

The idea of a European Economic Area and the Maastricht Agreement of December 1991 received full support from the

Belgian government because monetary stability and a united internal market would boost investment by multinational enterprises established in Belgium and exports to the EC countries. In 1991 about 75 per cent of Belgium's exports went to EC countries of which Germany (24 per cent) had become by far the most important trading partner. Meanwhile all sectors of the Belgian economy were opened up to foreign competition. That was also the case with the financial sector (banks and insurance companies) and with the food processing industry and agriculture (Demblon et al. 1990: 79–86). Even enterprises in the Belgian distribution sector (Grand Bazar–Innovation–Bon Marché – GIB, Delhaize) internationalized and acquired subsidiaries abroad, especially in the USA, or allied with French groups (Cora). But traditional industrial product groups like textiles, heavy chemicals, metal products and steel, and automobiles still dominated the balance of trade making the Belgian economy extremely vulnerable to any recession in the neighbouring countries, especially in Germany (see Table 10.6).

Table 10.6 Belgian trade balance, 1991
(in billion Belgian francs)

	Export		Import	
	Value	*%*	*Value*	*%*
Fishery/agricultural products	93.0	2.3	203.5	4.9
Energy	177.8	4.4	368.6	8.9
Minerals	551.6	13.7	412.6	10.0
Chemicals	623.3	15.5	509.7	12.4
Electrical/metal products	1,240.3	30.8	1,452.1	35.2
Foodstuffs	321.4	8.0	229.5	5.6
Textiles/clothing	281.5	7.0	233.3	5.7
Diamonds	273.2	6.8	–	–
Others	461.9	11.5	710.3	17.2
Total	4,024.0	100.0	4,119.6	100.0

Source: De Belgische economie in 1991: 40

Although the EC is still a long way from becoming the political union to which its founders aspired and its progress had been markedly lopsided, its influence has become of crucial importance for Belgian politics. The EC has reinforced centrifugal tendencies which had been contained during the previous decades by compromises worked out by federalists and Belgian unionists who were both present in the traditional political parties and the trade unions. Moreover, the neo-corporatist patterns of interest intermediation with their strongly centralized structures prevailed in the past over regionalist tendencies because many trade union leaders and entrepreneurs were convinced of the virtues of a united labour front. Nonetheless, centrifugal forces reinforced their influence on public opinion and forced the political parties to adapt their strategy.

When in 1993 the Dehaene government succeeded in reforming the Constitution, Belgium had become a federal state with directly elected regional parliaments appointing their own regional governments. But as soon as these reforms were carried out discussions started about a further decentralization and the establishing of a confederal state. Especially Flemish politicians and opinion-makers discovered that transfer payments from Flanders to Wallonia could only be stopped when Flanders acquired its complete financial and fiscal autonomy. Thus solidarity between Flemings and Walloons became the subject of a bargaining process between the two communities. In this case a further sub-dividing of the remaining central institutions, such as the National Bank, the Belgian Army, the diplomatic service, etc., and a complete disintegration of Belgium had to be taken into consideration. Although the King and the French-speaking pressure groups were opposed to this trend, centrifugal tendencies were reinforced by economic decline in Wallonia and better performances by the Flemish economy.

Because of the weakening of the traditional French-speaking bourgeoisie and the disappearance of the French language from public life in Flanders the viability of a Belgian State with its francophone predominance was undermined. With its bourgeoisie the Belgian State was fading away as a support for all centralizing forces traditionally symbolized by the King, the Belgian financial groups and the aristocracy. Because Wallonia and Flanders had acquired their own political and cultural identity, their political leaders were longing for a political power base in their own region. Thus they were losing interest in Belgian political affairs. This process was accelerated by the decline of heavy industry in Wallonia, by the decolonialization in Africa and by the growing economic influence of multinational capital in Belgium. This decline of Belgian capitalism was completed by an overall decline of the Belgian holding companies. During the 1980s all important Belgian holding companies lost their autonomy or were acquired by French groups. By taking in 1988 a majority stake in the SGB, the French group Compagnie Financière de Suez superseded the Belgian bourgeoisie as collective portfolio investor. In selling the SGB, the Belgian bourgeoisie also had danced its last tango.

BIBLIOGRAPHY

Allard P., Beaud, M., Bellon, B., Lévy, A.-M. and Lienart, S. (1978) *Dictionnaire des groupes industriels et financiers en France*, Paris: Editions du Seuil.

L'Année sociale (1960–92) Brussels: Institut de Sociologie, Université Libre de Bruxelles (1960–3); Editions de l'Institut de Sociologie, Université Libre de Bruxelles (1964–80); Editions de l'Université de Bruxelles (1981–92).

Aszkenazy, H. (1971) *Les grandes sociétés européennes*, Brussels: CRISP.

Bairoch, P., Deldycke, T., Limbor, J. and Vandenabeele, G. (1966) *L'Economie belge et internationale*, Brussels: Université Libre de Bruxelles.

— and Vandenabeele, G. (1968) *L'Economie belge et internationale*, Brussels: Université Libre de Bruxelles.

De Bankcommissie 1935–1960 (1960) Brussels: Bankcommissie.

Baudhuin, F. (1945) *L'Economie belge sous l'occupation 1940–1944*, Brussels: Etablissements Emile Bruylant.

— (1946) *Histoire économique de la Belgique 1914–1939*, Brussels: Etablissements Emile Bruylant. 2 vols.

— (1958) *Histoire économique de la Belgique 1945–1956*, Brussels: Etablissements Emile Bruylant.

— (1970) *Histoire économique de la Belgique 1957–1968*, Brussels: Etablissements Emile Bruylant.

Baumier, J. (1988) *La galaxie Paribas*, Paris: Plon.

Bekx, P., Cartrysse, R., Verbist, P. and Vulsteke, P. (1983) *Les consommations d'énergie dans l'industrie II: Modélisation et prévision*, Brussels: Bureau du Plan.

Belart, U., Keller, T. and Heinertz, E.B. (n.d.) *Opkomst en ondergang van Ivar Kreuger*, Amsterdam: Allert de Lange.

België. Basisstatistieken, 1965–1974 (1976) Brussels: Belgisch Instituut voor Voorlichting en Documentatie.

Belgique, pays en voie de sous-développement: Pour une restructuration démocratique de l'économie précédé du Manifeste du GEM (1978) Brussels: Du Monde Entier and Fondation J. Jacquemotte. Also published as *België naar de onderontwikkeling: Voor een demokratische herstrukturering van de ekonomie, voorafgegaan door het Manifest van de GEM* (1978) Louvain: Kritak.

De Belgische economie in . . . [annual publication] (1975–91) Brussels: Ministerie van Economische Zaken.

Belgische Petroleum Federatie (1978–91) *Jaarverslagen*, Brussels.

Bell Telephone Manufacturing Company 1882–1982 (1982) Antwerp: Bell Telephone Mfg Co. NV.

Berger, P. (1925) *La Belgique: Ouvrage de géographie économique*, Brussels: Librairie Falk Fils.

Bogaert, E.-W. (1945) *La construction navale en Belgique*, Brussels: Office de Publicité.

Bouman, J. (1956) *Anton Philips*, Amsterdam: Meulenhoff.

Bouvier, P. (1965) *L'accession du Congo belge à l'indépendance: Essai d'analyse sociologique. Colloque du Centre national d'étude des problèmes sociaux de l'industralisation en Afrique noire*, Brussels: Editions de l'Institut de Sociologie, Université Libre de Bruxelles.

Bruck, C. (1988) *The Predators' Ball: The Junk Bond Raiders and the Man Who Staked Them*, New York: Simon & Schuster.

Buitengewoon Congres BSP van 4 en 5 juli 1959, Verslagen BSP (1959) Brussels: BSP.

Buitenlandse investeringen in België (1979) Brussels: Ministerie van Economische Zaken, 2 vols.

Bulletin mensuel du commerce avec les pays étrangers (1919–39) Brussels, Ministère des Finances de Belgique.

Burk, K. (1989) *Morgan Grenfell 1838–1988: The Biography of a Merchant Bank*, Oxford: Oxford University Press.

Bussière, E. (1984) 'La sidérurgie belge durant l'entre-deux-guerres: le cas d'Ougrée–Marihaye (1919–1939)', *Revue belge d'histoire contemporaine* 15(3–4):303–80.

Buyens, F., De Haes, L., Hogenkamp, B. and Meynen, A. (1985) *Vechten voor onze rechten, 60–61, de staking tegen de Eenheidswet*, Louvain: Kritak.

Cantillon, B., Peeters, J. and De Ridder, E. (1987) *Atlas van de sociale zekerheid in België: Kostprijs – financiering – doelmatigheid*, Louvain and Amersfoort: Acco.

Capron, M. (1979) 'Sud-Luxembourg: une réconversion sabotée?', *La Revue nouvelle* 70(12): 525–39.

—— (1981) 'La crise sidérurgique en Belgique et en France', *Contradictions* 27–8: 65–104.

—— (1981–2) 'Le Dossier sidérurgique', *Contradictions* 30: 91–144.

—— (1987) 'The state, the regions and industrial redevelopment: The challenge of the Belgian steel crisis', in Y. Mény and V. Wright (eds) *The Politics of Steel: Western Europe and the Steel Industry in the Crisis Years (1974–1984)*, Berlin and New York: Walter de Gruyter.

Carbonelle, C. (1987) *Jacques de Staercke. Opdracht: ondernemen*, Tielt: Lannoo.

Carton, A., Henrotte, J., Śabic, F. and de Wasseige, Y. (1976) *Emploi et politique de développement en Wallonie*, Brussels: Editions Vie Ouvrière.

Cartrysse, R., Devulder, Y., Rigaux, D. and Verbiest, P. (1984)

Energieverbruik in de nijverheid: Historische ontwikkeling, modelbouw en prognoses. Syntheserapport, Brussels: Planbureau.

Cassiers, I. (1989) *Croissance, crise et régulation en économie ouverte: La Belgique entre les deux guerres*, Brussels: De Boeck–Wesmael.

Chlepner, B.-S. (1930) *Le marché financier depuis cent ans*, Bruxelles: Librairie Falk.

—— (1972) *Cent ans d'histoire sociale en Belgique*, Brussels: Editions de l'Université de Bruxelles.

Chomé, J. (1960) *La crise congolaise*, Brussels: Editions de Remarques Congolaises.

Compagnie Maritime Belge (Lloyd Royal) Antwerpen 1895–1945 (1947) Antwerp.

Congo 1885–1960. Socialistische stellingen (n.d.) Brussels: E. Vandervelde-Instituut de Brouckère-Stichting.

Conjunctuurbrief (1980–92) Brussels: Ministerie van Economische Zaken.

Cottenier, J., De Boosere, P. and Gounet, T. (1989) *De Generale 1822–1992*, Berchem: EPO.

Cut in Antwerp: Antwerpen, wereldcentrum voor diamant (1982) Antwerp: Uitgave HRD.

Cuypers, P. (1988) *Het bod op België: Carlo de Benedetti's greep naar de Generale Maatschappij*, Wommelgem: Uitgeverij Den Gulden Engel.

Daems, H. (1978) *The Holding Company and Corporate Control*, Leyden and Boston: Martinus Nijhoff.

De Bock, W., Coeck, J., Goossens, P. and Mthombeni, M. (1978) *Suikerbossie: België en Zuidelijk Afrika*, Brussels and Amsterdam: Manteau.

De Boeck, A. (1989) 'La SOFINA (Société de Transports et d'Entreprises Industrielles), 1989–1914', in M. Dumoulin (ed.) *Présences belges dans le monde à l'aube du XXe siècle*, Louvain-la-Neuve: Academia and Brussels: Univers-Cité.

La Décision politique en Belgique (1965) Paris: Librairie Armand Colin.

Declercq, G. and Vanneste, O. (1954) *Structurele werkloosheid in West-Vlaanderen: Een regionaal–economische studie*, Roeselare: NV Bank van Roeselare.

Degroote, A., Franssen, P., Hobin, V., Kruithof, J., Laureys, F., Lever, L. and Vranken, J. (1983) *Inleveren*, Berchem: EPO.

De Haes, L. (1978) *Het wangedrag van de multinationals*, Louvain: Kritak.

De Jong, L. (1979) 'Londen', in *Het Koninkrijk der Nederlanden in de Tweede Wereldoorlog*, The Hague: Martinus Nijhoff.

De Jonghe, A. (1972) *Hitler en het politieke lot van België*, Antwerp: De Nederlandsche Boekhandel.

Delaet, J.-L. (1986) 'La mécanisation de la verrerie à vitres à Charleroi dans la première moitié du XXe siècle', in G. Kurgan-Van Hentenryk and J. Stengers (eds) *L'innovation technologique: Facteur de changement (XIXe–XXe siècles)*, Brussels: Editions de l'Université de Bruxelles.

Delbovier, M., Corten, A., Creutz, E., Piraux, M., Englebert, J., Dechamps, J., Persoons, F. and Hallet, J. (1969) *Une Wallonie pour les travailleurs*, Brussels: Editions Vie Ouvrière.

Deleeck, H. (1992) *De architectuur van de welvaartsstaat*, Louvain: Acco.

De Leener, G. (1946) *Un grand belge, Ernest Solvay*, Brussels: Office de Publicité.

Deloof, J. (1979) *De tijd is veel veranderd: Een kroniek over honderd jaar in en om Bekaert te Zwevegem*, Zwevegem: Bekaert and Tielt: Lannoo.

Delpérée, F. (1983) *Chroniques de crise 1977–1982*, Brussels: CRISP.

De Man, H. (1935) *De uitvoering van het Plan van den Arbeid*, Antwerp and The Hague: De Sikkel & Servire.

Demany, F. (1946) *On a volé 64 milliards! L'Histoire de la Banque d'Emission*, Brussels.

—— (1959) *SOS Congo (Chronique d'un soulèvement)*, Brussels: Labor.

Demblon, D., Aertsen, J., Goeteyn, L., Groessens, G. and Van Doninck, B. (1990) *100 jaar boeren*, Berchem: EPO.

Depoortere, R. (1989) 'L'évaluation des dommages subis par l'industrie belge au cours de la première guerre mondiale', *Revue belge de philologie et d'histoire* 67(4): 748–69.

De Preter, R. (1983) *De 200 rijkste families: Geld en macht in de wereld van de holdings en de miljonairs*, Berchem: EPO.

Deprez, R. (1963) *La grande grève (décembre 1960–janvier 1961): Ses origines, son déroulement, ses leçons*, Brussels: Fondation J. Jacquemotte.

De Ridder, H. (1983) *De keien van de Wetstraat*, Louvain: Davidsfonds.

—— (1986) *Geen winnaars in de Wetstraat*, Louvain: Davidsfonds.

—— (1989) *Sire, geef me honderd dagen*, Louvain: Davidsfonds.

—— (1991) *Omtrent Wilfried Martens*, Tielt: Lannoo.

De Smet, L., Keeris, H. and Vlassenbroek, W. (1971) *Panorama van de wereld: België Luxemburg*, Roermond: J.J. Romen & Zonen.

Dethomas, B. and Fralon, J.-A. (1989) *Les milliards de l'orgueil: L'affaire de la Société Générale de Belgique*, Paris: Gallimard.

Dewachter, A. (1992) *Besluitvorming in politiek België*, Louvain and Amersfoort: ACCO.

De Waele, M. (1983) *Staal: Een monster zonder waarde?*, Antwerp: Kluwer.

Dierckx, K. (1989) 'De NMKN: 70 jaar steun aan de Belgische economie', *Documentatieblad* 2: 121–36.

Dodge, P. (1966) *Beyond Marxism: The Faith and Works of Hendrik de Man*, The Hague: Martinus Nijhoff.

Dossier 'Question Royale' (1974) Brussels: CRISP.

Dubois, L. (1988) *Lafarge Coppée 150 ans d'industrie: Une mémoire pour demain*, Paris: Belfond.

Durviaux, R. (1947) *La banque mixte, origine et soutien de l'expansion économique de la Belgique*, Brussels: Etablissements Emile Bruylant.

De economische toekomst van België: Een verslag aan de Koning Boudewijnstichting (1981) Brussels.

Een eeuw vestiging in België 1872–1972 (1972) Brussels: Bank van Parijs en de Nederlanden België.

Ekonomische berichten (1984–92) Brussels: Paribas Bank België.

L'Electronucléaire en France (1975) Paris: Editions du Seuil.

Empain, Baron E.J. (1985) *La vie en jeu*, Paris: J.C. Lattès.

Een energie-onderneming in de samenleving (1984) Antwerp: Verenigde Energiebedrijven van het Scheldeland–EBES NV.

Er is opnieuw een toekomst (1985) Brussels: PVV.

Evalenko, R. (1968) *Régime économique de la Belgique*, Brussels and Louvain: Vander.

Faire face à la crise: Rénover et agir 1. Congrès des 27 et 28 mars 1982 Bruxelles, PS (1982) Brussels: Institut Emile Vandervelde.

Féaux, V. (1963) *Cinq semaines de lutte sociale: La grève de l'hiver 1960–1961*, Bruxelles: Editions de l'Institut de Sociologie de l'Université Libre de Bruxelles.

Fitzmaurice, J. (1983) *The Politics of Belgium: Crisis and Compromise in a Plural Society*, London: C. Hurst & Company.

Gandois, J. (1986) *Operatie Staal: Het relaas van een crisismanager*, Tielt: Lannoo.

Geerts, L. (1979) *De bezetting van RBP*, Louvain: Kritak.

Gerard, E. (1985) *De Katholieke Partij in crisis: Partijpolitiek leven in België (1918–1940)*, Louvain: Kritak.

Gérard-Libois, J. and Gotovitch, J. (n.d.) *L'An 40: La Belgique occupée*, Brussels: Pol-His.

—— (1983) *Léopold III: Le non-retour*, Brussels: CRISP.

Gérard-Libois, J. and Lewin, R. (1992) *La Belgique entre dans la guerre froide et l'Europe (1947–53)*, Brussels: CRISP.

Gillingham, J. (1977) *Belgian Business in the Nazi New Order*, Ghent: Jan Dhondt Foundation.

—— (1991) *Coal, Steel, and the Rebirth of Europe, 1945–1955: The Germans and French from Ruhr Conflict to Economic Community*, Cambridge: Cambridge University Press.

Gotovitch, J. (1981) *De Belgische socialisten in Londen*, Antwerp: Standaard.

—— (1983) *Sous la Régence: Résistance et pouvoir*, Brussels: CRISP.

Govaert, S. (1985) 'Leysonitis. De onstuitbare opgang van André Leysen', *De nieuwe maand* 28(2), 13–22.

Groueff, S. (1967) *Manhattan Project: The Untold Story of the Making of the Atomic Bomb*, New York: Bantam Books.

Gutt, C. (1971) *La Belgique au carrefour 1940–1944*, Paris: Fayard.

Hahn, C.H. (1953) *Der Schuman-Plan*, Munich: Richard Pflaum.

Halsberghe, E. and Van den Bulcke, D. (1981) *Werkgelegenheid en multinationale ondernemingen: Een evaluatie van tien jaar buitenlandse investeringen en desinvesteringen in de Belgische industrie*, Ghent: SERUG.

Hancké, B. (1991) 'The crisis of national unions: Belgian labor in decline', *Politics and Society* 19(4): 463–87.

Hansenne, M. (1985) *Emploi: Les scénarios du possible*, Paris and Gembloux: Duculot.

Haven van Antwerpen: Beknopte Gids (n.d.), Antwerp: Stad Antwerpen.

Henau, B. (1993) 'De leidende economische kringen en de oplossingen voor de crisis, 1930–1940', in *1940 België, een maatschappij in crisis en oorlog – Belgique, une société en crise, un pays en guerre*, Brussels: NCWO II/CREHSGM.

Herremans, J. (ed.) (1988) *Het Belgische bedrijfsleven: Een doorlichting van de belangrijkste economische activiteiten*. Brussels: VBO and INBEL.

—— (1990) *Het Belgische bedrijfsleven: Een actualisering van de sectoriële gegevens*, Brussels: VBO.

Hoflack, K. (1989) *Theo Lefèvre, staatsman*, Antwerp and Baarn: Hadewijch.

Hofmans, G. (1992) 'Het probleem van de ekonomische kollaboratie. De houding van de Groep de Launoit tijdens de tweede wereldoorlog', *Bijdragen – Cahiers Navorsings- en Studiecentrum voor de Geschiedenis van de Tweede Wereldoorlog* 15: 5–52.

Hogg, R.L. (1986) *Structural Rigidities and Policy Inertia in Inter-War Belgium*, Brussels: Koninklijke Academie voor Wetenschappen, Letteren en Schone Kunsten van België, Klasse der Letteren.

Hulpiau, R. (1945) *De economische evolutie der Belgische cementindustrie tusschen 1920 en 1940*, Antwerp and The Hague: Standaard.

Huysse, L. and Dhondt, S. (1991) *Onverwerkt verleden: Collaboratie en repressie in België 1942–1952*, Louvain: Kritak.

'De invloed van de internationale economische integratie en samenwerking op de Belgische landbouw' (1968) *Internationale Spectator* 22(19): 1603–767.

Jacobs, D. (1988) *Gereguleerd staal: Nationale en internationale economische regulering in de Westeuropese staalindustrie 1750–1950*, Enschede: Sneldruk.

Janssen, D. (1981) *Discours inaugural du nouveau président de la FEB*, Brussels: Fédération des Entreprises de Belgique.

Joye, P. (1960) *Les trusts en Belgique: La concentration capitaliste*, Brussels: Société Populaire d'Editions.

—— (1984), 'L'agroalimentaire. Trusts et holdings en Belgique', *Cahiers marxistes* 123: 2–11.

Kalb, M.G. (1982) *The Congo Cables: The Cold War in Africa – From Eisenhower to Kennedy*, New York: Macmillan.

Keulemans, D. (1989) 'De institutionalisering van het sociaal-economisch overleg: De wet van 20 september 1948 houdende organisatie van het bedrijfsleven', in E. Witte, J.C. Burgelman, and P. Stouthuysen (eds) *Tussen restauratie en vernieuwing: Aspecten van de naoorlogse Belgische politiek (1944–1950)*, Brussels: VUB Press.

Kindleberger, C.P. (1967) *Europe's Postwar Growth: The Role of Labor Supply*, Cambridge, Mass.: Harvard University Press.

Krul, N.G. (1964) *La politique conjoncturelle en Belgique, aux Pays-Bas et en Suisse*, Geneva: Librairie Droz.

Kruyt, J.P. (1932) *België: Boeren en arbeiders sedert den Wereldoorlog*, Groningen-Batavia: P. Noordhoff.

Kuisel, R.F. (1981) *Capitalism and the State in Modern France*, Cambridge: Cambridge University Press.

Lamfalussy, A. (1961) *Investment and Growth: The Case of Belgium*, London: Macmillan.

Lamy, R. (1990) *Narration authentique d'une OPA: Bataille pour la Société Générale*, Gembloux: Duculot.

Lanning, G. and Mueller, M. (1979) *Africa Undermined: Mining*

Companies and the Underdevelopment of Africa, Harmondsworth: Penguin.

Laureyssens, J. (1984) 'La Société Genstar: Histoire d'une réussite belge au Canada', in G. Kurgan-Van Hentenryk and J. Laureyssens (eds) *Un siécle d'investissements belges au Canada*, Brussels: Editions de l'Université Libre de Bruxelles.

Lekime, F. (1992) *La mangeuse de cuivre: La saga de l'Union Minière du Haut-Katanga 1906–1966*, Brussels: Didier Hatier.

Lemoine, R. (1929) 'The Banking System of Belgium', in H. Parker Willis and B.H. Beckhart (eds) *Foreign Banking Systems*, New York: Henry Holt & Co.

Lentzen, E. and Vincent, A. (1981) *Les groupes d'entreprises en 1980: Les principales opérations de restructuration*, Brussels: CRISP.

Leysen, A. (1984) *Krisissen zijn uitdagingen: Vrijmoedige overwegingen van een ondernemer*, Tielt and Weesp: Lannoo.

Liefmann, R. (1932) *Cartels, Concerns and Trusts*, New York: Arno Press.

Loeb, N. (1965) *Le patronat industriel belge et la CEE*, Brussels: Editions de l'Institut de Sociologie de l'Université Libre de Bruxelles.

Luykx, T. (1967) *Geschiedenis van de economische bewustwording in Vlaanderen 1926–1966*, Antwerp: De Nederlandsche Boekhandel.

—— (1972) *Dr Alfons Van de Perre en zijn tijd (1872–1925)*, Antwerp and Utrecht: Standaard.

Luyten, D. (1990) 'Het katholieke patronaat en het korporatisme in de jaren dertig en tijdens de bezetting', *Cahiers – Bijdragen – Centre de Recherches et d'Etudes historiques de la Seconde Guerre Mondiale* 13: 91–148.

Mabille, X. (1986) *Histoire politique de la Belgique: Facteurs et acteurs de changement*, Brussels: CRISP.

McKay, J. (1970) *Pioneers for Profit: Foreign Entrepreneurship and Russian Industrialization 1885–1913*, Chicago: Chicago University Press.

Manifest van Kortrijk: Handvest van het modern liberalisme (1982) Brussels: PVV.

Marks, S. (1981) *Innocent Abroad: Belgium at the Paris Peace Conference of 1919*, Chapel Hill: University of North Carolina Press.

Martens, W. (1985) *Parole donnée*, Brussels: Didier Hartier.

Maurel, A. (1992) *Le Congo de la colonisation belge à l'indépendance*, Paris: L'Harmattan.

Meynen, A. (1978) 'De grote werkstaking 1960–1961', *Belgische tijdschrift voor nieuwste geschiedenis* 9(3–4): 481–513.

Michel, H. (1936) *La dévaluation belge: Une opération aussi délicate que décevante*, Paris: Imprimerie du Palais.

Michel, R. (1971) *Les investissements américains en Belgique*, Brussels: CRISP.

Milward, A.S. (1984) *The Reconstruction of Western Europe 1945–51*, London: Methuen.

Moden, J. and Sloover, J. (1980) *Le patronat belge: Discours et idéologie (1973–1980)*, Brussels: CRISP.

Mommen, A. (1982) *De teloorgang van de Belgische bourgeoisie*, Louvain: Kritak.

—— (1985) 'Albert Frère redt Groep Brussel-Lambert', *De nieuwe maand* 28(6): 36–45.

—— (1987) *Een tunnel zonder einde: Het neo-liberalisme van Martens V en VI*, Antwerp: Kluwer.

Moons, J. (1957) *De economische structuur van de Kempische steenkolennijverheid*, Hasselt: Limburgse Economische Raad.

Moreau, R. (1984) *Combat syndical et conscience wallonne: Du syndicalisme clandestin au Mouvement Populaire Wallon 1943–1963*, Liège: Editions de la Fondation André Renard, Brussels: Editions Vie Ouvrière and Mt-s.-Marchienne: Institut Jules Destrée.

Morphologie des groupes financiers (1966) Bruxelles: CRISP.

Nationale Bank van België (1974–92) *Verslagen*, Brussels: Nationale Bank van België.

De nationale rekeningen van België 1963–1971 (1972) Brussels: NIS.

Neuville, J. (1981) *La lutte ouvrière pour la maîtrise du temps: La conquête des 8 heures et la revendication des 40 heures*, Brussels: Editions Vie Ouvrière.

—— and Yerna, J. (1990) *Le choc de l'hiver '60–'61: Les grèves contre la loi unique*, Brussels: CRISP.

NMNS 1988 (1989), Brussels.

Norris, W. (1987) *The Man Who Fell from the Sky*, New York: Viking.

Nova, W. (1970) *Dossier pour un gouvernment wallon: Fédéralisme et perspectives économiques*, Liège: Editions de la Fondation André Renard.

OECD (1979–92) *OECD Economic Surveys Belgium Luxemburg*, Paris: OECD.

Olyslager, P.M. (1947) *De localiseering der Belgische nijverheid*, Antwerp and The Hague: Standaard.

OMGUS. *Ermittlungen gegen die Deutsche Bank* (1985) Nördlingen: Franz Greno.

OMGUS. *Ermittlungen gegen die Dresdner Bank* (1986) Nördlingen: Franz Greno.

'De overheidshulp aan bedrijven' (1987) *Tijdschrift van de Nationale Bank* 62(1):5–28.

Pasture, P. and Mampuys, J. (1990) *In de ban van het getal: Ledenanalyse van het ACV 1900–1990*, Louvain: Hoger Instituut voor de Arbeid-KU Leuven.

Peeters, S., Blomme, J., Buyst, E., Goossens, M., Houbrechts, G., Nackaerts, P., Peeters, S., Pepermans, G. and Schroeven, C. (1986) *Reconstruction of the Belgian National Income, 1920–1939: Methodology and Results*, Louvain: Katholieke Universiteit Leuven (Centrum voor Economische Studiën).

Phlips, L. (1962) *De l'intégration des marchés*, Louvain and Paris: Nauwelaerts.

Priorité 100,000 emplois. Un objectif pour le rassemblement. Quelle Wallonie? Quel socialisme? Un objectif pour le rassemblement des progressistes (1975) Liège: Editions de la Fondation André Renard and Brussels: Editions Vie Ouvrière.

Quaden, G. (1984) *La crise des finances publiques*, Liège: CIRIEC.

—— (ed.) (1987) *L'économie belge dans la crise*, Brussels: Labor.

Quelle Wallonie? Quel socialisme? Les bases d'un rassemblement des progressistes (1971) Liège: Editions de la Fondation André Renard and Brussels: Editions Vie Ouvrière.

Quévit, M. (1978) *Les causes du déclin wallon: L'influence du pouvoir politique et des groupes financiers sur le développement régional*, Brussels: Editions Vie Ouvrière.

Raes, K. (1983) *Aan hen de keuze? Een kritisch essay over de ideologie van het neo-liberaal bezitsindividualisme*, Ghent: Masereelfonds.

Raid sur la Générale (1988) Brussels: Edition de l'Echo de la Bourse.

Ranieri, L. (1985) *Emile Francqui, ou l'intelligence créatrice 1863–1935*, Gembloux: Duculot.

Régime fiscal des personnes physiques sous la nouvelle législation. Loi du 20 novembre 1962 (1963) Brussels: Banque de la Société Générale de Belgique.

Reuchlin, H. (1978) 'Handelsvaart', in R. Baetens, P.M. Bosscher and H. Reuchlin (eds) *Maritieme geschiedenis der Nederlanden*, Bussum: De Boer Maritiem.

Rigaux, D. (1983) *Energieverbruik in de industrie: Evolutie per sektor (1970–1981)*, Brussels: Planbureau.

Rijksdienst voor Arbeidsvoorziening (1992) *Jaarverslag*, Brussels.

Scholliers, P. (1985) *Loonindexering en sociale vrede. Koopkracht en klassenstrijd in België tijdens het Interbellum*, Brussels: Vrije Universiteit Brussel (Centrum voor Hedendaagse Sociale Geschiedenis).

—— (1993) 'Strijd rond de koopkracht 1930–1945', in: *1940 België, een maatschappij in crisis en oorlog – Belgique, une société en crise, un pays en guerre*, Brussels: NCWO II/CREHSGM.

Siaens, A. (1985) *Le prince et la conjoncture: Les sources politiques d'instabilité et de déclin*, Paris and Gembloux: Duculot.

Slomp, H. and Van Mierlo, T. (1984) *Arbeidsverhoudingen in België*, Utrecht and Antwerp: Spectrum. 2 vols.

Smets, D. and Rens, J. (1976) *Historique du Centre Syndical Belge à Londres 1941–1944*, Brussels: FGTB.

Een socialistisch plan voor het ekonomisch herstel (1981) Brussels: SEVI.

—— (1972) *Société Générale de Belgique*, Brussels: Société Générale de Belgique.

Société Générale Belgique (1979–87) *Jaarverslag*, Brussels.

SOS Sidérurgie (1978) Brussels: Du Monde Entier and Fondation J. Jacquemotte.

Spaak, P.-H. (1969) *Combats inachevés*, Paris: Fayard, 2 vols.

SP–alternatief, samen sterk voor vrede en werk (1983) Brussels: SEVI.

Statistieken – Statistiques (1970–1991) (1992) Brussels: FABRIMETAL.

Stengers, J. (1989) *Congo: Mythes et réalités. 100 ans d'histoire*, Gembloux: Duculot.

Stouthuysen, R. (1980) *Mutatiebeleid: noodzaak voor een zinvolle ekonomische toekomst*, Hasselt: Vlaams Ekonomisch Verbond.

Tableau annuel du commerce avec les pay étrangers (1919–31) Brussels: Ministère des Finances de Belgique.

Trappeniers, F. (1967) *Les avantages comparatifs dans le Marché Commun Européen*, Louvain and Paris: Nauwelaerts.

Troisième rapport relatif au problème des investissements (1948), Brussels: A. Goemaere.

Turani, G. (1988) *L'ingegnere: Carlo De Benedetti e l'assalto ai cieli della finanza*, n.p.: Sperling & Kupfer Editori.

Union Minière du Haut-Katanga, 1906–1956 (1956) Brussels: Editions L. Cuyvers.

Van Audenhove, M. (1980) *De grote economische crisis van de jaren dertig*, Brussels: Gemeentekrediet van België.

Van Broekhoven, E. and Bosman, E. (1981) *Energie in België*, Antwerp: Standaard Uitgeverij.

Vandenabeele, G., Gelders, H. and Serepfanoglu, S. (1969) *L'économie belge et internationale*, Brussels: Université Libre de Bruxelles.

Van den Bulcke, D. (1981) *Industriële herstrukturering en multinationale ondernemingen in de Belgische economie*, Brussels: Ministerie van Economische Zaken.

De Slovere, J., Van de Walle, E. and Konings-Steel, K. (1971) *De buiten-landse ondernemingen in de Belgische industrie: Een algemeen-, regionaal-, en bedrijfseconomisch onderzoek*, Ghent: SERUG.

Vanden Driessche, M. (1988) *Poker d'enfer: OPA sur la Générale de Belgique*, Paris: Fayard and Marabout.

Van den Wijngaert, M. (1990) *L'économie belge sous l'occupation: La politique d'Alexandre Galopin, gouverneur de la Société Générale*, Gembloux: Duculot.

Vandeputte, R. (1979) *Léon-A. Bekaert: Een groot man. Een goed mens*, Tielt: Lannoo.

—— (1982) *Ministre sans pouvoir*, Brussels: CRISP.

—— (1985) *Economische geschiedenis van België 1944–1984*, Tielt: Lannoo.

Vanderlinden, J. (1985) *La crise congolaise*, Brussels: Editions Complexe.

Van der Rest, P. (1962) *Onderzoek naar de economische ontwikkeling van de gebieden van Charleroi, het Centrum en de Borinage, inleiding door*, Luxembourg: Europese Gemeenschap voor Kolen en Staal.

Van der Valk, H. (1932) *De betrekkingen tusschen banken en industrie in België*, Haarlem: De Erven F. Bohn.

Van der Wee, H. (1986) *Prosperity and Upheaval: The World Economy 1945–1980*, New York: Viking.

—— and Tavernier, K. (1975) *De Nationale Bank van België en het monetaire gebeuren tussen de twee wereldoorlogen*, Brussels: Nationale Bank van België.

—— and Verbreyt, M. (1985) *Mensen maken geschiedenis: De Kredietbank en de economische opgang van Vlaanderen 1935–1985*, Brussels: Kredietbank.

Van de Velde, M. (1936) *Economie belge et Congo belge*, Antwerp: Lloyd Anversois.

Van Haver, G. (1983) *Onmacht der verdeelden: Katholieken in Vlaanderen tussen demokratie en fascisme, 1920–1940*, Berchem: EPO.

Van Molle, L. (1986) 'Innovation technologique et changement social: le cas de l'agriculture belge, XIXe et XXe siècles', in G. Kurgan-van Hentenryk and J. Stengers (eds) *L'Innovation technologique: facteur de changement (XIXe–XXe siècles)*, Brussels: Editions de l'Université de Bruxelles.

Van Molle, L. (1990) *Ieder voor allen: De Belgische Boerenbond 1890–1990*, Louvain: Universitaire Pers Leuven and Belgische Boerenbond.

Vanthemsche, G. (1978) 'De val van de regering Poullet–Vandervelde: een 'samenzwering der bankiers'?', *Belgisch tijdschrift voor nieuwste geschiedenis* 9(1–2), 165–214.

—— (1980) 'De politieke en economische context van de Belgische bankwetgevingen van 1934 en 1935', *Revue de la Banque* 8–9: 31–50.

—— (1987) 'De economische actie van de Belgische Staat tijdens de crisis van de jaren 1930, *Res Publica* 29(2): 127–51.

—— (1989) *De werkloosheid in België 1929–1940*, Berchem: EPO.

—— (1990) 'Unemployment insurance in interwar Belgium', *International Review of Social History* 29(2): 349–76.

Verduyn, L. (1992) *Beaulieu pleit onschuldig*, Louvain: Kritak.

Verhoeyen, E. (1993) *België bezet 1940–1944*, Brussels: BRTN Educatieve Uitgaven.

Verlaeten, M.P. (1979) *Enkele beschouwingen over de uitvoer van België*, Brussels: Ministerie van Economische Zaken.

Het verlies aan levenskracht van de Belgische economie in het voorbije decennium (1981) Brussels: Nationale Bank van België.

Verreet, E. and Van Overtveldt, J. (1991) *Fons Verplaetse: De meester van het herstel*, Zellik: Roularta Books.

Vints, L. (1989) *P.J. Broekx en de christelijke arbeidersbeweging in Limburg 1881–1968*, Louvain: Universitaire Pers and KADOC.

Voor de regering van morgen: Het memorandum van het Verbond van Belgische Ondernemingen aan de formateur (1979) Brussels: Verbond van Belgische Ondernemingen.

Warner, G. (1978) *La crise politique belge de novembre 1944: Un coup d'état manqué?*, Brussels: CRISP.

Weissman, S.R. (1974) *American Foreign Policy in the Congo 1960–1964*, Ithaca: Cornell University Press.

Willame, J.-C. (1972) *Patrimonialism and Political Change in the Congo*, Stanford: Stanford University Press.

Witte, E. (1989) 'Tussen restauratie en vernieuwing: Een introductie op de Belgische politieke evolutie tussen 1944 en 1950', in E. Witte, J.C. Burgelman and P. Southuysen (eds) *Tussen restauratie en vernieuwing. Aspecten van de naoorlogse Belgische politiek (1944–1950)*, Brussels: VUB-Press.

Young, C. (1965) *Politics in the Congo: Decolonization and Independence*, Oxford: Oxford University Press.

INDEX

236